NHOJ

A MEMOIR THAT STARTED BACKWARDS

N H O J

JOHN LAZENBY

\Bᵇ\
Biteback Publishing

First published in Great Britain in 2025 by
Biteback Publishing Ltd, London
Copyright © John Lazenby 2025

ISBN 978-1-78590-809-5

10 9 8 7 6 5 4 3 2 1

A CIP catalogue record for this book is available from the British Library.

Set in Minion Pro

Printed and bound in Great Britain by
CPI Group (UK) Ltd, Croydon CR0 4YY

FSC
www.fsc.org
MIX
Paper | Supporting
responsible forestry
FSC® C171272

To Sharon and Jean
'If wishes were horses…'

CONTENTS

PART I

CHAPTER ONE

A JUVENILE GUNPOWDER PLOT

In the summer of 1961, just a few months after my seventh birthday, I almost killed my grandmother.

It was an accident, of course. I certainly never harboured any murderous intentions towards her. But there were no mitigating factors in this case and no excuses. I committed an act of such reckless stupidity that I, and only I, know how close I came – a couple of millimetres, a hair's breadth – to doing the unthinkable.

As far as my family was aware, the firework I smuggled off the top shelf of the larder that Sunday, while my grandmother slept soundly in a garden chair, soared as high as any twelve-inch skyrocket could soar. It tattooed the sky with sparks and climbed effortlessly on a triumphant, coruscating arc into the cornfield next door. That unexpected show was alarming enough in itself. But what no one knew was that for the first fateful, warp-speed seconds of its flight, the skyrocket had hurtled unerringly towards my grandmother's head.

Obviously, that wasn't part of the plan – not that I paid much attention to planning. My actions were mostly random, done on an impulse or an instinct, for no other reasons than they were fun and exciting. On this occasion, I wanted to cause a bit of a stir – a sensation – to fire up a Sunday so stupefyingly slow it had almost ceased to exist. Starved of movement and momentum, the twin elements that drove my life, I was physically incapable of sitting still for longer than a few minutes at a time. The urge to do something, to make something happen, was an irresistible force beyond my control. Unfortunately, there was also a part of me that delighted in seeking out trouble and with little concern for the consequences.

So, I thought it would be fun to launch the skyrocket, wait for the loud, crackling explosion at the top of its arc, like a ripple of applause falling slowly to earth, and then watch the expressions of horror on my parents' faces. A juvenile gunpowder plot, in other words. Except that it turned into my horror instead.

The skyrocket had been left over from Bonfire Night – the last firework standing – and placed in cold storage on the top shelf with its stick peeping over the edge, tantalisingly out of reach yet tantalisingly attainable. If I hadn't known better, I almost would have believed that my parents were trying to encourage me. It was impossible to miss it, and whenever I went into the larder, I automatically glanced up to see if it was still there. I knew the stick would eventually pull me in; it was always pointing at me for one thing. It was only a question of time.

The irony of my impeccably bad timing was that my father had just persuaded my grandmother to give up driving in the hope of preserving her health and safety – and that of the residents of the greater Sussex area. She was a strong-minded woman and it was no small victory, achieved after months of battling. If she wasn't passing cars on blind bends, she was taking her eyes off the road to look at something or wave to someone she thought she recognised. Usually, her red Talbot Sunbeam was travelling too fast for that to be even a possibility. It was a minor miracle she hadn't killed herself or anyone else. Her final act behind the wheel was to cause an embarrassing incident in the picturesque village of Ditchling beneath the South Downs – although, typically, she always claimed it wasn't her fault. She removed the paint off a row of stationary vehicles in the tiny high street, leaving a jagged strip along the side of each one, so similar that it looked as if they had all been struck by an identical streak of lightning. The cacophonous scream of metal on metal brought people hurrying out of shops and doorways to see who or what had ruined Ditchling's sleepy idyll.

'It's for your own good, Mother,' my father told her when he confiscated her keys a few days later. Her racing days were over.

My troubles, meanwhile, were only just beginning.

The removal of the rocket from the larder that Sunday could not have gone more smoothly, though. Using an upturned crate to stand on, I had no difficulty lifting it off the top shelf, reaching up and slowly lowering it down, not daring to take my eyes off it for a second. It reeled me in with its dark-red cone and streamlined cardboard body, covered in red paper peppered with white stars. It was solid to the touch but lighter than I'd expected, the gunpowder so tightly packed it felt as if the slightest jiggle or vibration might cause it to ignite in my hands. I had already selected an empty jar and hidden a box of matches in my pocket. Now all I had to do was sneak outside without being detected.

I checked the coast was clear. My mother and my aunt were in the kitchen, newspapers spread out on the table, their voices competing with the sound of *Family Favourites* on the radio. The Sunday roast was already cooking away, flooding the house with its enticing aroma. My father was on the other side of the garden halfway up a ladder, clipping the front hedge. My grandmother was asleep under a straw hat in the back garden and my sister was in her room. The door stood open and I slipped through it.

Safely outside, I placed the rocket in the jar on a small patch of lawn to the right of the door, out of view. In front of me was a low, scrubby hedge with an opening carved out of the middle and a brick path winding through it into the back garden, where I could see my grandmother asleep in a deckchair. She had her back to me, a cardigan draped around her shoulders, her chin resting on her chest, her grey hair escaping from under a straw hat borrowed from my mother. I took care to aim the tip of the cone well away from her and pulled out the box of matches. At first it occurred to me that the sides of the jar were too low for the rocket, which refused to stand up straight; it insisted on tilting to one side and I had to keep repositioning it so the cone was repointed at the sky. But I couldn't go back inside and find another launch pad – that would be too risky. I told myself the jar would just have to do.

I took one last quick look around: no clouds, no breeze, the trees motionless beneath a bright sun and a vast, taut blue sky. Perfect rocket weather. I struck the match, lit the touch paper and, as I had seen my father do, immediately took two or three urgent steps back, waiting for the fizzle and hiss before ignition. And that was when fate tilted in the wrong direction.

Seconds later, there was a loud whistling noise like escaping steam and the rocket lifted off with a jolt, knocking over the jar in the same movement. The cone had slipped down again before take-off, and for one moment I thought it would fly into the hedge and no further, to be left sputtering and trapped, mangled among its thick stems. The rocket that never got off the ground. Instead, it somehow blasted its way through the top of the hedge and flew on, trailing sparks and paper while maintaining its low trajectory.

But there was something else, something far more horrible to contemplate than any collision with a hedge: the rocket, having been buffeted off course, was now arrowing straight for the back of my grandmother's straw hat.

I watched as if hypnotised, unable to do anything in those excruciating seconds except clench my fists as tight as I could and pray as though my life depended on it. I had never felt the need to pray before, but then I had never done anything as stupid as this. I didn't just pray, I pleaded, 'Please God, please God, please…' I pleaded so hard that I snapped the match clean in two in my fist and didn't give the pin-sharp stab of heat in my palm a second thought. I pleaded so hard that I barely noticed the gentle breeze that came out of nowhere and ruffled my hair.

However, in that moment something miraculous happened. The cone of the rocket rose fractionally and lifted over the top of the straw hat, scarcely disturbing it as it did so, and started to climb. Not even the high-pitched keening of its whistle as it passed overhead could rouse her from her sleep.

The taste of pure relief and renewed energy that surged through my body was overpowering – the shift from terror and blind panic to joy and elation was so rapid it was dizzying, like shedding a skin and growing another in the space of seconds. I couldn't believe my eyes or my luck. I tried in vain to follow the flight of the rocket but lost its trail somewhere in the intense blue sky and dazzling sun, as though it had burned a hole in the horizon and disappeared through it. But a loud bang somewhere above the cornfield, accompanied by the unmistakable echo of crackling applause, told me all I needed to know.

Not even my grandmother could sleep through that, and she suddenly rose unsteadily and urgently to her feet, using the wooden frame of the deckchair to lever herself up to see where the bang had come from, its echo still reverberating. But, having woken with a jump, the effort seemed too much for her and she instantly flopped back into the canvas sling of the chair. The impact loosened the wooden slat at the rear of the chair and, in almost slow motion, both she and it collapsed in an undignified heap on the grass.

That final clap of thunder also triggered a flurry of activity as my mother and my aunt, followed by my father, converged on me from opposite ends of the garden. In the confusion that followed, I spotted Ajax, our fox terrier, sprint a succession of increasingly demented laps of the lawn and realised I had forgotten all about his terror of fireworks in my haste. He appeared to be trying to purge the sound from his head. I, however, remained rooted to the spot, the empty jar lying on its side by my feet. I needed only to glance at my mother to register the disappointment in her eyes. I watched my father disentangle my grandmother from the deckchair, reassemble it, wedge the wooden slat into place with his foot and gently sit her back down again before running over to where we were standing. He still had the hedge clippers in his hand. My mother opened her mouth as if to say something, but it was my father who spoke first. He had a habit of starting conversations with a question: what did you do that for? Has anyone seen my shoes? Why do you think that's funny? Or maybe it was just whenever he talked to me.

On this occasion, he demanded, 'What have you done, John?' There was a tone in his voice that I hadn't heard before and it caught me off guard. I wanted to tell them: at least the rocket didn't bury itself in the hedge, at least it flew, at least it didn't hit my grandmother. But I realised it was pointless. They wouldn't have known what I was talking about, so I said nothing.

I felt the broken match embedded in my palm and tasted the

cordite that hung on the air all around me, like a bad lie. The fallout had begun.

• • •

There was that word again. SPELLED. At least, that's how it sounded to my seven-year-old ears. When I first heard it, I thought it might have been spilled – 'John's been spilled' – which was news to me because as far as I could tell, I was thoroughly intact and all in one piece. But no, I knew my mother's voice too well: the diction was so precise, so clear, it could have cut crystal. 'John's been SPELLED.' That was what she said. Definitely.

I had no clue what it meant, having heard it for the first time only moments ago, yet I had already convinced myself there was something unusual about it, something special. I even repeated it several times under my breath just to make sure. I'd always loved the sound of words from an early age, which if nothing else ex-plained my instant fascination with SPELLED – that and the fact it had been mentioned in the same breath as my name. Usually, if I didn't know the meaning of a word, I would try to 'read' it by its sound alone because that was all I had to go on and SPELLED chimed perfectly with me. Perhaps it was the obvious connotations of magic that made it seem so alive, so full of hope and promise. If that was true, then I was already bewitched by it.

And there was another thing: my mother had mentioned it three times in the past few minutes, taking extra care on each occasion to wring the last drop of importance out of it. This word would soon make itself known to me, I told myself.

I was sitting at the top of the stairs, listening to my mother and my aunt indulge in their late-evening ritual of drinks, cigarettes and idle chat in the kitchen. Or perhaps not so idle, in this instance. It was well past my bedtime and as usual, I found it impossible to sleep. From the top of the stairs, I could see down to the back door and the hallway, which led directly into the kitchen. The kitchen itself, though, was hidden from view. If I sidled halfway down the stairs and craned my neck through the banisters to my right, I could see into it – just – but the stairs creaked and groaned like the timbers of an old ghost ship, even under my insubstantial weight, and would have given me away long before then.

Anyway, I didn't need to see into the kitchen to know that everything was in its place. The room bathed in light and laughter, my mother and my aunt seated at the big wooden table by the window overlooking the front garden, the ashtray filling up, the stash of bottles with their colourful labels and unpronounceable (to me) names – gin, Dubonnet, vermouth, Martini, Cinzano Bianco – arranged along the bench at the far end of the room; the concoctions and potions that made their breath hotter than a furnace. I didn't need to see into the kitchen to recognise the music of their voices that I loved to listen to when I couldn't sleep.

It wasn't just that their voices were comforting and reassuring. It was more the way their words buzzed and bounced off each other; it was how they dropped their voices for dramatic effect whenever they imparted a secret piece of information or made a rude comment about an acquaintance, even though they thought no one was listening. I loved the way their conversations pinballed between topics and mingled with the warm cigarette smoke that floated upstairs. Their favourite cigarettes were Du Maurier, a Canadian brand that came in a distinctive lipstick-red cardboard box, complete with a hinged lid. They always tapped their cigarettes on the lid two or three times before lighting up. I knew their mannerisms by heart.

Even as young as I was, I could tell they were a formidable double act and one you underestimated at your peril. Strong willed, quick witted, amusing, intelligent – not to mention tall and strikingly beautiful into the bargain – they were a match for anyone and appeared to me to be all but invincible. They had a cold and reserved side to them too when pushed, and my aunt could be embarrassingly icy to anyone she disliked; they could rumble a phoney in seconds flat and send them packing for good measure. But mainly, they were fun and carefree, endlessly so, and rarely needed an invitation to let their hair down.

One of the big hit songs of that time was Chubby Checker's 'Let's Twist Again'. The dance craze had erupted almost overnight, and the record stayed in the charts for a marathon thirty-four weeks, from the deep of one winter to the start of another. Often, when it came on the kitchen radio, they would turn it up as loud as it could go and start to twist, hooked on its joyous, up-tempo beat. My younger sister, Gina, and I gleefully joined in, giving it everything we had, laughing and singing along to the words while they danced around us, competing with each other to see who could pull off the most outrageous moves. They swivelled their hips, worked their arms and swung their bodies down to the floor and up again like they were drying their backs with a towel, their cigarettes pursed in their lips. On one occasion, my father paused in the doorway and stared at us in blank disbelief before being beaten back by the loud music. He had the air of a man who had just been locked out of his own house.

'Have you all gone mad?' he sighed.

'What?' we yelled in unison, barely turning our heads in his direction.

'Have you all gone mad?' he repeated at the top of his voice.

'Oh, Richard, stop being so stuffy and come and join us,' my mother shouted after him.

If nothing else, I was just glad to have them on my side.

And there it was again. *That* word. I heard my aunt stretch it out as far as it would go, like it was a piece of elastic, until it almost snapped back on itself. SPELLED. This time, she punctuated the sentence with 'Oh, Donty' and what sounded like a sigh or a long exhalation of air or perhaps a flicker of amusement. I couldn't be sure.

That was me. I was Donty. My aunt barely used my real name, unless maybe I'd been rude to her and she wanted to show me her displeasure, in which case she'd make it sound like it was something unpleasant she needed to remove from her shoe. Otherwise, it had been Donty for as long as I could remember. Donty was part of my aunt's restless quest to invent nicknames for us all and had soon caught on with the rest of the family, which was only fair I suppose because as a baby I'd called her Dow, being unable to pronounce her name, Daphne. It's funny how some names stick, and others don't, and Dow would stay with her for the rest of her life – not just within the family but with the many guests and visitors who stayed at our house over the years, my school friends among them. I even felt a glimmer of pride at the way Dow tripped off their tongues so naturally.

She had moved in with us a year earlier, invading the house with her humour and vitality, her quirkiness, her piano playing and passion for betting on the horses. From then on, our days were soundtracked by the rhythm of the racing results on the radio and the familiar roll call of place names: Towcester (pronounced toaster because, I assumed, it was where the first one had been invented), Wincanton, Uttoxeter, Redcar, Bangor-on-Dee or, closer to home,

Plumpton. Within a matter of weeks, it felt as though she had always lived with us.

I had no idea how long I'd been sitting there at the top of the stairs when I was alerted by sudden movement in the kitchen: the high-pitched scraping of a chair on the floor, the jingle of car keys. It was my mother readying herself to collect my father from the train station. 'Oh, heavens, look at the time,' she said, draining her drink. My mother, Virginia, was late for most things but often seemed unduly surprised by the fact. This was how their ritual usually ended, with her struggling into her coat and dashing for the door, all in one fumbling movement. Dow called out goodnight, picked up her half-full glass and her cigarettes and wandered off to her end of the house, well accustomed to the hurried curtailment of these evenings. It was my cue to leave too and tiptoeing cautiously across the landing into my bedroom, I slipped back under the covers. I always slept with my door open, and within seconds I heard the loud, disembodied roar of laughter and muffled voices from Dow's television.

Sometimes I would lie awake and listen to two televisions, my aunt's and my parents', vie for my attention from opposite ends of the house. Different channels, jarringly at odds but in magnificent stereo: gunfire, horses' hooves, the ricochet of bullets, a sudden surge of music, audience applause, heated debate. The fragments of sound collided, splintered, merged and embedded themselves in my mind, shifting like a kaleidoscope until it was impossible to dislodge them.

On this night, though, I must have dropped off earlier than usual because the next thing I recall was being woken by my father polishing his shoes in the kitchen – a task he performed without fail, last thing before bed every night of the working week. The substitution of one ritual for another. The brushstrokes alternated between long monotonous strokes or short jabbing movements, depending on his mood, often lasting for minutes on end. On this occasion, the strokes appeared particularly fast and relentless, like windscreen wipers battling a torrential rain. It was as though he wanted to make his shoes disappear, to expunge them, to remove a deadweight from his shoulders, and I lay there willing him to stop.

My father was a creature of habit, who regularly mowed the lawn in a cardigan and tie, even on blazing summer days, until the sweat ran down his face and my mother had to go outside and order him to rest. He spent a lifetime struggling, and failing, to throw off the burden of his upbringing. Ultimately, his life pivoted on two deathbed promises, one he had made to his father, the other to his father-in-law. The first of those promises and the most onerous, to abandon a career in the Royal Navy and take over the running of the family business – a job for which he was almost entirely un-suited – bound him to a path of such overwhelming responsibility and expectation that he could neither step off it nor leave it behind. The only option open to him was to see that path to its conclusion before it broke him.

He belonged to an old-fashioned club, one that was dwindling in numbers even then, in which a man of his word could no more go against that word once it had been given than he could betray a gentleman's handshake once it had been made. The casual ease with which many verbal agreements and handshakes were ripped up by so-called trusted business partners, colleagues and associates never failed to sadden him. He dreamed of freedom, of escape, but realised it was futile and remained to the end of his days a prisoner, chained to an innate sense of duty. I knew nothing of the finer points of this as a small boy, only that the repeated brushstrokes, back and forth while I lay above him in the darkness, were lonelier than any sound I had heard. For years afterwards, I always associated the pungent whiff of Kiwi shoe polish with sadness and regret.

When his shoes were eventually buffed and shined to perfection, he placed them on a sheet of newspaper and inserted a pair of wooden shoe trees – an act, mercifully, that took seconds rather than minutes. Patiently, I waited for him to shut the kitchen door, switch off the light and go upstairs to bed. But even this relatively simple procedure turned into a trial while he triple-checked each plug and appliance, muttering 'off, off, off' under his breath, moving his hands in a beckoning motion as he did so, like a conductor summoning one last supreme crescendo from the orchestra. The relief I felt when he was done and finally turned out the light was enormous.

In the silence that lingered after he had vacated the kitchen and gone to bed, my thoughts returned to the word SPELLED and I tried to replay some of the conversation I'd heard earlier that evening. But I couldn't stop my mind from racing; it was as if the atmosphere had suddenly shifted, propelled by my father's frantic brushstrokes to be replaced by one of nagging doubt and probing uncertainty. Any confidence I had in SPELLED evaporated faster than a dream, along with my own confidence. What if I had mistaken it for another word altogether? The meaning of it remained a mystery to me after all, as did so many things at that time in my life. I knew I couldn't risk asking my mother or Dow what it meant either, for fear of giving myself away. Things had been strained with my mother since the episode with the rocket and I was desperate to get back into her good books. And another thing: why was I the one who'd been SPELLED, whatever it meant?

My head hummed with unanswerable questions.

CHAPTER TWO

THAT IS NOT A
SERIOUS QUESTION

By the age of seven, I could write only one word without the assistance or input of someone else, and that word was my name. But as it turned out, I couldn't even do that correctly. I wrote it as NHOJ, although I was the solitary person in the classroom who failed to recognise there was a problem with that. My teachers at St Peter's Court in Burgess Hill, Sussex, the preparatory school where I had been a day boy for nearly a year and a half, were left to impatiently point out to me the anomaly of my back-to-front writing.

One teacher suggested that I was suffering from what he described as a rare form of word blindness. He made it sound as though it were irreversible. But as far as I could tell, it didn't mean I was blind – it simply meant that the way I saw letters and numbers was not the way others viewed them. As I spent most of my time at school going backwards, according to my teachers, it didn't come as any great surprise to me. Naturally, reading was an impossibility for me as well; the peaks of the words and letters were just too hard to climb. I often wondered what it was that everyone else was seeing that I wasn't or what it was they had, in abundance, that I lacked.

Another teacher assured my parents that I would grow out of this condition in time, like sucking my thumb. My father, I noticed, seemed curiously comforted by that news. The general consensus, however, was that my deficiencies with the written word were the product of nothing other than a deep-rooted laziness, dangerously fused with a chronic lack of concentration.

If anything, I was even more befuddled by numbers and repeatedly failed to master the most rudimentary of mathematical sums. If $9 + 8 = 17$, for example, I would inexplicably arrive at an answer of 71 – much to the consternation of my teacher and the open-mouthed incredulity of my fellow pupils, most of whom couldn't decide whether I was being funny or just plain stupid. Yet to my eyes, the numbers looked exactly as they were supposed to look – as did the order of the letters NHOJ – and no amount of concentration on my part was going to reverse them. The simple truth was that I didn't understand what I was doing wrong or why I was always getting left behind by the others, always bottom of the class – that lonely, empty place to be. Sometimes it felt as though I was being suspended in mid-air, caught between two worlds: mine and the one I didn't belong in. But as no one had volunteered a plausible explanation for my problem or a ready-made solution to reverse the process, I assumed it couldn't be all that serious. My mother had always instilled in me the importance of being an optimist in life, so, without too much ado, I decided it wasn't worth losing any sleep over. Not that I slept much anyway.

The first time I wrote my name was on the outside of my bedroom door at home. I would have been six or seven. I proudly scrawled NHOJ in sky-blue crayon, and I remember my parents chuckling warmly at me in an amused, matter-of-fact manner as if to suggest it was an easy mistake to make on my part, nothing more. *Typical*

Donty. I drew a figure alongside it with a cowboy hat, a six-shooter and spurs, which was supposed to be me; someone was always brandishing a gun or hurling a spear in my pictures. Art was one of the few things I was any good at and I had a small mountain of school exercise books to prove it, littered with drawings and little else. Rather like the pen lines and marks on a wall that indicate the changing height of a child and stay for ever as part of the fabric of the family home, so my mother was reluctant to erase my name from the door. It was still there when my parents sold the house in 1981. I think, in a funny kind of way, she saw it as a symbol of my growth and her unfading belief in me.

I have since learned that it is not uncommon for children to place letters and numbers in reverse order when first being taught to write. Sometimes this will happen for no other reason than they are struggling to memorise the alphabet and the individual shapes of letters. The teacher who told my parents that I would grow out of it in time was right in a way, though I suspect he was saying only what they wanted to hear. Reversed writing is usually done by children between the ages of three and seven and, more often than not, by left-handers like me. The technical term for it is mirror writing because the characters appear correct when reflected in a mirror. As I was able to write only one word at the age of seven – it was as if I had got stuck at NHOJ and could go no further – I obviously wouldn't have required much of a mirror.

In 1961, such thinking was unheard of at St Peter's Court. The back-to-front writing of my name, coupled with my failure to recognise the disparity, prompted more frustration than concern among my teachers. I was the conundrum that no one knew what to do with, the pupil who baffled and irked his teachers in equal measure, the irritant under their skin or, to put it another way, the problem no one wanted to solve. Unfortunately, the teacher I appeared to annoy the most was the headmaster, Mr Gent, a deeply serious man who, among other things, taught Latin to the senior boys – a subject that might have proved fatal to him if he'd had the misfortune to teach it to me. The few who still retained a sliver of a will to help me trotted out the same old mantras they had since the day I first arrived at school: if I concentrated hard, sat still, paid attention in class and stopped myself from being so easily distracted and distracting others in the process, I would start to make some progress with my studies. Clearly, though, they too had given up on me, really.

Concentration, concentration and more concentration. It was the prescribed cure-all for any child experiencing learning difficulties in the classroom at that time and represented a perfect distillation of my early school days. This dusty remedy had never failed hundreds of pupils before me, I was repeatedly told, so why should I be any different? Yet I was beginning to wonder if there might not be something just a bit different about me.

It didn't help that I spectacularly missed the point of school. It barely occurred to me that I was there to work. I saw it primarily as a place for making new friends, for broadening my circle of acquaintances, for outings and fun and games – a social whirl, in other words. Whatever else I lacked at school, I certainly didn't lack friends. Lessons were merely an obstruction to all that jollity. I was always the last one back into class after morning or afternoon breaks and regularly had to be called or fetched inside by one teacher or another. I was forever trying to persuade the others to stay outside in the grounds with me and once even tried to stage a sit-in in the sandpit. On my own, of course – the others soon dutifully returned to their desks. The teacher eventually coaxed me back inside by allowing me to draw pictures for the rest of the lesson. As art was the only means I had of expressing myself in the classroom – I spent my whole time thinking in pictures – it swiftly did the trick. I was frequently left to my own devices by my teachers and, conveniently for them, drawing kept me occupied and prevented me from disturbing the class and taxing their patience.

My cause wasn't helped by my unruly appearance. My tie was always halfway round my neck, my shoelaces permanently undone, my hair in urgent need of a comb and there were invariably mud stains on my face and kneecaps. Mysteriously, I often ended up with a ring of mud around my nose, like a smear of warpaint. My mother made sure I went off to school each morning looking appropriately smart and presentable, and I returned home in the afternoon as if I had just run a cross-country race over the marshes, having crawled across the finishing line on my hands and knees. My charcoal-grey cap, which I was supposed to wear at all times outside the school grounds, was lost to the winds. I mislaid more school caps than any person had a right to.

My untidiness went hand in hand with my inability to memorise anything that didn't interest me, and I seemed incapable of doing the everyday things others did: follow instructions, process information, obey the rules, stay out of scraps, tell my right from my left, knot my tie, do up my shoelaces. Mr Gent would routinely stop me to point out a trailing lace or to straighten my tie like a fussy tailor. Each time, I received a shake of the head and a tired sigh, as if it was all too much trouble for him. His pinch of patience had run out a long time ago, and it came as no surprise when he finally snapped and lost his temper with me, in a school lecture of all things.

The subject of the lecture was deep-sea diving, and as an avid fan of the American action television series *Sea Hunt*, starring Lloyd

Bridges as a crime-fighting former naval frogman, I was instantly gripped. School lectures had always been a bugbear for me, mainly because they were agonisingly boring and that was if I could even understand them. Many of the lecturers were so dull and monotone they almost brought their own dust into the room with them; the school seemed to have a special knack for finding these people. If that wasn't bad enough – especially for somebody like me who found it physically uncomfortable to sit still – the hard wooden seats numbed and immobilised your backside in minutes. It usually required all my reserves of willpower not to dismantle my chair in front of everybody. Later, I would learn to cultivate the art of looking alert and attentive in lectures, while my mind flew off on other tangents. I lost count of the amount of tries I scored down the left wing for England or the number of times I flattened Geoff Boycott's off stump, opening the bowling for Sussex against Yorkshire, and watched him trudge disconsolately back to the pavilion. But on this occasion, time sped by.

The lecturer had a serious manner about him – as you might expect from a man who did such a dangerous and thrilling job – but not disagreeably so, and he commanded our interest and attention throughout. If at any stage my mind showed signs of wandering, there was always the rubber diving suit on display or the collection of oxygen cylinders, flippers, speargun, mask, snorkel and various other pieces of underwater equipment to keep me focused. He had completed expeditions to some of the world's most perilous diving sites – Florida, Bermuda and the Great Barrier Reef in Australia, where he had explored all manner of shipwrecks, including a Second World War American submarine armed to the teeth, its torpedoes still loaded in the open hatches, awaiting an order that never came. There was an impressive intake of air from the floor at that fact. It certainly startled me and has lodged in my mind ever since, a typical example of the kind of information I retained as a child. After some enthusiastic applause at the end of the lecture, we were asked by Mr Gent to raise our hands if we had a question. I immediately launched mine into the air and eagerly tried to catch the lecturer's eye, as if pointing out some imaginary speck on the ceiling. Because I was sitting in the front row, it wasn't exactly hard for him to miss me.

'The boy there,' he said, gesturing expectantly in my direction.

'Have you watched *Sea Hunt*?' I blurted.

Laughter was never far from the surface during school lectures, mainly because of the overbearing seriousness of the subject, the comical creak of wooden chairs or the fact the lecturer was often too portentous for his or her own good. If they delivered a throwaway line or made some rare attempt at humour, however vague, it would invariably generate a gale of laughter it didn't merit, purely by way of alleviating the tension. But my question brought the house down.

A wave of laughter rolled down from the back seats and appeared to engulf the room; it then withdrew like backwash, only to intensify again. The lecturer, meanwhile, looked as if someone had cut off his oxygen supply – something that was always happening to Lloyd Bridges's character in the programme, usually because of some act of villainy. Mr Gent, who had clapped his hand to his brow when he heard my question, could stand it no more and sprang to his feet, his face an incandescent purple. The laughter stopped but not quite as abruptly as he might have hoped, and he stared down the last few gigglers and snorters, challenging them to meet his gaze, to defy him.

'That is *not* a serious question,' he announced once the room had fallen into silence. 'This has been a fascinating lecture – I'm sure you all agree.' Some boys nodded; my ears burned as if someone had singed the tips of them. 'But Mr Bancroft has not travelled all the way from Plymouth to St Peter's Court today to answer questions about a television show. Certainly not. He is here to discuss the very serious and intriguing topic of deep-sea diving, to expand our knowledge, our understanding. And what an excellent job he has done of it too.' There were more nods of appreciation. After a suitable pause, he turned his attention to the back of the room, where the prefects and senior boys were seated. 'Now let's have some proper questions. Patterson, I'm sure that you have a question for Mr Bancroft.'

Indeed he did, impeccably delivered, and I had to sit there and endure it while listening to the lecturer's measured, detailed response. Afterwards, I was pulled aside by Mr Gent, who still looked on the brink of combustion, and informed I was to be banned from asking any further questions at lectures, school outings, functions or any other events that involved members of the public. 'You're an embarrassment to the whole school and we can't have it,' he told me. 'Not only that, but I've just had to apologise profusely to Mr Bancroft for the disturbance you caused. From now on I want you to keep your mouth closed and your opinions to yourself. Is that understood?'

Once again, I was at a loss to know what I had done wrong. I was hurt and confused at the way my question had been torpedoed out of existence, but there was nothing I could do other than bottle my frustration, wait for the feeling to pass and continue to muddle through. Nevertheless, a thought had occurred to me, one I didn't dare dwell on for too long: maybe it wasn't just words and numbers that I saw back to front. Maybe it was the world I inhabited as a whole.

Even at the age of seven I had a fascination for detail, albeit one that existed purely on my own terms. I was supremely disinterested in the specialist subjects of my teachers but constantly absorbed in the distinct quirks and characteristics of their personalities. How I must have exasperated them. So little of what they tried to teach me stayed in my head, yet if something caught my imagination – be it some obscure, inessential fact, which mattered to nobody but me, or one of my teacher's trademark traits or foibles – I could recall it with almost photographic clarity. Perhaps that's why Mr Gent, with his brilliantined dark hair and enigmatic half smile, as though he could never quite bring himself to go the full distance, has remained so sharply in focus for me. The same could also be said for Mr Farquharson and Mr Rattray who, apart from sounding like a firm of dubious Dickensian solicitors, were two of St Peter's Court's more compelling characters.

In fact, Mr Farquharson was a geography teacher who, fittingly, had travelled from another continent, having spent most of his life in South Africa. He always wore tweed jackets with leather elbow pads and drove a seemingly indestructible 1940s black Ford Popular, his pride and joy. It was, he could not resist reminding us, 'built to last'. He had scant regard for the modern cars that our parents drove and made no secret of it, tutting or shaking his head in mock despair at those monstrosities, as he referred to them, convincing us they would all fall apart within a few years. 'Destined for the scrapyard,' was how he described them. He was also a former airline pilot, which made him something of a rarity among schoolteachers. He would probably have been in his late fifties or early sixties, but his ashen-grey hair made him look much older to my young eyes. There were even rumours he had fought as an airman in the First World War, and I was frequently tempted to ask him if he had flown biplanes but, sensibly, resisted on this occasion.

Mr Rattray – whose name I took literally to mean a tray of rats – was a younger man, an English and history teacher who also happened to be a volunteer fireman, a role he performed with excessive dedication. When the siren sounded in town, he would drop whatever he was doing, even if he was in the middle of class, and without so much as an explanation set off at the speed of an Olympic sprinter for the fire station a couple of streets away, his tie flying out behind him like a flame. All he needed was a baton in his hand to complete the picture.

I have another defining image of Mr Rattray, however. It was during one of his English lessons that I felt truly uplifted for the first time in a classroom – awakened, if you like – and that was when the poem 'King John's Christmas' by A. A. Milne was read out to us. I had never felt so engaged and alive in a class before, and for once I was fully present in the moment, not zoning out or idly drawing. The fact that I shared the same name as the subject of the poem undoubtedly helped pique my interest and curiosity. But it was the rhythm, the gathering pace of the words, the images they painted and how they rhymed that left the deepest imprint on me. I experienced an affection for King John that I hadn't expected – I was overjoyed when, in the poem, his wish for a red, india-rubber ball was granted. My fragile dreams, like sails, instantly filled with fresh hope. I almost believed the words were written about me and, for one glorious moment, I felt freed from the four walls of the classroom. I loved it so much I even asked him to read it out again. My request was declined, but the rhyming words, once planted inside my head, continued to breathe and grow.

It was unquestionably a breakthrough for me – I had finally connected. But I wasn't flying for long. As the days and weeks of the Christmas term of 1961 ticked down, an event was taking place behind the scenes that would change my life in ways I could never have foreseen. Unbeknownst to me, Mr Gent had invited my parents to the school to 'discuss John's future', although in his mind my fate was already sealed and had been for some time. I was blissfully unaware of any such encounter, of course, my eyes fixed unwaveringly on the Christmas holidays that were just around the corner. But some painful truths were faced in that meeting, some harsh words exchanged, a point of no return reached, some deep breaths taken and, finally, a verdict delivered.

• • •

It was almost the end of the Christmas holidays and I had still to discover the meaning of the word SPELLED. Within a few days, however, my infatuation with the word was to be overtaken by events and the arrival of a far more devastating revelation, to the point that it would cease to matter to me altogether. It never once occurred to me that there might have been a connection between SPELLED and the sudden whirlwind that blew my small world inside out, causing it to unravel uncontrollably before my eyes. It all happened so fast, the ground ripped from under my feet without any explanation.

I suppose I should have seen it coming. After all, the signs were everywhere if I had just bothered to take them in: the way my parents and Dow were suddenly unable to look me in the eye or hold my gaze, the whispers in the kitchen, how their words froze on their tongues whenever I walked in, the absence of any conversation about the start of next term… Even I knew the Christmas holidays couldn't last for ever. And where was my school uniform? Normally by this time it would have been brought out of the wardrobe, any missing buttons sewn on, any last-minute alterations made, yet another school cap ordered. If my mother had forgotten, which seemed unlikely but possible, I wasn't going to be the one to remind her. How could I have failed to hear the footfall of change among all that?

When I finally learned the truth about SPELLED several years later (my parents tried to keep it from me for as long as they could), I wasn't in the slightest bit surprised. I'd somehow managed to build up a word that didn't exist – at least not in the sense I hoped it had. It was like finding a lump of coal and mistaking it for a bar of gold; I couldn't have got it any more wrong if I'd tried. Nor did it surprise me that I had misheard and confused it for another word. And not just any word either, however similar they might have sounded to my ears. This one had a meaning that was all too vivid and real. For the record: that word was *expelled*.

I was seven years old and I had been expelled from school. My principal crime, among many? I was apparently unteachable.

CHAPTER THREE

IT WILL BE JUST LIKE
A HOLIDAY

It was a new year and I was about to discover just how unteachable I was. In many ways, 'unteachable' could not have been a
more apt description of me at that time, seeing as I already thought
of myself as an *un*-person. After all, my teachers at St Peter's Court
were forever pointing out how untidy I was, how unintelligent, un-
knowledgeable and unmanageable, along with several words I had
yet to learn the meaning of: unpredictable, unobservant, uncooper-
ative, unfathomable. To my mind, unteachable would have been no
better or worse than any of the others – it was just another word, an
addition to the expanding constellation of terms and expressions
that were regularly used to describe me.

Fortunately, unteachable or any similar-sounding words couldn't
have been further from my mind on a chilly afternoon in early January 1962 when I set off with my parents for the mysterious seaside
resort of Broadstairs in Kent. I say mysterious because my parents
had announced, out of the blue and in a most roundabout way, that
we were going there for a holiday. What my mother said was that
'it will be just like a holiday going to Broadstairs'. As far as I was

concerned, that was as good as saying we *were* going on a holiday and nothing could persuade me otherwise. I was even wearing a new outfit, carefully chosen by my mother 'for special occasions', as she put it: a pale grey-flannel jacket, matching shorts, a light-blue shirt and black lace-up shoes. It was still two months until my eighth birthday, and the next special occasion I could think of was my sister's sixth birthday at the end of January... but whatever this occasion was, at least I didn't have to wear my charcoal-grey St Peter's Court blazer with its canary-yellow piping any more. Or my cap, for that matter.

Two days earlier, my parents had announced that I would not be returning to St Peter's Court for the start of the next term – news I was still struggling to make sense of. Mostly, I worried that I might not see any of my friends again. In the same breath, I expected to be told the name of my new school and braced myself for the inevitable revelation but nothing was said. I experienced a rush of relief and wondered whether I would have to attend another school ever again. My parents, meanwhile, had become weirdly obsessed with Broadstairs and could talk of little else, cramming my head with more facts about the town than I knew what to do with, including mention of a hotel where I naturally assumed we'd be staying. It soon took my mind off my friends at St Peter's Court. Despite my limited experience of hotels, I loved the hustle and bustle of them and imagined big, wooden revolving doors that made a well-oiled sound, like a deck of cards being cut and shuffled, with every spin and turn they took.

On the morning of our departure, however, my parents success-fully evaded and deflected any questions I had about the holiday or the hotel. They even managed to see off my attempts to separate them in the hope of catching one or the other (especially my father) unawares, and my best efforts to wheedle an answer out of them or pick up on a clue fell disappointingly flat. I had to admit it did seem an odd time to be going to the seaside for a holiday – not that I was complaining, though. There was already snow in the air when we drove away from home – wispy, feathery snowflakes that billowed around in circles in the wind and melted the instant they touched the ground. Rather like my questions.

'How long are we going to be staying in Broadstairs?'

'I told you, it's a surprise,' my mother repeated for about the fifth time that day.

'What kind of surprise?'

'Well, it wouldn't be a surprise if I told you that now, would it?' she answered, barely changing the tone of her voice while she concentrated on her driving, the windscreen wipers making short work of the snowflakes.

At which point, I tried a different tack: 'Why do I have to wear this new outfit? It's really itchy.'

'Because where we're going, they like you to look smart. That's why.'

'Who's they?'

'You'll find out for yourself soon enough.'

'But why does it have to be a surprise, Mum?' I asked again, more out of desperation than anything. Whereupon my father briskly changed the subject.

My annoying inquisitiveness had nothing to do with the fact that I didn't trust my parents. Of course, I did; I trusted them implicitly. For one thing, they were always warning me about the awful repercussions that awaited me if I told too many lies, which, apart from anything else, assured me that they were nothing if not truthful. It was also clear to me that I was getting precisely nowhere with my incessant questioning. If this was a game of patience and persistence, then I was losing it hands down. I decided there was nothing else for it but to sit back, enjoy the ride and wait for the surprise that lay in store.

Thanks to my parents, I already knew that Broadstairs boasted a famous ice cream parlour called Morelli's Gelato, as well as an amusement arcade, a golden crescent of sand known as Viking Bay (there was also a replica Viking longboat on the beach at a place called Pegwell Bay further along the coast), a small harbour, an even smaller pier bedecked with carvings from wrecked ships and an ancient, ghostly edifice named Bleak House, which glowered out to sea, its brick blacker than beach tar. I couldn't deny that Broadstairs sounded an interesting place, if not a little strange, and wanted to go exploring as soon as we arrived.

And yet no sooner had we crossed the Sussex-Kent border than I started to feel a slight uneasiness, an instinct that something wasn't quite as it should be. Perhaps it was because my parents were behaving like actors rehearsing lines for a play and they'd been doing this in my company and without let-up since the start of the Christmas holidays. Perhaps it was the furtive glances they had exchanged with Dow before we drove off. Perhaps it was nothing, perhaps it was my imagination. But as the journey progressed, the feeling continued to gnaw at me and wouldn't go away.

Invariably on long car journeys, my parents took it in turns to share the driving duties and at the halfway point they changed over. Before setting off again, my mother brought out the scotch eggs and we had a small roadside picnic. If there was an occasion that didn't call for scotch eggs, my mother had yet to find it. My father, for some reason, always wore his hat in the passenger seat, and he took it off once he was behind the wheel and pulled on his driving gloves, buttoning them at the wrist. There was no doubt in my mind who was the more capable driver of the two. My mother was always comfortable when driving, instinctive, relaxed and rarely flustered; our Vanden Plas positively purred along when she was at the wheel. To say that my father was a cautious driver would be to put it mildly – he was cautious almost to the point of parody. He drove as though he had a boot full of dynamite and the slightest jolt or bump in the road could have catastrophic consequences. Before overtaking he would compute, assess and evaluate the angles, the space, the distance, the risks, the merits, the seconds, the milliseconds, and then, when every bone in my body was screaming at him to complete the manoeuvre, he would decide against it.

It reminded me of the numerous run-ins he had with my grandmother over her driving. On one occasion during Sunday lunch, my grandmother announced that she had managed to complete the 24-mile journey from Eastbourne to Brighton in only twenty minutes, despite having been advised by my father to allow for a time of at least forty-five minutes. The image of her driving in a pair of racing goggles came into my head. 'Twenty minutes,' she repeated in case some of us had missed it the first time around, while shooting a withering glance in his direction.

'It's nothing to be proud of, Mother,' my father remarked quietly.

'It's Eastbourne to Brighton,' she exclaimed, the exasperation in her voice at full throttle. 'Not London to Brighton, for goodness' sake.'

He patiently explained that he had factored in the additional time to account for any potential traffic delays, breakdowns or red lights on what, after all, was a busy coast road. 'What's the point of asking for my advice, Mother, if all you do is ignore it?'

She looked at him incredulously. 'What red lights?'

My father didn't reply – instead he wore the expression of a man who'd just discovered he had a flat tyre. He would, however, go on to have the last word a few weeks later as it turned out, following my grandmother's debacle in Ditchling high street.

My attention was suddenly diverted by my father switching on the car radio, and my heart sank instantly. It was the worst programme in the world, not to mention the most depressing: *Sing Something Simple*. My father's favourite. Thirty minutes of utter torture that made me want to press my hands tightly over my ears and keep them there until it was over. I wasn't normally prone to car sickness, but I had only to hear the syrupy, mawkish opening bars of the title song to feel distinctly queasy and lightheaded. 'We invite you to *Sing Something Simple*, a collection of favourite songs, old and new, sung by the Cliff Adams Singers, accompanied by Jack Emblow on the accordion,' the announcer intoned, his voice almost oozing out of the radio like over-ripe cheese. For many years, I thought Jack Emblow's name was actually Jack Envelope.

Every song sounded the same to me, as if they had somehow been stuck together by the gooeyness of it all, the only variation being that each one seemed slightly more depressing than the previous one. At the same time, the high-pitched accordion skipped and skit-tered between the sugared voices, adding another layer of schmaltz to the mix while sounding strangely like a herd of goats imbibing laughing gas. I'm sure, looking back, that my mother also listened to *Sing Something Simple* through gritted teeth – her record collection brimmed with the likes of Frank Sinatra, Nat King Cole and Louis Armstrong, among others, and it would have sounded to her like musical marzipan. Her love for music was such that it couldn't help but rub off on me. In fact, to improve the odds of that happening, she had played Beethoven's *Symphony No. 5* relentlessly to me in the last few months before I was born – something my father appeared to be systematically trying to reverse.

By this time in the journey, I had that feeling you get in your stomach when you've eaten too much cake too quickly and you know at some point very soon you are going to pay for it. I was about to ask my father to stop the car – the asphyxiating combination of *Sing Something Simple*, the scotch eggs and the highly scented aroma of the upholstery was making me feel more nauseous by the second – when we turned into a driveway and crunched loudly over the gravel towards a huge red and brown brick building. For a moment, I imagined we were driving over Jack Envelope's whining accordion.

A man and a woman were standing on an island of grass in the middle of the drive, and on hearing our engine they stared directly at us; the man had his hands clasped firmly behind his back and they both craned their necks to see inside the car as we drove by. I saw my mother smile at them and my father lift a gloved hand off the wheel in recognition. The building appeared to visibly grow before my eyes as we drove towards it, until it filled the entire windscreen. We parked alongside a line of cars opposite an arched, wooden front door that was formidable enough to have kept a battering ram at bay. I guessed this was the hotel, though it might just as easily have been Bleak House. Tangled ivy sprawled across the brick, swaying in the wind and making an eerie swishing noise; on some parts of the brickwork, the ivy had climbed two or three storeys high and looked like monstrous Victorian side-whiskers.

The man and the woman walked over to the car and my parents climbed out to meet them; my mother motioned to me to do the same and I followed reluctantly, still feeling a bit groggy. The man, whom I assumed was the hotel manager, had a bristling, silver military moustache and matching, neatly parted silver hair combed across his forehead, with a loose strand that dipped over one eye. The woman had iron-grey hair and wore what looked like a doctor's white coat, with a small watch clipped to its top pocket and a row of biros on display. But it was her mottled, red face that was the most noticeable thing about her; on closer inspection, I saw she had a purple blotch on both cheeks that seemed to connect all the various dots and veins mapping her skin.

The pair introduced themselves to my parents, shook hands and exchanged some practised pleasantries. When they had finished, my father put his hand on my shoulder. 'And this is John.' They didn't shake hands with me, but the man looked me up and down for several seconds.

'No tie, I see,' he said.

'Oh, we can easily put that right,' my mother replied, a little too hurriedly for my liking. And then, like an amateur conjuror, she reached into the pocket of her coat and produced a navy-blue tie. She proceeded to put it on me, doing up the top button of my shirt and knotting it expertly before flattening down the collar with a pat of the hand. 'There,' she said, stepping back and looking approvingly at me, staring deeply into my eyes and holding my gaze as she did so. 'That looks better, doesn't it?' I couldn't help but detect a slight awkwardness about her, as if she were not just rehearsing lines for a play but acting them out.

'He's not properly dressed without one,' the man added crisply.

There was a brief, uncomfortable pause in the conversation after that, until the woman asked if I would like to go inside and see where I'd be sleeping. She gave me a smile that lasted for all of two seconds but produced a curious ripple effect on her face, like a pebble breaking the surface of a pond. I nodded, stopped scuffing the gravel aimlessly around with the soles of my new shoes and followed her.

'You'd better take your overnight case with you if you're going inside, John,' my mother called, opening the boot and handing the small case to me. There was the same lingering look as before. I walked away carrying the case, but my mother called out again, this time to the woman. 'One thing: John likes to have a glass of Ribena before bedtime, would it be possible to arrange that for him?' My mother had a habit of blurting out things that embarrassed me. We were remarkably alike in that regard, both impulsive, both blurters, which was probably why I always felt so self-conscious when she did it. *A glass of Ribena before bedtime.* The man turned and watched me intently, his hands still behind his back. Why would she say something like that?

'Of course we will, Mrs Lazenby,' the woman replied, and I saw my mother's face soften and relax. 'A glass of Ribena, that will be no trouble at all.'

We walked in through the front door and the woman slammed the mighty oak frame behind us. It closed with a resounding thud and a small clink of metal, like someone throwing away a key.

In front of me, at the far end of the corridor, was a long window with a sweeping view of playing fields, goalposts and what looked like a cricket pavilion. The far perimeter of the fields was skirted by houses, bare trees, overgrown grass and a ragged assortment of garden fences, which served as a straggling boundary line. For some unknown reason it reminded me of a graveyard. There was no view of the sea. A black-and-white-tiled hallway stretched before me like a giant chequerboard and to my left was a highly polished, steep wooden staircase, which we now started to climb, passing what I took to be other guests on their way down. There was a strong smell of burned food and disinfectant. I could make out the sound of running footsteps and boys' voices at the end of a distant corridor somewhere within the building; their voices were sometimes muffled, sometimes distinct, as if a door was being repeatedly opened and shut or someone was playing with the dial on a radio.

After reaching the first floor, we turned left and I followed the woman down a long corridor before continuing up two more flights of stairs and a dimly lit passage. Not a word passed between us. As we climbed, the stairs became narrower with more twists and turns to negotiate, the carpets gave way to brown linoleum or, in some places, rickety floorboards and everything looked dingier and dustier, as if we had somehow entered another building. Finally, I found myself in a room with a collection of iron beds, a traveller's trunk at the foot of each bed and a wooden chair at the head. There were no pictures on the walls. In the centre of the room was a washstand containing plastic bowls, tooth mugs and towels. A bare light bulb hung from the ceiling. It was like no hotel room I had ever seen – not that I'd seen that many, of course.

'This is your dormitory,' the woman said at last. It was a word I had never heard before. 'And here's your bed.' She indicated it by rapping her knuckles on the scratched iron frame. It made a dull, dead sound. I recognised a pair of my striped pyjamas from home, neatly folded on top of the pillow, my dressing gown draped over the back of the chair, my slippers tucked beneath it. I looked at the trunk; it was green with wooden slats across the lid and the corners and there was writing on it. I wished I'd been able to read the bold, black lettering. It might have provided a clue to what all this meant, some answers to the flood of questions that were forming in my mind faster than I could keep up with them. How did my clothes get here? And without me knowing a single thing about it? Was this the surprise my parents had talked about? Why were there so many other beds in the room? What sort of place was this, apart from one where I had to wear a tie while on holiday? How long were we intending to stay here? As for my trunk… I didn't even know I had a trunk. And what was inside it anyway?

I was about to put that very question to the woman when I felt her turn and look at me. 'Oh, in case you were wondering, we don't do Ribena here before bedtime,' she said. I wasn't wondering – I had more important things to occupy my mind. 'So you can put that idea out of your head.' This time there was an unmistakable edge, a coldness to her voice. The change in tone was so abrupt, so immediate, it brought me up with a jolt and I swung around to meet her gaze. Her face gave nothing away – a mask of blotches and veins except for the challenging glint in her eyes. I stared back at it, open-mouthed, unable to say anything. And with that, she turned smartly on her heel and walked off, the soft pulse of her shoes on the linoleum disappearing down the corridor.

I was startled by what I'd heard and for a minute, I wasn't sure what to do next. It was so unexpected that I even wondered if it was something I'd done, something I'd said – yet I'd hardly spoken a word to her. I looked around the room again, at the empty beds, the vast trunks, and a shiver coursed through me. In that split-second, I knew I couldn't stay in the room a moment longer. I left my over-night case on the bed – it would slow me down too much – dashed out the door, ran the length of the corridor and started downstairs as fast as my legs could propel me. As I descended each flight, each turn of the stairs, I was clinging to the one thing I believed in and trusted above all else: my parents.

In my anxiety to get downstairs, I narrowly avoided a collision with a group of boys who were dressed identically to me. I didn't even think about them or why we were all wearing the same clothes because I had no intention of staying in this place, whatever it might be. I couldn't wait to find my parents, to tell them what a terrible idea of theirs this was. I re-emerged breathless in the hallway. The front door was partially open and I accelerated through the gap. But our car was nowhere to be seen.

I almost skidded to a halt in the gravel, staring in a mixture of shock and disbelief at the empty space where I'd last seen it parked no longer than ten minutes ago. Most of the other cars had vanished too or were in the process of driving away. I could hear my heart beating faster, a feeling of panic mounting inside me. My mouth suddenly had a dry, funny taste to it, and when I tried to swallow nothing happened.

They wouldn't have gone, not without saying goodbye, of course they wouldn't. But why had our car disappeared? I ran blindly to the edge of the drive, looking left and right at the unbroken line of traffic on the road. The cars all had their headlights on now, a bewildering blur of white and amber beams whizzing past me like tennis balls, causing my head to spin and turning the sleet into tinsel specks. I willed our car to appear out of nowhere, to pull reassuringly into the drive, my parents to climb out with smiles on their faces, with some simple explanation, something that made perfect sense of it all. But there was no sign of them, only the ceaseless churn of engines, and with every passing set of headlights, my situation grew more hopeless, more desperate.

The cold was beginning to numb my feet and hands, so I gave up after a while and ran back towards the front door, which was still half open. Perhaps someone inside would know where my parents were, perhaps that's where my simple explanation lay. I didn't have to look far. The man with the moustache was standing at the end of the hallway with a bell in his hand, as if he was poised to ring it. The odour of burned food and disinfectant had been replaced by noxious oil fumes, the air thick with the heat and sound of scalding, clinking radiators. He stopped, almost in mid-motion, and looked surprised to see me emerge through the gap in the door.

'What do you think you're doing, boy?'

'Where are my parents?' I panted.

'Driving home, I would imagine.' His words were jagged and sharp, like the woman in the white coat. 'You're not allowed outside at this hour.' I saw him glance at his watch.

'When are they coming back?'

He glared at me, as though I had accidentally trodden on his foot or knocked into him or, even worse, poked my tongue out at him. 'I've told you; they've gone.' And he rang the bell, wielding it with such force that the loose strand of hair at the front bobbed and danced frenziedly over his eye in rhythm with the deafening clang.

I waited for him to finish and tried again, even though I could scarcely hear my own voice. 'But they wouldn't leave without me, we're supposed to be going on holiday to a hotel... this hotel, I think,' I added doubtfully. My voice trailed away; I could see that it was useless.

'Don't you have a dormitory to go to, boy? I suggest you take yourself upstairs and get ready for bed. Otherwise, you'll be late for lights out on your first night. Don't just stand there. Hurry up.'

I wanted to tell him that I didn't usually go to bed at this time, but I knew it was not intended as a suggestion and I had no other choice but to return to that awful room. I turned to begin the long ascent. 'Not those stairs,' he shouted, and I froze on the spot. 'Those are staff only – yours are down there.' And he pointed to the end of a corridor that led off the hallway. I followed the direction of his finger, where a throng of boys was noisily stampeding and elbowing their way up a twisting flight of stone steps.

I quickly attached myself to the back of the throng and started to climb. All the way up, my heart was swinging like a fist inside my chest and each step felt more mountainous than the last. The words 'They've gone' kept repeating in my head, exhausting me, forcing me to stop and catch my breath every few seconds, as if all the pain I'd ever felt had been delivered in one excruciating blow. Invariably, someone clattered into my back or smacked into me going in the opposite direction and I spun like a turnstile at a football match.

Eventually, I reached the top of the stairs and walked down the corridor back to the room where minutes earlier I thought I had made good my escape. I could hear voices as I got nearer and had to summon one last sliver of courage and strength before setting foot inside. I kept my head down and, not daring to look around or catch anyone's eye, made straight for the bed. Luckily, no one spoke to me, although there was a faint lull in the conversation and I sensed a couple of heads turn in my direction. Someone had moved my overnight case and placed it beside the chair, but I couldn't bring myself to open it. I sat down on the bed and stared hard at my shoes. There was still a part of me, even at this late hour, which believed my parents would return. They were cutting it fine, though, leaving it to the last minute as usual.

I managed to sneak a glance around the room. I could see that the boys were about the same age as me, possibly a little older but not by much. I recognised some of them as the ones I'd nearly run into earlier on the stairs. Most were already in bed, or in their dressing gowns and slippers, and a couple were boisterously discussing a film they had seen during the holidays, *The Alamo*. I heard them mention Davy Crockett, a name that would have resonated with any seven-year-old boy at that time. Not long after, the man with the moustache appeared in the doorway and the atmosphere instantly shifted. He informed the room he would return in five minutes for lights out and anybody yet to change into his pyjamas had better do so now. I noticed I was the only one still in his clothes and realised that his words were directed solely at me. In that moment, a feeling of sudden dread swept over me. I was going to have to undress in front of others. Something I had never done before.

As embarrassed and awkward as I felt, I jumped to my feet and removed my tie by pulling it over my head, still knotted. I hadn't successfully learned to untie one yet, let alone tie one, and this method not only saved time but would allow me to reuse it again in the morning. I did the same with my shoelaces, hoping with every bone in my body that the boys weren't looking at me. I took off my shirt, my trembling fingers fumbling with the buttons and, keeping my back to the room, put on my dressing gown before clumsily tearing off the rest of my clothes and replacing them with my pyjamas. I threw everything onto the chair and climbed into bed – or at least I would have climbed into bed had I been able to draw back the top sheet and blanket. They appeared stuck fast, immovable, almost as though they had been nailed down. I forced one leg inside, kept the other on the floor and was attempting to somehow prise the sheet and blanket apart, while also removing my dressing gown, when the boy in the bed directly opposite me asked my name.

'John,' I replied, trying to give the impression that this was quite normal behaviour for me.

'No, your name – you know, your *proper* name.'

'He means your surname,' one of the others interjected.

My face must have appeared as blank as my mind.

'Your *last* name.'

'Oh… Lazenby.'

The boy opposite me looked bemused. 'What sort of name is that?'

I finally succeeded in getting enough purchase on the blanket to loosen it and in doing so, lifted my other leg into the bed. 'Viking,' I said, quick as a flash, even surprising myself.

I remembered how my father had proudly explained that our name was of Scandinavian origin. We were descended from the Vikings, or the Norsemen as he often called them, and most of our ancestors had settled in the north of England. 'There's nothing unusual about the name Lazenby in Yorkshire or Cumbria,' he had told me. 'Take a look in a phone book up there one day, you'll find hundreds of us.'

If the boy opposite me was planning to make another comment about my name, he thought better of it because at that exact moment the man returned and any conversation automatically stopped. He marched straight over to the windows and opened them as wide as they would go. No boy was to attempt to close them, regardless of the weather, he warned us. The curtains billowed crazily in the wind, the light bulb swayed alarmingly on its cord and leaves, twigs, branches and scraps of paper blew in. The wind was so loud it appeared to be howling from inside the room, like someone blowing on stretched cellophane. At this point, I thought the man might say a few cheery, consoling words to us: a joke, a funny story, anything to brighten the mood. But it was too much to hope for. He said a perfunctory goodnight, flicked the light switch and closed the door without waiting for our reply, plunging the room into an impenetrable darkness.

And that was when I knew my parents wouldn't be returning.

Within seconds my body was racked with uncontrollable sobs.

I didn't want to cry, but the tears gushed out of me in an unstoppable flow that I had no idea how to stem; they soaked the front of my pyjamas and streamed down the back of my throat until I was forced to drink them. Sometimes when I cried at home, which was rare, I would do it just for effect or out of frustration, to get my own way with something, and would have to scrunch my eyes as tight as I could to even squeeze out a tear. But this was like a torrent. It was impossible not to sniff too, though I did my best to stifle the sound with my sleeve so as not to alert the others. Part of the reason that everything kept pouring down my throat, I quickly discovered, was my pillow. It was so flat and flimsy it made my head feel too big for my body. I tried to pummel some shape into it, but I might as well have pummelled the air for all the good it did. It was a useless pancake of a pillow, a pie with all its stuffing removed.

'Who's blubbing?' I recognised the voice; it was the boy in the bed opposite me. 'Someone's crying, I can hear you. Come on, who is it?'

I sat up, with tears glistening on my cheeks. 'Well, it's not me, for one,' I said and swiftly lay down again, in case the darkness was nothing more than an illusion. My head promptly sank through the pillow where its middle should have been. A sad shadow of a Viking.

Perhaps if I lay completely still and resolutely refused to sniff, the boys would soon lose interest. The occasional snippet of conversation passed between them after that, about what they'd done during the holidays, the films they'd seen, the television programmes they'd watched – *Bonanza, Rawhide, Danger Man* – all of which I knew and loved and all of which made my heart ache more. But mostly they had little appetite for talking and, if anything, seemed happy to be left to their own thoughts. No one said they wished they were at home or mentioned whether they felt sad about that or not. I could have joined in with them if they had, except they might have had trouble shutting me up. I longed for the safety and comfort, the certainty of home. I instantly missed the conversations in the kitchen, where I could eavesdrop to my heart's content. I missed my bedroom, where I could sleep with the door open to the accompaniment of two televisions. I missed Dow, I missed my sister – as much as anything, I missed Ajax and our cat, Bill, and wondered if they missed me as much as I missed them. I even missed the sound of my father polishing his shoes and, on this night of all nights, pondered whether his brushstrokes would be slow and deliberate or fast and relentless.

It wasn't too long before, one by one, the other boys began to drop off, and I detected a subtle change in the pattern of their breathing. Soon I was the last one left awake, adrift with only the chaos of my thoughts for company. I listened to the occasional snore, the odd, garbled word from someone muttering in their sleep. I heard the windowpanes rattle and chatter in their frames and the wind deposit some more of the night's debris into the room as if it were a giant dustbin. How could anyone expect me to sleep locked in the suffocating, starchy grip of these sheets, with a pillow that had no middle, with these strangers I hadn't clapped eyes on until a few minutes ago, with twigs and leaves flying past my head at regular intervals? How I envied the other boys their knack of being able to fall asleep so casually, of not having to feel thunderstruck or devastated like me – alone, lost, confused and scared.

I even tried to convince myself that I hated my parents in the hope it might make me feel better in some way. Yet I couldn't hate them, no matter how badly I wanted to; I just hated what they seemed to have done to me. I hated the pain of being heartbroken, of being tricked and betrayed, of not knowing when or if I would ever see them or our home again. I hated the fact they had left me in this place without saying goodbye. And that was when it hit me: the word that perfectly described my life, the word that summed up the latest *un*-person I had inevitably become.

Unwanted.

CHAPTER FOUR

WAS HE SHOT OR BAYONETED?

No sooner had my eyes snapped open the next morning than I was wide awake, alert and alive to every sound and movement. Of course, I knew instantly where I was and would have given anything to have come slowly to the surface, to have found myself back at home where I belonged. I took a quick look around the room. It appeared to have shrunk somehow in the morning light, narrower, more hemmed in, the beds crammed closer together, the washstand and the trunks taking up every inch of space. It didn't surprise me that I was the only one awake or that my head already thrummed with terrifying thoughts of what the new day might bring.

What surprised me about my first night in this place was that I'd managed to sleep at all. I hadn't expected that; I had expected to see in the grey dawn instead. Besides, I didn't think you could sleep through sorrow that raw. But at a meeting point somewhere between pain and exhaustion, I must have grown tired of trying to stay awake, or used up all my tears, and eventually dropped off. It wasn't a deep sleep – it was fitful and fretful, almost as if I knew I was sleeping, pinned in these sheets, in a strange bed, a strange room, miles from home. The events of the day were so indelibly stamped on my mind that I relived them over and over in my dreams… and in those dreams, my parents were always driving away from me. On one occasion, my mother glanced back at me and I caught the sadness in her eyes.

One of my first thoughts on waking, once I established that the day had dawned much like any other, was of my bedroom at home. I pictured my empty, unslept-in bed and wondered if my drawing books, which I'd meant to bring to Broadstairs but had forgotten at the last moment, were still strewn across it. I couldn't imagine I would have any use for them here. It was agony to think of life carrying on at home as though nothing had happened, the everyday routines, the rituals – but just not with me. I looked around again at the other beds, at the motionless forms inside them; most of the boys had pulled their blankets over their heads during the night and burrowed under the sheets to keep themselves warm. The curtains were still flapping wildly in the wind like the wings of some monstrous bird, and I'd half-expected to see snowflakes whirling around the room, to find a sifting of snow on our blankets, a dusting on the floorboards. Instead, the occasional leaf fluttered harmlessly past my bed before floating down to join the shifting carpet of leaves and twigs.

I lay there for several minutes waiting for something to happen, for someone to wake up and distract me from my thoughts. It struck me there was no feeling quite as odd as waking up in a room full of strangers, apart perhaps from falling asleep in one. I was mulling this over when I heard a sound of spongy footsteps on the linoleum outside and immediately sat up. The footsteps drew closer, the door opened wide and the woman in the white coat bustled in. She switched on the light, almost blinding me with its stark white glare, drew back the curtains and slammed the windows shut. In a frenzy, the wind hammered against them to be let back in, before the sound slowly dropped to a moan. She then passed through the room, rapping her knuckles brusquely on each bed frame as she went. 'Time to get up. Wake up. Rouse yourselves,' she repeated, until she stopped abruptly at the foot of mine. 'There's no sleeping in here,' she said, although it must have been as clear as day to her that I was the only one fully awake, sitting up in bed, not buried beneath the sheets. I could tell at once she had it in for me, but as desperate as I felt, I tried to give her a look that said, *I'm already awake in case you hadn't noticed.* No doubt it failed miserably.

She was followed into the room by two older boys in their dressing gowns and slippers, each carrying an enamel jug of steaming hot water. They proceeded to pour the water into the plastic bowls in the washstand, filling them almost halfway. The pair could not have appeared any more disinterested in their task if they tried. One of them, wearing a silk dressing gown with a long, knitted scarf twined flamboyantly around his neck, clearly considered it so far beneath his dignity that he maintained an expression of total disdain throughout, as if he had just been assigned to the worst job in the world. They didn't look at anyone or utter a word and on completion of the chore promptly disappeared, leaving clouds of steam floating in the freezing air like a signature of their disapproval.

When they had gone, the other boys struggled out of bed and stumbled over to the washstand, stretching, yawning and rubbing their eyes. I swiftly followed their lead, taking my place at the one unoccupied basin, aware that the woman was watching my every move. Still half asleep, they removed their pyjama tops, dipped their flannels in the water and gingerly applied them to their faces, necks and armpits. One boy squeezed his wet flannel over his head and let the water drip into the basin before towelling it dry. 'Don't forget to use your soap, all of you,' I heard the woman say.

My first mistake of the day – the first of many, if you discount climbing out of bed – was to urgently splash a handful of boiling water into my face and nearly scald myself. I felt the burning rivulets of water run down my chest. For several seconds I was unable to open my eyes and blindly groped around, fumbling for a towel that wasn't there.

'Did your mother forget to provide you with a flannel and towel then?' the woman asked, making no effort to disguise the scorn in her voice.

I couldn't imagine that she would be talking to anyone else. 'I don't know… I don't think so,' I replied, not daring to open my eyes until the stabbing pain had subsided.

'I expect you'll find what you're looking for in your overnight case,' she said. 'That's if you can even be bothered to open it.'

I managed to feel my way over to the bed without tripping over my trunk and, still dripping water, opened the case and rummaged around inside. Sure enough, I found a towel and a sponge bag. I heard the woman give a grunt, as if to say *I told you so*. I rubbed my eyes with the towel. It smelled unmistakably of home and I held it tightly against my face, breathing it in as deeply as I could, inhaling the comforting aroma. Miraculously, when I opened my eyes a few seconds later, I could still see. The sponge bag contained a flannel, a bar of soap, a toothbrush, toothpaste, tooth mug, a hairbrush and a comb. I went to close the case but something else inside, something shiny, caught my eye and to my surprise I pulled out a book.

It was an illustrated history book, about the size and thickness of an annual. I eagerly flicked through the colourful images: Roman soldiers, ancient Britons and Vikings jumped out at me, the smell of the new print rising with them from the fresh, crisp pages. I was sure it was a present from my mother; she was always finding books for me, ones with pictures. This was her way of letting me know she was thinking of me, she still cared, she hadn't forgotten me. I felt a surge of hope and thumbed through the remaining pages, the years disappearing in a blur, the images flying wondrously before my eyes.

The final picture was of a space rocket being launched in a blaze of orange fire, the stars and stripes clearly visible on its fuselage. I had heard enough on the radio about what was called the space race to know that the US launched its rockets from Cape Canaveral. I also knew that a Russian astronaut – I could see his smiling face but couldn't remember his name – had completed a single orbit around the Earth in April 1961 to become the first man to enter space.* That summer crackled incessantly with news of the space race, and I spent much of it running between the kitchen and the garden, always keeping an ear out for the latest on the radio. Everyone seemed to be saying that Russia would beat the US and win the race to land the first man on the moon. Sometimes when I lay on the grass and looked up at the infinite sky, I almost believed I could taste rocket fuel on the tip of my tongue.

'You haven't got time for that now. Put the book away,' the woman snapped, bringing me back to earth with a jolt. 'Hurry up and finish washing and then put your clothes on. If you've not washed and dressed and made your bed by the time I return, there'll be trouble.' It appeared to me that I was already in trouble, but I quickly closed the book and did as I was told. 'Breakfast is in five minutes. This school doesn't revolve around you, whatever you might think.'

So that was it. *I was at school.* The words resounded unhappily inside my head for a moment or two while I tried to take them in

---

* His name was Yuri Alekseyevich Gagarin.

and then turned into a thunderclap – several thunderclaps – that re-verberated through me like an aftershock. If I had still been unsure of where I was when I woke that morning, I certainly knew now. I suppose I would have found out soon enough at some point or other during the day. In truth, perhaps a part of me already suspect-ed; I just didn't want to admit it. To have done so would have meant having to accept that my parents had lied to me, had pretended to take me on a holiday that didn't exist, had abandoned me… at a boarding school, as it now turned out. And somewhere deep down inside, I still couldn't bring myself to believe that.

I washed in a daze, brushed my teeth, rinsed my mouth in hot water and put on my clothes in the same frantic, fumbling manner with which I'd torn them off the night before. Typically, I didn't run a comb through my hair – it never would have occurred to me to do so. I wondered if I'd ever get used to dressing and undressing in front of others. This was the first time I had attempted to make a bed, but as the sheets were still tightly tucked in, there didn't seem a lot for me to do other than smooth out the wrinkles on the blan-ket and thump the pillow a few times. It was impossible to think straight. My brain was moving too fast for my body, or was it the other way around?

'Matron will go mad when she sees that,' one of the boys said, pointing to my bed. I looked around at the other beds – they matched each other perfectly, without a crease to be seen.

'You'd better do something about your tie as well,' another chipped in. I fetched it from somewhere around my left shoulder and tried to tighten the knot, but it appeared to be stuck.

'Who's matron?' I asked.

'That's Mrs Rudd – you know, the woman who doesn't like you,' the boy who slept in the bed next to me explained. He couldn't resist a smile, I noticed. Somewhere on a floor below a bell had started to ring incessantly. 'That's the bell for breakfast,' he added and started towards the door. 'Come on, matron will be back any second. If you want to have something to eat, you'd better follow us. It won't be very nice, mind.'

'Yeah, don't say we didn't warn you,' another called.

As if on cue, Mrs Rudd reappeared in the doorway just as I was hurrying out. The others had already taken off down the corridor and I could hear them shouting to each other as they clattered down the stairs.

'Just a minute,' she said. 'Where do you think you're going? You haven't made your bed yet, and you can't go to breakfast with your tie looking like that. Come back here.' But I didn't stop, I just kept running.

On reaching the dining hall, I was immediately confronted by a sea of faces and didn't know where to put myself until I spotted some of the boys from my dormitory near the back of the room, seated at one of six long wooden tables. I went over and joined them. They were too busy talking among themselves to pay much attention to me, but at least no one told me to go and sit somewhere else. The conversation of some seventy boys or more, all talking at the same time and at the same intensity and volume, roared in my ears. I felt as if a freight train was bearing down on me. I sat at the end of the table next to a tall window and looked out at a concrete playing area, a set of cricket stumps, a pair of goalposts chalked on the red brick wall in front of me, the boundary of the playing fields just visible out of the corner of my eye. Inside, there was a wide serving hatch at one end of the hall and a fireplace with luminous green tiles and a collection of battered, dented cups and trophies arranged along the mantlepiece at the other. I wondered what you had to do to win one of those cups. Oddly, a vase of artificial flowers stood in the middle of each table, looking almost as out of place as me.

Breakfast consisted of scrambled egg on fried bread, wheeled to the tables on a fleet of ancient, rattling trolleys. The plates were handed to the boy at the head of each table and then passed down the line. No one was allowed to touch their food until everyone had been served and the man with the moustache had said grace. And then came the roar again. At first, I thought it was a race to see who could finish their meal first and quickly joined in, though I wasn't in the slightest bit hungry. The smell of it made me feel faintly sick too. I had barely cut into the fried bread when, to my horror, the whole thing suddenly disintegrated in a shower of fragments, most of which flew across the table, with one landing on the plate of the boy opposite me. I watched it touch down with precision, like a miniature space capsule, in the middle of his scrambled egg – a trick I could not have repeated had I attempted it a hundred times over. For about a minute, I was unable to take my eyes off it. Thankfully, it must have happened too fast for anyone to notice, particularly the boy opposite, who had been in earnest conversation with the person on his left at the time. Nonetheless, I was in two minds as to whether I should point it out to him or just pretend it hadn't happened. In the end it didn't matter because he turned back to his plate, picked up the fragment on the end of his fork, put it into his mouth and swallowed it down with a dollop of egg.

I felt relieved and more at ease after that potential embarrassment had been avoided, and when no one was looking, helped myself to a slice of toast. But it was too soggy and the square of butter that came with it too hard to spread. I didn't want to send another item of food flying across the table, so gave up on it. The cloudy grey tea, poured from a big copper teapot by a member of the kitchen staff, had warm milk mixed with it and was so weak it was virtually taste-less – even with the four or five spoonfuls of sugar I heaped into it.

I spent the rest of breakfast listening to the swerve and flow of the conversation. It seemed to have no end or beginning that I could see but just swept round and round, in constant forward movement, like cars trying to knock each other off a racetrack. So much of what was said went over my head anyway – the names, the nicknames – though nearly everyone had something to say, usually at the same time, about the new term, the lessons and the food. None of it was good, none of it reassuring. I learned that French and Latin lessons were hated without exception, feared even, and the very thought of having to attend one already filled me with instant dread. If the small flame of hope that this was not a school still flickered feebly inside me, it was ruthlessly snuffed out in the minutes that followed.

'I've forgotten how terrible the food tastes,' one boy said and pre-tended to push his plate away in disgust.

'I haven't,' another laughed. 'You can't forget something that bad.'

One boy, who appeared to be a couple of years older than the others, announced that at his last school there had been a choice of cereals – cornflakes or shredded wheat – for breakfast, followed by what he somewhat pompously described as a properly cooked hot meal.

'Welcome to Hildersham House,' he was told, and everyone laughed.

I naturally assumed that Hildersham House must be the name of my new school and repeated it countless times under my breath – *Hil-der-sham House, Hil-der-sham House* – until I had lodged it firmly in my brain.

'At least there's only ten weeks this term, not twelve,' somebody else piped up. 'That's a relief, anyway. It's those last two weeks that always get to you.'

'That's true, but the Easter holidays are shorter too,' the boy opposite me replied, using the side of his knife like a brush to entice the remnants of fried bread onto his fork. 'So, it doesn't make much difference really.' He could have been reading from a train timetable for all the enthusiasm he summoned.

I had never thought much about time when I was at St Peter's Court. For a start, I didn't have any need to. I was a day boy and everything was done for me. I saw my parents every day, I went home at the end of each afternoon and watched television, usually westerns, in the evenings before going to bed and usually without a care in the world. Time didn't matter. I knew some days were longer than others, especially during certain lessons, but that was about it. Even so, I couldn't believe anybody would think ten weeks was a short amount of time, a cause for celebration, and worried how I'd ever manage to survive that long on my own. Ten weeks felt like a year to me; it made me dizzy just to think about it. It was like Mount Everest.

'Who's the new boy over there?' someone asked and I saw a row of heads automatically swivel in my direction. They might just as well have pointed at me.

'Oh, him,' one of the boys from my dormitory shrugged. 'He's named after some Viking.'

The boy who asked the question didn't appear to have an answer to that and the conversation moved rapidly on, the cars still careening endlessly around the track.

• • •

There was one piece of good news, at least, for me to digest with my breakfast: there were no lessons during the first two days of a new term. This fact was confirmed before we left the dining hall by the man with the moustache – or the headmaster, Mr Snowden, as I now knew him. These two days were to be spent wisely, he advised us, so that all boys were back in the routine, reacquainted with their surroundings, refreshed and raring to go once the real business of school began again. 'I would suggest therefore, looking around the room, that some of you might want to shake the cobwebs from your heads.' The comment prompted a rustle of nervous laughter. This was followed by an announcement that school assembly, which all boys had to attend, would be held at midday in the recreation hall.

We were filing out after breakfast – I was following close on the heels of the others from my dormitory, making sure I didn't get left behind this time – when I heard someone call my name. A woman was sitting on the window seat in the main hall, the playing fields stretching away behind her like a carpet slowly unfurling into the distance. I took in the white hair fastened into a bun, the glasses dangling from a chain around her neck, a soft, inquisitive expression on her face. She raised a hand and beckoned me over.

'You're new here, aren't you?' she asked, putting on her glasses to observe me in closer detail.

'Yes,' I told her.

'I thought so.' She introduced herself as Mrs Blackman, the wife of the deputy headmaster, and pointed to a tall town house, just visible through the open door, on the other side of the road directly opposite. It was almost completely submerged beneath a deep green cascade of ivy. 'That's us, just across the way there. How are you settling in?'

'OK,' I replied. But there was something about the flatness of my voice, the dismal echo of it inside my head and the expression on her face that made me want to repeat myself. 'Yes, OK,' I tried again, introducing a little more energy into my tone but being careful not to overdo it.

She leaned forward slightly. 'Are you homesick?' The question took me by surprise and I looked askance at her, unsure of how I should respond.

I hadn't heard the word before but that wasn't what worried me – it was the fact that it felt so unnatural, so abnormal to my ears. I had always thought of home before as a place of joy, of hope and warmth, safety, kindness, love and laughter – an abundance of laughter – not one of sickness, dread, fear, pain or sadness. The thought was destabilising, but I didn't have the word for that yet, either.

'I'm asking because of your eyes,' she said, mistaking my silence for reticence and staring at me intently through her glasses. 'Have you been crying?'

'No.' The word was out of my mouth before I could stop it.

'They look very red and raw to me, puffy too.'

'Oh, that… Mum says that's because I'm always staying awake,' I asserted, as confidently as I could.

She seemed bemused by my reply for a moment. 'Do you mean that you don't sleep at night?'

'Hardly ever… well, sometimes… not very much.'

'I certainly hope that's not true. You'll need all your sleep here, especially when lessons and games start.'

I had already noted during our brief exchange how often she put on her glasses and then removed them, a process she repeated with almost bewildering regularity; it was as if she didn't like what she was seeing at first but then felt compelled to take another look. Even when she wasn't wearing her glasses, she was holding them permanently at the ready rather than letting them dangle free, so she could whisk them on and off at a moment's notice. Sometimes she just lifted them to her eyes without putting them on and held them there for a few seconds, like she was watching a ship in the distance through a pair of binoculars. More disconcertingly, perhaps, she had a habit of nodding her head while she talked and listened, a gentle swaying motion that gave the impression she was travelling on a train. It was so noticeable that I wondered whether I wasn't supposed to nod back at her.

'That's most irregular,' she continued after a lengthy pause. 'We can't have boys not sleeping.' She removed her glasses again, breathed on the lenses and looked quizzically at me for several seconds. She was warm yet strangely distant at the same time. 'Anyway, boys have always slept exceptionally well here – they remark on it. It's the sea air that does it, of course. You see, you'll be no different.'

I realised I hadn't seen or heard the sea since my arrival. 'How far is the sea?' I asked, suddenly snapping to attention.

'Not so far, about twenty minutes by foot, but you have to walk briskly,' she said, waving a hand in its direction. 'You'll be taking plenty of walks there this term, don't you worry about that – two walks a week and one on Sunday.'

So, the sea did exist – it wasn't just another lie, conveniently made up by my parents to soften the blow before they enacted their getaway plan. 'And Bleak House?' I asked. 'Is that there as well?'

'Bleak House?' She frowned. The glasses were back on in an instant. 'No one's ever asked me that before. Yes, that's still there – at least it was the last time I looked. Why?'

Who knows how long our strange, halting conversation might have lasted had one of the boys from my dormitory not arrived at that moment to inform me that I was to report at once to matron. I think Mrs Blackman appeared more relieved than me at his intervention.

When I returned to the dormitory, it was to discover there was no sign of Mrs Rudd or anyone else for that matter, but my blanket, sheets and pillow were reduced to a crumpled state on the floor. The bottom of the mattress was hanging off the side of the bed, the top wedged among the bed springs like someone clinging to a life raft. In my hurry to get down to breakfast, I had stupidly left my new book on the bed and it had also been flung onto the heap, along with my pyjamas, dressing gown and slippers. I rescued the book and put it on my chair, having first examined it for any signs of damage. I was just retrieving my pyjamas, dressing gown and slippers when I heard Mrs Rudd enter the room.

'Oh, so you've finally deigned to make an appearance, have you?' She didn't wait for a response or an explanation but informed me that from now on I was to report to her each morning before breakfast with my hair combed, my tie knotted, my laces done up and my bed properly made. 'Until I'm satisfied that you look respectable and you've learned to make your bed like the other boys. We can't have another repeat of your performance today. Now pick up those two sheets and hand them to me. We make our beds with hospital corners here. Do you know what hospital corners are?'

I didn't even know what homesickness was, what hope would I have with hospital corners? But whatever they were, and they sounded deeply unpleasant to me, they couldn't have been any worse than the images I was already conjuring in my mind. All I could think of were bandages and blood – gallons of blood – probably because the last time I went to hospital, to have several stitches inserted in an ugly cut at the back of my head, my shirt was awash with it.

She straightened the mattress and shook out the sheets. 'I'll show you how to make a bed with hospital corners and then I want you to do it. I won't demonstrate it again, so pay attention and watch carefully – you've wasted enough of my time today as it is.' She laid the sheet over the bed, erased any creases with her hand, gave the end of it a hefty tug and tucked it in under the base of the mattress. 'It's so simple even you could do it.' If I had learned anything in my short life to date, it was that nothing was ever as simple as people made it out to be.

And so it proved. One moment she was explaining how the over-hang of the top sheet must always be equal on both sides, which was confusing enough as I had no idea what an overhang was, the next she was making a fold in the bottom of the sheet and placing it on top of the mattress to form a 45-degree angle from the corner of the bed. I had even less idea of what a 45-degree angle was. It was at that precise point in the procedure that I felt my concentration waver and my mind start to switch off. I recognised the signs instantly: a haze formed in front of my eyes, my head emptied faster than a basin of water, her words and actions blurred into one... and before I knew it, the demonstration was over.

'And that's a hospital corner,' she announced, gesticulating at her handiwork. I found myself staring at what I could only describe as a line in a sheet. For a minute, I wondered whether I hadn't missed something glaringly obvious and looked hard at it again. No, it was most definitely a line in a sheet – an extremely straight line to be exact. Whatever else I was expecting, it wasn't that. 'You could put a shilling in there,' she said, pinching the edge of it between her thumb and forefinger, 'and it wouldn't fall out, it's that tight.' So that would explain why I needed a hammer and chisel to climb in and out of bed. 'Now, are there any questions?'

I had one burning question: why? But I didn't dare ask it. 'No,' I muttered, and realised that I still had no clue as to why they were called hospital corners.

She gave a grunt of disbelief and tugged the sheets apart again, leaving them scrunched up in a ball at the end of the bed. 'In that case, I'll be back in ten minutes, when I'll expect to find your bed remade in the correct fashion.'

Despite her optimistic expectations, I spent the next few hours embroiled in a long, painful battle with a pair of sheets, an experience that was made even more excruciating by the frequent appearances of Mrs Rudd every ten minutes or so. Sometimes she would pass comment on my abject attempts to create a hospital corner – 'that's a flap, not a hospital corner'; 'you could stick half a house in there, there's so much room'; 'that's an apology for a straight line'; 'if I can pull it apart, it's not a hospital corner' – other times, she would drag the sheets off the bed, deposit them on the floor with almost undisguised glee and say nothing, except 'Start again'. On another occasion, frustration got the better of her and she snatched the sheet out of my hand. 'Give it here,' she said gruffly. She redemonstrated a 45-degree angle but still to no avail. 'Didn't your parents teach you anything?'

The one time I managed a passable resemblance to a hospital corner – admittedly, more by accident than design – it also failed the test. 'You've done only one side of the bed,' she pointed out. 'Do it again.' It had never occurred to me that I needed to do both sides. By which time, I felt sick enough to be in a hospital.

In the end, I was spared from any further humiliation by the bell – its harsh clang sounding a welcome note of release for once. 'That's the bell for school assembly,' she said, returning to the room. 'You'd better run along or knowing you, you'll be late for that as well.' I dropped what I was doing and made off downstairs as quickly as I could, with my bed still unmade and Mrs Rudd's voice repeating like a machine gun in my ears. Somehow, I knew I had not heard the last of hospital corners.

I was not late for assembly on this occasion and found my way there by following the first group of boys I bumped into. The recreation hall was situated outside in a barn-like building, no more than a dozen paces from the school, connected by a small, roofed walkway. The room had a woody, dusty quality to it and a smell that reminded me of our garden shed at home. We sat in metal chairs with canvas seats and backs, beneath rows of honours boards with gold lettering and a column of high windows, through which the light trickled onto us. Mr Snowden stood behind a lectern and addressed the room from a raised wooden stage, the staff seated on either side of him. The majority wore the archetypal uniform of the independent schoolteacher: tweed jackets with elbow pads, the occasional flourish of a silk handkerchief flowing from a top pocket, a club tie, grey flannel trousers, brown leather or suede shoes. Some sat with their arms folded, some stared rigidly ahead and one or two reached into their jacket pockets for the reassurance of a pipe, which they cradled lovingly in their hands or filled with tobacco, longing for the moment when they could relax and light up again in the comfort of the common room. It was almost as though they belonged to some wandering troupe of school masters.

There were three who didn't fit the mould, however, and I could not take my eyes off two of them at first because they dressed so differently: a stout woman in a dark-blue overcoat and a beret, who we learned taught music, and a man with longish greying hair swept back behind his ears, a brown corduroy jacket and black jeans with the bottoms rolled up, who was the art teacher. The third was a young woman in a skirt and green cardigan who sat with her hands in her lap at the far end of the stage, a slight gap between her and the others as if she had deliberately distanced herself from them.

I heard my name read out as one of a handful of new boys, along with a new member of staff who was introduced to us as Miss Shepherd. The young woman I had noticed briefly got to her feet and gave us all a beaming smile, so bright that I was surprised to find myself grinning back at her. After that, I spent most of the time drifting in and out of what was being said or looking idly around, until Mr Snowden asked for a show of hands from any boys interested in joining the boxing club. I saw several hands go up and watched as a couple of boys exchanged challenging, knowing looks with each other, smacking their fists playfully in their palms as they did so. Before I knew what I'd done, my hand was in the air too.

I heard one or two boys whisper and snigger in the seats behind me but thought nothing of it. Mr Snowden nodded approvingly at the number of hands and made a note of each name as he went. I couldn't help but notice that every boy with his hand up was at least two or three times bigger than me; some were as old as twelve or thirteen and in some cases appeared even older. Gradually, he worked his way down to me – the only boy with his hand still held aloft. But instead of making a note of my name as he had done with the others, he stopped abruptly, returned his pen to his inside jacket pocket with an air of finality and proceeded to turn to the next item on his agenda. 'The places that remain out of bounds to all boys this term are as follows...'

I could not understand why he had chosen to ignore me. At first, I wondered if he might not have seen me, though that seemed unlikely considering he had looked straight at me before putting away

his pen. Perhaps he would take a note of my name at a later stage
– though that seemed unlikely too. I tried to sit up taller, stretched
my arm as high as it could go and puffed out my chest, if such a
thing was possible. I knew that my father had boxed at school and I
reckoned if he could do it, so could I. 'You learn a lot about yourself
in a boxing ring,' he told me once, intriguingly. By this time, I was
starting to squirm in my seat. I sensed heads turn in my direction
and detected the unmistakable sound of suppressed laughter. The
staff, who had scarcely registered a flicker of movement until this
point, began to shuffle uncomfortably in their seats or vigorously
cross and uncross their legs. Meanwhile, the boy seated directly
behind me inserted his hand into the gap in the back of my chair
and, for no apparent reason, grabbed my elbow to try to force my
arm down. In my efforts to keep it upright, a small tussle developed
between us. I managed to wrench it free just as Mr Snowden looked
up from his notes.

'Would the boy with his hand up please desist from doing so
before his arm drops off,' he said. There was a smattering of laughter. 'As far as I am aware – and do correct me if I'm wrong – boxing
has yet to introduce a weight division for someone of his size. Let
alone find a suitable opponent for him.' There was more laughter,
though at no stage was it anything other than polite. A few of the
staff even permitted themselves a wry smile. Still, it felt like a private
joke in which I was not included. Reluctantly, I lowered my arm. At
that moment, my eyes alighted on a boy sitting in the row in front
of me. He was certainly smaller than me, lighter too. It crossed my
mind that if I could somehow persuade him to take up boxing, we
could maybe have our very own title fight: the belt for the school's
smallest boy, perhaps. 'My advice to you', Mr Snowden continued,

addressing me in person for the first time, 'is to volunteer again in two or three years' time, when hopefully you will have grown bigger.'

His words were delivered with all the force of a knockout blow. My boxing career was over before it had begun.

• • •

I had about as much understanding of the concept of staying under the radar, keeping my head down or making myself invisible as I had of writing my own name correctly or capturing lightning in a bottle. I was wholly unprepared for the unfamiliarity of my new surroundings and my inability to adapt, to respond accordingly, was matched only by my impulsivity, my capacity to attract unwanted attention to myself at almost every turn and usually in the most inappropriate moments. I was not even one full day into my new life at boarding school and it seemed I wasn't finished yet. To tell the truth, I was only warming up.

On the final afternoon before the start of lessons, Mrs Blackman conducted the new boys on a guided tour of the school. It started in the classrooms – complete with their vast blackboards and rows of ancient wooden desks with attached seats, like battle-scarred chariots – and concluded in the chapel. A dark, solemn place, the chapel was sealed off from the rest of the school by a huge pair of oak doors, which were kept permanently locked when it was not in use. Inside, it smelled in equal parts of furniture polish and dust. The sounds coming from outside dissolved within seconds as Mrs Blackman shepherded us past ranks of empty pews, precarious stacks of hymn books and piled-up cassocks. I took in the stained-glass windows, the lectern carved in the shape of a golden eagle – the pale light glinting wanly off its outstretched wings – and the soaring, wood-and-metal pipe organ, which, because of its bewildering assortment of pedals, levers, switches, knobs and buttons, could easily have passed for a time machine.

On our way out, Mrs Blackman stopped in a small recess at the rear of the chapel where a ceremonial army helmet and a sword were hanging on the wall, next to a wooden plaque. She instructed us to gather round. The helmet and sword belonged to Mr Snowden's uncle, who had been killed in the First World War while serving with the 1st Battalion of the Hertfordshire Territorial Force, she explained. Lieutenant Harcourt John Snowden was a school master too – a time-honoured family tradition – and had been a pupil at Hildersham House almost seventy years ago. We learned that he and his regiment had fought with distinction at the Battle of Ypres in November 1914, and she repeated the name slowly to make sure that we remembered it: Y-p-r-e-s.

'Now who thinks they can say Ypres?' she enquired.

'Ypres, Ypres,' we trilled back at her, like fledglings that had fallen out of their nests.

'Good,' she replied. 'And can anybody tell me which country Ypres is in?' There was an abrupt pause. 'Nobody?'

I wasn't thinking about her question. I gazed up again at the black helmet, at its silver fittings, the deadly sharp spike on top, the insignia on the front, the chin strap. I even noticed that a thin film of dust had collected on the surface of the helmet. I looked again at the mighty sword sleeping in its scabbard of khaki-brown leather, at the intricate pattern on the brass hilt, and could contain my curiosity no longer.

'Was he shot or bayoneted?' I asked.

Mrs Blackman, who had been reaching for the glasses around her neck in preparation for providing the answer to her question, gave a short gasp, let her glasses dangle free and placed her hand on her throat. You could have heard dust falling in the silence that followed while we all waited on her next breath, open-mouthed, like a small huddle of ghosts in the gloom of the recess.

'Well...' she said finally, putting her glasses back on and staring hard at me; she was not so much nodding her head this time as shaking it.

'When he was killed, I mean,' I added quickly.

'I'm thoroughly aware of what you meant,' she said, seeming to recover her composure. 'I heard it the first time, thank you, and do not need to hear it again. None of us do. Once is quite enough.' And she held out the flat of her hand to me, as if to reinforce the point before I could open my mouth again. 'We do not ask questions like that and we most certainly do not ask them in a place of prayer and contemplation. Lieutenant Snowden made the supreme sacrifice for his country and that is all we need to know.' Whereupon she ushered us out of the chapel and back into the light.

And so it was that a day later, a letter of complaint about my conduct, penned by Mrs Blackman, was winging its way to my parents in Sussex. It appeared my enquiry about the death of Mr Snowden's uncle had triggered a succession of alarm bells within the walls of the school – something that needed to be urgently addressed. To me, it was no different from any of the details or facts I craved in my life at that time. To Mrs Blackman, though, my unfortunate question, as she put it, not only displayed an 'unhealthy enthusiasm for the means of Lieutenant Snowden's death' but what she feared might prove an 'undue interest in all things violent' on my part. 'The question was, I am afraid to have to inform you, bloodthirsty in the extreme,' she wrote to my parents.

To their credit, whatever my parents thought about my failings – and they were myriad – they knew that a penchant for violence was not one of them. It was no secret I loved westerns and war films too, when I was allowed to watch them, but what boy didn't? Much later, my mother admitted to me that they had laughed off the letter and filed it away as a curiosity, thinking nothing more of it; my parents' reactions never ceased to surprise me. Indeed, their filing system proved so efficient that I didn't discover it for another five decades – the powder-blue headed notepaper still as crisp and new as the day it had been written.

The irony of Mrs Blackman's concerns about my bloodthirsty tendencies would become all too apparent during the coming days and weeks of my first term at boarding school. Not that I knew the meaning of irony back then, of course, but I certainly knew a beating when I saw one. I was about to learn that it was not me who had the unquenchable thirst for 'all things violent'.

CHAPTER FIVE

STOP!

The next few weeks did not exactly fly by like the wind-torn pages of a calendar in one of the old black and white movies that regularly screened on Sunday afternoon TV, but at least I had a sense of time moving, a rhythm to the passing days. I stopped crying after lights out too, and my yearning for home – a deadweight of sorrow that weighed on my chest last thing at night and first thing in the morning – suddenly lifted. Home was no longer the first thought in my head. I could breathe again. Even the nights, when the gaps in the conversation grew steadily longer until everyone but me had fallen asleep, were not quite so daunting.

However, in acquiring this new-found freedom, I couldn't help but feel as if I had entered into a strange pact with some dark force or other – the kind that exacts a price for every wish granted – because no sooner had I stopped missing everyone at home than I felt guilty I wasn't missing them enough.

Fortunately, I didn't have time to dwell on it for long and soon had other things to occupy my mind – when I wasn't losing myself down the endless corridors that tunnelled and twisted their way through the building, that is. Some of these had yet more corridors leading off them, making it almost impossible to tell whether you were at the head or the tail of the snake. They may have been easy to get lost in – for me, at least – but they also made for perfect running tracks. Like the others, I sprinted everywhere, and the corridors, the passageways, the stairs, the ceilings above our heads resounded all day with the churn of our running feet. Occasionally, Mr Snowden appeared and ordered boys to stop running, and the sound ceased for a minute, as if catching its breath, before inevitably starting up again. I had been at Hildersham House for nearly three weeks before I noticed that the noise was always at its loudest whenever I was sitting at my desk. It wasn't until I looked down one day that I realised that the sound was my own feet drumming on the spot, in perpetual motion, beating a restless tattoo on the floorboards. Sometimes it felt as if I was running to catch up with myself, with my pounding heart and senses.

By this time, I had learned to tie my laces and successfully knot my tie, even though I was still countless corridors behind the others in terms of what I could or couldn't do. My hospital corners, for instance, remained a work in progress, to put it mildly. If Mrs Rudd was prepared to cut me some slack with my appearance – even she had her good days – there was no such leniency or margin for error when it came to her obsession with my bed-making skills. It had to be exact, immaculate, or else she would repeat the two words I dreaded the most: 'Start again.' Invariably, this would result in her tugging the bed clothes unceremoniously to the floor. Sometimes it felt as if my days began and ended with hospital corners. Every morning, I would try to perfect sheets that were as tight as Fort Knox, in her words, and then later attempt to breach the fortress's defences just so I could climb into bed at night.

I had my own obsessions, too. On my many journeys around the school during those first few weeks, I was constantly intrigued by the number of ringing telephones I heard – in Mr Snowden's study, the sitting room off the main hall, the school office. They were never quiet, never still – sometimes they were left to ring off the hook for minutes on end. As my mind routinely spiralled between hope and despair, I even managed to convince myself it was my parents calling. On those days, I waited outside the door at every opportunity in the hope they might want to hear my voice again or have a quick word with me. In truth, I couldn't understand why it had taken them this long. Better still, I told myself, they had relented, they couldn't bear to be without me or to keep up the pretence a day longer; they were coming to collect me and all would be forgiven.

In my imagination, Mr Snowden would open his study door and deliver the happy news. 'That's your parents I've just been speaking to on the phone, boy. Apparently, they've decided to take you home.' I could feel the excitement ignite inside me and imagined the words he would use. 'Go and find matron at once and start packing your things – they're arriving this afternoon to collect you.' But he never did and they never did. The reality was that I was on my own, and whenever he walked out of his study after taking a phone call, it was to find me standing in his way, looking up expectantly.

'You again. What are you waiting out here for, boy?'

'Nothing, sir.'

And he brushed past me. 'Well, don't get in people's way then.'

Another obsession of mine revolved around the length of the Easter term and how quickly or slowly ten weeks would pass. I would ask the question of anyone who had the misfortune to engage with me, both boys and teachers, in my desperation to learn the answer. Of course, the pessimists, of which there were any number at Hildersham House, delighted in telling me it would be painfully slow. 'You'll wonder if it will ever end,' one explained. The optimists assured me it would soon start to speed up: 'It goes faster after week five,' I was informed. 'How much longer until week five?' I replied. The majority of those I questioned, including Mr Snowden, merely looked at me as if I were a buffoon and walked off without bothering to reply.

Undoubtedly, the best piece of advice I received came from one of the boys in my dormitory, James Teague. 'The term definitely won't go any quicker if you keep asking that question,' he pointed out assertively when I interrogated him about the length of ten weeks. 'You've got to stop thinking about it – thinking about it makes it go slower. If you want to make it go faster, don't think about it any more.' Even I could understand the logic behind that.

Teague was barely eight years old yet he unerringly knew the answer to most things. He could also talk about subjects he knew precisely nothing about and still make you believe every word, even if at times he was clearly making it up as he went along. If we guessed as much, we made no attempt to stop him, mainly because his words were so reassuring. Perhaps it was because his elder brother was a prefect at Hildersham House that he appeared so self-assured and in the know, so much older and wiser than the rest of us. He had an inexhaustible fund of stories at his fingertips too – especially when they concerned his father's wartime exploits, where he often appeared to be fighting on different fronts and in different campaigns all at the same time, like the heroes from the comic books we devoured.

On one memorable occasion, as he told it, his father was at home on leave from the army when a German Heinkel bomber flew low towards his house, returning from a raid. He had been dozing in a deckchair, but on hearing the unmistakable drone of the aeroplane's engine, he raced indoors, fetched his rifle from his kitbag and crouched down in the garden, the butt of the Lee-Enfield 303 nestled into his shoulder. When it came into range, he took careful aim, squeezed the trigger, and downed the bomber with a single shot. I can remember the disappointment I felt when, no more than a week later, I overheard him tell the same story to another group of boys. In this version, the Heinkel had spectacularly transformed into a Stuka dive bomber, which then engaged in a ferocious fire fight with his father above the garden, until he eventually disposed of it – with his final bullet.

For my part, I told the others that my parents had never said goodbye to me after depositing me at the school like an unwanted parcel, hurriedly driving away the moment my back was turned. 'I bet your parents all said goodbye to you... mine told me we were going on a holiday,' I said, delivering it like a punchline. I suppose that I hoped in some way it might make me look bigger in their eyes. I had no clue what they thought about my story because they greeted it with a long, awkward silence, which might have drifted into next week if I hadn't piped up 'Not that I care, of course'. I never mentioned it again and nor did they.

Nonetheless, Teague's words about the ten weeks were exactly what I needed to hear. He taught me a valuable lesson that day, and I made sure that I never looked too far ahead or back for the rest of the term. I didn't have enough room in my head for much else anyway. And just as he had predicted, time indeed started to speed up, the days so full and fast they virtually pinballed off the walls, the events and outings unfolding so rapidly around me that, for the first time in my life, I struggled to stay awake at night. There were games of rugby, which resembled disorderly egg-hunts played on mud slicks, and there were walks to the beach in crocodile formation, past the permanently scowling Bleak House and a wind-whipped sea, which was either milky white or cloudy grey, the colour of school tea. And, of course, there were lessons – lessons in the mornings and again in the afternoons, followed by prep in the evenings. In fact, it was just as well that I had finally started to sleep because my frustration in the classroom, or more specifically my inability to read or write, had returned to torment me and I would soon need all the strength I could muster.

It was hardly a secret that I was the only boy in the school who was illiterate. It was there for all to see when we attended chapel on at least three occasions during the week and every Sunday. The sight of me tornadoing through the pages of my prayer book in search of the hymn number, set to peals of thunder from the organ, was already a familiar and distracting part of the service. The letters, words and numbers spun so fast before my eyes – a blizzard of bewildering and unrecognisable shapes – that it was all I could do to stop myself from ripping out the pages in frustration. Sometimes a boy would take pity on me and show me the correct page or surreptitiously swap his prayer book with mine when no one was looking, whereupon I would pretend to sing along, making up the words that I couldn't read. But others, aware of Mr Snowden's steely glare or too embarrassed to be seen standing next to me, refused to lend a helping hand or even look my way. Usually, I was still flicking my way through the pages when the organ suddenly and unexpectedly squealed to a halt, like someone slamming on the brakes in a car, and the hymn was over.

Mr Snowden's patience was already at breaking point. Unable to ignore my frenzied page-turning a moment longer, he had taken to coming down the aisle, snatching the book from me, turning to the hymn and prodding his finger angrily at the page. 'There, hymn 236, boy – it's not that difficult to find.' His voice was so loud it momentarily drowned out the singing. Things reached a spectacularly low point for me when on another occasion, in the middle of a hymn, he grabbed my book and rotated it 180 degrees, making it evident to anyone who was watching – often the entire congregation, apart from the organist – that I had been holding it upside down.

After that, I devised a plan to try to save myself from further embarrassment. I was already learning to survive as best I could by any means or trick I could employ – an instinct I would hone meticulously over the coming years. So, before the next service in the chapel, I asked one of the boys to show me where the 'Magnificat' and the 'Nunc Dimittis' were in my prayer book. As both psalms regularly appeared in the service, I realised that if I dog-eared the respective pages, I could then turn to them at a moment's notice without having to spin relentlessly through my book and catch Mr Snowden's gimlet eye in the process. Of course, the hymns would remain a lottery and I would still have to fly by the seat of my pants whenever their numbers were called out, but hopefully this would help to limit the damage, divert attention from myself and, more crucially, keep Mr Snowden at arm's length. The plan went like clockwork – though most of the time I had no idea whether it was the 'Magnificat' or the 'Nunc Dimittis' I was pretending to sing along to.

Unfortunately, no matter how hard I concentrated in the classroom or prayed in the chapel, I could not make the words and letters dance to my tune; I could not make the connection between them. Their meaning remained hidden from me. Numbers were equally baffling – the longer I looked at them, the more cluttered my head became. I knew that the teachers' scribbled chalk marks on the blackboard were made of letters and letters formed words, yet if anything, I felt further away from unlocking the mystery than I'd ever done, from telling them apart, from untangling the rows of knots I regularly saw before my eyes – as numerous as the ones I tied myself into. I was no nearer to finding the key, the password, the secret command or trick, or whatever it was I was missing. I just knew I was missing something. Worse, I couldn't even ask my teachers what that was because I had no idea how to describe it to them.

Perhaps it would turn out to be something so ordinary, so straightforward, that when the answer finally revealed itself to me, I would be stunned by the simplicity of it, by the fact it had been staring me in the face all along. But what if it was even more complicated than I thought? And what if it never revealed itself to me?

All I could do was watch the other boys in my form, hope to learn their secrets and marvel at how clever they were. Clever didn't even really cut it in the case of Teague, who thrived on the competitive nature of the lessons. He appeared to know the exact question the teachers were going to ask even before they did and had his answers prepared well in advance. Not only that, but he kept the teachers on their toes by asking his own questions. From the minute I met the others, I could tell they were cleverer than me (which wasn't difficult) – though, to be fair, most had a head start on me, having been at the school for a term or two by the time I showed up. Their quick thinking and their fast minds left me in a spin. I was used to getting left behind in class, of course, but not like this. The distance between us had already grown into a yawning gap, as wide as a canyon.

More than anything, I wanted to be like them: to see the world through their eyes, to be able to make perfect sense of what was written on the blackboard or in my textbook; to play by their rules for a change, to expect things to come naturally, as easily as breathing; or to experience the gift of concentration. Just the individual handwriting styles of the teachers were enough to throw me – the long loops, flourishes and swirls further complicating the jumbled-up patterns I saw on the blackboard and adding yet another layer of confusion to my muddled mind. Sometimes I wished for nothing more than to see words and letters sit still, to stay fixed in one place and not to switch positions all the time like figures flitting across a football pitch. It didn't seem too much to ask.

One of the first things I learned about the others, apart from the fact they were a completely different breed from me, was that some already had their careers decided for them – their futures mapped out, their places in the world assured. Most even knew the name of the next school they were going to. As the sons of politicians, diplomats, doctors, lawyers, businessmen, bankers or tycoons – or in Teague's case, from farming stock – they knew as early as the age of seven or younger that they'd be following in their fathers' footsteps. They could tell you, almost down to the last detail, what they'd be doing for the rest of their lives (Teague, naturally, was to become a farmer), as if their future selves were being assembled and slotted effortlessly into place like the parts of a machine – a winning machine at that. No wonder they displayed such an overwhelming sense of certainty. The odd boy out that I was, I couldn't tell you what the next hour held in store for me or how I'd even get through it. It was hardly surprising that I felt like a trespasser within the school walls or that I spent so much of my time seeking refuge in my drawings. It was all I had.

In those moments, Miss Shepherd, our form teacher, would often pull up a chair and sit next to me. She showed a keen interest in what I was drawing or painting and was quick to encourage me to use my natural gift, as she described it. This gift, I soon learned, was my imagination. 'It's one of the things that makes you special. You must never be afraid to use it.' Special was not a word I'd ever expected anyone to say about me. Put simply, it was the best thing anyone had ever said to me. When a couple of the others poked fun at me for always drawing pictures in class, she chided them gently: 'You might wish you had his imagination one day.' It was the first time anyone had stuck up for me in a classroom or found anything remotely good to say about me. Unlike the other teachers I had known, she appeared curiously unconcerned by my failings, oblivious almost, and made no effort to try to change me, to force me to fit in. It was as though she understood how I ticked, which was another first for me. My head and body felt lighter when I was with her, unburdened by the dread, fear, frustration or panic I frequently felt inside.

But not everyone was so appreciative or accepting of my 'natural gift'. One of those who had little time for my drawings, and even less time for me, was Mr Foden, the history and geography teacher. In fact, everything about me seemed to infuriate him. This troubled me no end because history and art were my favourite subjects and the only occasions when I genuinely looked forward to being in a classroom, when my attention flamed and rarely wavered. Matters between us eventually came to a head after a lesson on one of the most significant moments in the course of English history, the Battle of Hastings.

I had listened enthralled while Mr Foden conveyed the full tumult of battle, the mighty crunch of armour, providing what amounted to a bird's-eye view of the deafening collision between the English and Norman armies. Afterwards, we were told to write down everything we had learned about these events, including William the Conqueror's accession to the English throne, and hand in our exercise books at the end of the lesson. A day or so later our books were returned with a flourish, propelled through the air towards us like they were balsa wood planes, as was Mr Foden's way. Each one was accompanied by its own distinct seal of approval, which involved as many variations of the word 'excellent' as he could conjure... until it came to mine. Mine remained hanging limply from his fingertips, as if he were dangling a dead rat by its tail and having to avert his nose from the stench.

'This,' he informed the class, opening the offending page for all to see, 'is what happens when boys fail to pay attention.' He nodded approvingly, like a conductor, a ringmaster, at the outburst of laughter that predictably followed. 'He has not only drawn a picture when we asked him for words, this imbecile has neglected to provide us with the date that changed the course of English history. The last time a foreign power successfully invaded these shores.' And he puffed out his chest, as though he had been personally responsible for repelling all such attempts. 'Remind him of that date please, gentlemen.'

'1066,' the class chorused in unison.

'And the month and day please, gentlemen.'

'October the fourteenth,' came the response, with even more gusto.

It was true that my drawing contained neither dates nor words – unless you counted the scrawled NHOJ at the bottom of it – yet I believed I'd perfectly captured the moment when the tide of battle turned in favour of the Normans. There were the English forces fatefully breaking formation behind their wall of kite-shaped shields to chase the fleeing invaders down Senlac Hill, only to be lured to their deaths at the hands of the French cavalry and a hail of arrows. There were the usual arms and legs flying in all directions, as men flailed, chopped, hacked and bludgeoned each other with broadswords, battle-axes and clubs. And there in the middle of this mayhem was King Harold himself – who had pleaded with his men to remain locked behind their tall shields – writhing in his death throes. If you had to be critical, the arrow embedded in his eye probably looked more like a large signpost pinioning him to the turf, but there was no mistaking the intent.

'This, gentlemen, is the work of an idiot,' Mr Foden concluded, to more laughter, and carelessly lobbed my exercise book back to me. It flew like an ungainly bird across the classroom, its pages flapping, before landing face down on my desk.

I won't pretend that the laughter didn't hurt. It did and lingered on for several days afterwards – a stabbing reminder of the mismatch that existed between us. I didn't blame them for laughing at me either. I would have probably done the same in their shoes. For a start, Mr Foden was one of those teachers who exerted a powerful influence over the class, who imposed his personality on everything he touched. Even the historical facts he dispensed bore the stamp of his character, making them, if nothing else, easy to remember. Boys were anxious to avoid his lacerating wit, to earn his good opinion, they wanted him to like them. I wanted him to like me too, but I knew that was a forlorn hope.

However, there was still one area where all boys shared common ground or remained on an even footing, and that was our fear of Mr Snowden. That fear united us like no other, it made us all equal, juniors and seniors alike, it gave us a sense of solidarity in a way that would not otherwise have existed. Unlike Mr Foden, who had his favourites, Mr Snowden did not discriminate and his temper threatened us all. His voice regularly boomed through the walls of his classroom into ours – sometimes he shouted in French or Latin, which if anything made it sound more terrifying, so loud that the air would tighten around us and bring our lesson to a standstill while we listened. It was like waiting for thunder to pass overhead. Miss Shepherd would either try to talk over him or to clap her hands and snap us back to attention, almost as if she were ridding the room of his energy.

Our contact with him in the classroom was limited to the occasional lesson of rudimentary French – where he appeared more amused than angry at our laughable attempts at pronunciation – but not Latin. We would study both subjects in more detail when we moved up a form, though I wondered how long that might take me. Nevertheless, we all knew what was coming down the track at some point, as if we were walking on thinning ice. We had heard about the beatings, the storm-force temper, his wildly fluctuating mood swings and how some boys measured their days by them. I had watched them troop out of his classroom at the end of a lesson ashen-faced like ghosts on many occasions. 'You can tell what mood he's in, the second he walks into a room,' one boy explained. 'You've got it coming, you wait.' Another remarked, 'You'd better hope you're good at cricket.' A comment that was completely lost on me at the time.

But for the moment, my troubles in the chapel apart, Mr Snowden hovered on the margins of our days like a shadow, rarely disturbing their flow. Until one night, after lights out, the thunder rolled in and exploded into the stillness of our dormitory.

• • •

I heard the footsteps advancing down the corridor – they were moving at a rapid pace without breaking stride. They were not stopping. Because our dormitory was situated at the end of the longest, farthest-flung corridor in the school, it always felt, especially in the deep of night, that everyone had forgotten about us tucked away here in the darkness. Which was why it was unusual to hear footsteps in the corridor after lights out. Unless, of course, they were coming into our room – though that would have been unusual too at this late hour.

But there was nowhere else for them to go – the linoleum in the corridor ran out just a few feet beyond our door, into a blank expanse of brick wall. A dead end. Perhaps it was the urgency, the speed of the footfall, that made me nervous, that made me think something wasn't right, that made me suddenly sit up in bed. I had little grasp of time and no idea how much had elapsed since lights out – an hour or two, maybe more – but as usual I was the only one still awake. And the footsteps kept coming.

I recognised them at once. During the day, those shoes made their own unmistakable noise on the tiles and floorboards, on the passageways between the classrooms, as if they were permanently crunching over splinters of broken glass, as if their soles consisted of sandpaper. Not even the springy linoleum of the corridor could muffle their identity.

The next thing I knew the dormitory door had burst open, and Mr Snowden was in the room, framed by a shaft of yellow light from the corridor. He flung the door into the back wall with such force that it rebounded off it, almost slamming shut. My initial response was to assume that I must have done something wrong, that I was the reason for this unwelcome intrusion. But instead of walking towards me, he turned abruptly, went over to Teague's bed in the opposite corner and stood above it. I heard him shout at Teague, something like 'You need to watch your tongue, boy' before driving his fist into my best friend's body.

There was a sickening thud as he connected with Teague's flesh, and he began to unleash his fury again and again in a flurry of vicious blows. The shock and the speed of it nearly knocked the breath out of me, and I couldn't begin to imagine the pain and fear Teague was feeling. He had been sleeping when he received the first punch and instantly cried out, scrabbling frantically with the sheets and bed covers to cushion the blows, trying to bury himself, flatten himself at the bottom of the bed like a hunted animal bolting for its burrow. I saw the silhouetted figure of Mr Snowden continue to pound him and heard, between the blows, the short, sharp grunts of his exertions. I watched in a mixture of horror and terror, which then turned into a burning anger, filling my body until I could stand it no more. As so often, I surprised myself with my reaction: suddenly I was screaming at Mr Snowden. I shouted 'Stop!' at the top of my voice and I might even have screamed it twice, the word sounding horribly loud inside my head.

He paused and looked in my direction but didn't appear to recognise me or take me in, as if he was unable to see through the fumes of his rage. No one else said anything. I noticed that his fists were still clenched and saw the faces of the others, frozen in horror. In that moment he took a couple of paces away from Teague's bed and turned towards mine, moving in a kind of dreadful slow motion. I didn't hesitate – I scrambled my sheets around me as Teague had done and dove for the bottom of the bed, lashing out at the hospital corners with my feet as I did so, like kicking in a door. At the bottom of the bed, I curled myself into a protective ball, enclosed my elbows around my head like a shield and tensed every bone in my shaking body. I wondered how I'd react when the first blow struck and the pain erupted inside me. I wondered if my bones would shatter. I didn't want to make a noise, so I scrunched some of the sheet into my mouth and waited... and waited.

My heart was hammering so hard that I never heard the door bang shut and I never heard Mr Snowden's footsteps retreat down the corridor. I might have stayed in that position all night if someone hadn't told me it was over, he had gone, and I could clamber out from under my fox hole in the sheets. It was pitch black again inside the dormitory when I returned to the surface and heard a low moaning sound coming from the end of Teague's bed.

I threw off my sheets and went over to him. 'Are you all right?' I asked. It sounded clumsy and stupid, but it was the only thing I could think of to say. I asked him again, and the moaning stopped briefly before resuming. Hardly any of us slept after that, and we lay awake listening to him groaning from the bottom of his bed until morning sneaked in, taking it in turns to go over to him – the centre of our collective attention – to ask how he was, to keep him company. He never replied to us, though often when we asked he fell quiet for a while, and we took that as an answer.

In the morning, it was all he could do to drag himself out of bed, put one foot in front of the other and stumble over to the washstand. It took him ages to undo the buttons on his pyjama top and ease it off, wincing with every movement before revealing a nightmarish tattoo of bruises on his back, arms and chest. We looked away and said nothing. We didn't want to stare. Afterwards, he barely looked at any of us either, avoiding our eyes at all costs, not wanting us to see what we already knew: his swagger was gone, his smile, his sense of fun, his stories were all switched off.

The others had taken to treating me differently too. It was as though they suddenly saw me in a different light. Undoubtedly, our worlds had been upended by what we witnessed that night. The foundations to mine had already been rocked beyond repair by my parents' decision to leave me here, but now I knew they would never feel stable again. How could any of us feel safe sleeping in a place where no one could hear you scream 'Stop!' at the top of your voice?

A few days later, Teague asked me to run away with him.

CHAPTER SIX

HOW LONG DO YOU THINK IT WILL TAKE TO GET TO AMERICA?

It was a full month before I managed to 'write' my first letter home. It may have been only six words and looked completely lost in the middle of the page – it also included two misspellings – but it was a start, nevertheless. They say that no journey can begin without taking the first step, no matter how tiny, how tentative. And that was my first step.

We had to write home once a week, every Sunday morning after chapel when a couple of hours were set aside for this specific task. Encouraged to fill both sides of the notepaper, the other boys crammed as much news into their letters as they could, as fast as they could, to ensure they had the rest of Sunday to themselves. This involved much hurried scribbling, head-scratching, chewing of pen tops and repeated nudging of each other's memories. 'What was the name of that person who gave the lecture on Africa again?' 'How many points did the first XV win by the other day?' It was not unusual for Mr Snowden to pace the classrooms in those moments – in a mood so openly good-natured it was almost disarming. He stopped just short of reminding us to tell our parents how much we were enjoying life at Hildersham House, but the message was loud and clear. His attempts at benevolence were more alarming than anything because we knew only too well what followed them.

During that time, my only means of communication with my parents was via my drawings, which were put in an envelope addressed by Miss Shepherd and posted on Monday mornings along with all the other school letters. The subject matter of my pictures seldom varied: I drew historic battle scenes, hundreds of them. Romans, Vikings, tanks, fighter planes, the Second World War, the Wild West. It wasn't that I couldn't draw anything else, it was just all I wanted to draw. At least there was nothing tentative about them.

Sometimes I even weaved them all into the same drawing. One Sunday, for example, I drew the US 7th Cavalry riding to the rescue of King Harold's army at the Battle of Hastings, streaming down Senlac Hill with their bugles blaring, in their dark-blue tunics, sky-blue trousers and yellow neckerchiefs. I was infatuated with the 7th Cavalry and in my reimagining of the battle, the Normans were routed, no match for the cavalrymen's Winchester repeating rifles or their superior horsemanship, as I wanted my picture to graphically illustrate.

In return, I received two letters a week, one from my parents (written by my mother) and the other from Dow, both of which Miss Shepherd read to me. My mother's letters hardly pulsed with news and almost always told me the same thing: all was well at home, she had left my room exactly as it was and everyone hoped I was enjoying life at school, after which they rapidly ran out of puff.

Dow's letters, by contrast, were all about Ajax and Bill and were therefore of far more interest to me. She spared no detail with her descriptions: Bill continued to bring mice to my room at night, even though I was no longer there, and Ajax still escaped through the holes in the hedge to chase the school children on their bicycles in the road. 'No sooner have we plugged one gap than he cunningly finds another escape route,' she wrote. 'We don't know how he does it. Luckily, he always comes trotting back to us. I do worry that he'll try to bring one of them crashing off their bikes one day – you know what he's like.' Dow's letters never failed to remind me just what it was I missed so much about home.

Meanwhile, I was busy hatching my own escape plan, though it was Teague, for obvious reasons, who managed most of the logistics; my role, it seemed, was just to keep him up to the mark. Naturally, we hadn't dared breathe a word of our pact to anyone and agreed never to talk about it unless we were on our own.

'When are we off?' I asked him, on one of those rare occasions when we had a moment to ourselves.

'Any day now,' he replied.

It had been any day now for a week or more, and I was starting to worry he might have got cold feet. Perhaps we both had. I was thrilled initially by the prospect of running away, and even suggested we might stow away on a boat and head for America – I was nothing if not ambitious – but with each passing day, I had become more apprehensive, more restless. To my dismay, Teague had still not recovered his spark, his zest, the things that made him who he was – it was as if his spirit had been drained, wrung dry by what had happened to him that night. 'Just make sure you're ready to go when I give the signal,' he told me. I couldn't help but detect the lack of enthusiasm in his voice, though.

However, before we disappeared across the Atlantic, I had a visit from my parents to worry about. It had arrived like a bolt out of the blue – mainly because a part of me had not expected to see them again. We were allowed to be visited by our parents twice during the ten-week Easter term, and this would be the first time I'd seen mine since they'd driven away without saying goodbye to me. To be honest, I wasn't sure I wanted to see them again. I wasn't even sure they would show up, for that matter.

'Supposing they don't come?' I asked Miss Shepherd after she'd read out my mother's letter informing me of the news.

I could tell it wasn't the reaction she had expected. 'Of course they will,' she said and gave me a look to suggest I should know better than to ask something like that. She showed me the letter, underlining the words with her finger so I could follow them, and repeated the sentence to me. 'They're looking forward to seeing you – it says so here.' I gazed at her tousled, light-brown hair, her sunny, reassuring smile and wanted to believe her with all my heart. But I worried that if I did, I would build up my hopes only to have them knocked down, *again*. The truth was I couldn't bring myself to trust my parents.

As my form teacher, Miss Shepherd regularly wrote notes to my parents and included them in my envelopes home. Her notes compensated for the absence of any words from me and no doubt helped to leaven the mood created by my darkly dramatic drawings. She always found a few snippets of news to impart and even something encouraging to say about me. 'John continues to be happy and well and has started to play a more active role in class.' A progress report, if you like, but without an awful lot of progress.

On this occasion, she wrote to my parents requesting that they provide me with some pocket money. 'John tells me that he doesn't have any. The other boys seem to have fifteen shillings, which they are allowed to spend at various intervals during the term. I think he feels a bit left out,' she explained. 'I know you are seeing John at the weekend and wondered if you could supply him with a similar amount, so I can set up an account for him. Thank you. Yours sincerely, Dorothy Shepherd.'

Before sealing the envelope and addressing it, she asked if there was anything I would like to say to my parents. She suggested that we could write it together or I could even attempt to write it on my own. 'It would be a nice way of showing them the strides you've been making,' she said.

She had recently devised a new of way of helping me to learn to read and write. This method involved her putting a pen or pencil between my thumb and forefinger, placing her hand over the top of mine and guiding it across the page, so that we could form some letters and words together. At first, I felt nothing: my hand was simply being manoeuvred across the page, mechanically almost, in a slow, crabbing movement, and I followed wherever she led. My heart was just not in it.

We practised the alphabet over and over again. We did exercises where I'd pick a letter from the alphabet and then we'd write down all the words I could think of beginning with that letter. However, if 'T' stood for teapot, for instance, my first inclination was always to want to draw it, not write it. Sometimes she would cut a letter out of cardboard, glue it onto some paper and ask me to trace it with my finger while I tried to memorise its shape by touch. 'Think of letters and words as your friends and they will soon make themselves known to you,' she'd say. 'Or why not try to imagine that you are drawing or painting them?' She was always encouraging me, always finding new ways to keep me focused and engaged. Mostly, though, all it seemed to do was remind me of how much I loved drawing – as if I needed any reminding of that – and how little I liked words and letters.

But then something unusual took place, something quite magical in fact. She was steering my hand across the page one day – I must have been concentrating uncommonly hard on this occasion – when, to my amazement, I discovered I had somehow completed the exercise without her hand on mine. She had let go of it midway through the sentence we were writing without me noticing, and I'd just carried on as if nothing had happened. I felt like a novice swimmer who strikes out from the shallow end on his own and completes an entire length of the swimming pool.

Afterwards, Miss Shepherd admitted to me that this was not the first time she had let go of my hand – but it was the first time I'd been aware of it. And there was another occasion when the magic sidled up to me almost unnoticed. Often, she would ask me to paint the letters we had written together, in as many different colours as possible. I told her I always painted the roof and stem of the 'T' brown because it was the same colour as our teapot at home and watched as a smile spread across her face. She was right, then. Words and letters were finally making themselves known to me.

For the first time, I had managed to form one or two of the elusive shapes by myself and recognised some of them, even if it was no more than a glimmer, a light blinking in the darkness. They had sat still on the page, they had answered my call, not shifting and merging before my eyes as they'd always done before. I felt a wave of hope rush over me, like the first time I heard the poem 'King John's Christmas' – except that on this occasion it came with a heightened sense of anticipation as the letters crystallised inside my head. I tingled from head to foot too, as if all the trapped energy I'd felt in every classroom I'd ever sat in had suddenly been released, like a pressure gauge. From then on, my heart didn't sink whenever Miss Shepherd suggested I practise my reading and writing. Instead, it felt strangely uplifted. I wanted to expand my knowledge, to take the next step and the next, to learn to write new words and experience their magnetic pull, to watch the letters fall into place like puzzle pieces. I wanted to feel the gentle pressure of her hand on mine, her kindness, her patience. I wanted to draw on her strength and know I was safe, even if it was only for a moment.

'Have you thought about what you'd like to write to your parents then?' she asked. 'You could tell them how much you're looking forward to seeing them again on Sunday.' She proceeded to draw some pencil lines with a ruler across the notepaper – this was to prevent my words from falling off the page in a clumsy arc – and handed me the pencil.

If there was one thing that I missed above all else, it was home: Ajax and Bill, the garden, my bedroom, the background sounds, a television, two televisions, the radio playing in the kitchen, laughter running like a tap. My home life felt more precious to me than anything, each memory a treasured one.

'It doesn't have to be perfect.' Miss Shepherd smiled, noticing my hesitation, my pencil poised awkwardly above the lines she'd drawn. 'It just has to come from you, that's all.'

So in the end, I wrote 'I whic i was at hom' and signed it 'from john'. The word 'love' was conspicuous by its absence, as was the word NHOJ. It was the first time I had ever spelled my name correctly.

• • •

Predictably, I was the last boy left standing on the small island of grass in the middle of the driveway.

Earlier the area had thronged with boys chatting and laughing, overjoyed at the prospect of seeing their parents again. They even managed to infuse me with their enthusiasm. The island had quickly thinned out, however, as a parade of cars started to arrive in the driveway, their tyres crackling expensively over the gravel. Soon our number had been whittled down to just me – a mere onlooker at the spectacle that followed. Some boys ran towards their parents' cars to be scooped up into their mothers' arms, some were kissed, others were hugged. A few shook hands with their parents as though they were meeting them for the first time, and one or two simply opened the car door and climbed in without saying a word as if they were getting into a taxi. Almost all, though, were driven off with an expression of sublime contentment on their faces, like a procession of little kings.

After a while, I stopped looking for my parents' car every time I heard an engine in case I was disappointed. I told myself that if I stopped looking, they'd be bound to turn up. If I wandered back indoors and refused to glance out of the window, perhaps that might do the trick. I was always playing these games. They never worked. I was wondering what I had done to deserve this again and why I never learned when I heard a top-floor window scrape open and saw Mr Snowden's head appear among the prongs of ivy.

'What are you still doing here, boy?' he roared. 'I take it your parents do realise they're supposed to be collecting you?'

'Yes, sir,' I said, nodding glumly up at him.

If they hadn't arrived in the next thirty minutes, he informed me, I would have no other choice but to accompany him to the golf course. The thought of having to watch Mr Snowden play golf all afternoon filled me with an indescribable dread. I imagined myself foraging for lost golf balls in the undergrowth or picking up litter or something equally ghastly. To be fair, he seemed similarly unenthused by the idea of having me along as company. 'The school will be locked up for the rest of the day – you can't stay here on your own. Come and find me if they're not here in half an hour.' And he slammed the window shut.

I was ready to accept my fate when a car suddenly pulled into the driveway and the distinctive battleship grey of my parents' Vanden Plas swept towards me containing two smiling faces. I actually breathed a sigh of relief. Naturally, my parents appeared quite oblivious to the fact that I was the only boy in sight. Perhaps they thought they were early. My father parked the car and climbed out, followed by my mother. I walked towards them. My father shook hands with me – I noticed he was still wearing his driving gloves – and we said hello. For one awful moment I thought my mother was going to lean in and kiss me, though at least there would have been no one to witness it, or my embarrassment, had she done so. Instead, she reached out a hand and squeezed my shoulder. 'You haven't been waiting here long, have you?' she asked.

'No,' I replied, and we all got into the car. The sickly aroma of the upholstery was in my nostrils before we'd even turned out of the driveway and onto the road.

Things did not get any better after that. In fact, as the day wore on, it increasingly felt as though two strangers had arrived to take me out. It was kind of these strangers, whoever they were, but in all honesty, I could have done without it. After driving around town for a while, we took an early lunch, during which I fidgeted endlessly and shuffled uncomfortably in my seat while my mother indulged her equivalent of fidgeting – keeping up a non-stop barrage of chatter. She seemed determined to prevent anyone else from talking, filling any void in the conversation with as many words as she could cram into it, which suited me as I had nothing much to say anyway.

Perhaps her incessant talking was on this occasion designed more to ward off any awkward, embarrassing questions that I might have. I was still desperate to understand why my parents had driven off without saying goodbye; I just didn't know how to bring it up. My father – apart from punctuating her sentences with the occasional lengthy sigh – did what he normally did in such situations, which was absolutely nothing, and continued to study the menu as if he were perusing the *Financial Times*, a paper he always read with more trepidation than joy.

Later, we had afternoon tea in a seafront hotel, where the tick of the clock on the restaurant mantlepiece almost drowned out the muttered conversations. The sea behind the glass was its usual cloudy grey colour, crested with foam. The chime of the clock at regular fifteen-minute intervals and the gentle rattle of cups and saucers made me long for the din and chaos of school. I wondered what would happen if I picked up my cup and threw it across the room, shattering it into a thousand pieces. Not long after suppressing that thought, my mother disappeared to reapply her make-up, leaving me alone with my father. We both looked at each other for several seconds.

'Are you enjoying playing rugby, John?' he asked at last, helping himself to another scone.

'Yes, very much,' I told him and watched a lump of strawberry jam slide off his scone and onto the tablecloth. 'I scored a try last week.'

'Well done. And have you started boxing yet?'

'We haven't started yet,' I lied. 'Soon, I hope… I think.'

'Good for you.'

It was while we were having this conversation that I spotted another boy from Hildersham House sitting with his parents in the corner of the restaurant by some potted palms. He was no more than a year or two older than me. We glanced at each other, sheepishly looked away and made sure not to catch each other's eye again, as if we were both too embarrassed to be seen out in public with our parents.

On Sundays in 1962, because all the shops were closed, there wasn't much else to do other than sit in tea rooms or hotel restaurants like this one. In summer, of course, there was always the beach with its golden crescent of sand but, for six or seven months of the year, it was a windswept, desolate, exceedingly cold place, where it was almost impossible to stand up without being blown over and where only the foolhardiest ventured. My parents sometimes managed to find a hotel with a television room and that helped to kill a few hours, though I remember Sunday afternoon programmes being about as depressing as the rows of darkened shops in the high street, which we regularly walked past for something to do.

At least when they finally dropped me off that evening, in time for school chapel, they said goodbye. I watched them disappear down the driveway and waved briefly but didn't know whether to feel sad or confused or both. All I knew was that after spending some five weeks apart from my parents, they had become somehow strange to me, and I wondered how that could have happened so fast. Halfway through evensong, with my thoughts turning to Monday morning and the organ thundering out 'For Those in Peril on the Sea', I was soon drowning in sorrow again.

If there was one thing I learned early on about my parents' visits, it was that they were always late, no matter what. During my stay at Hildersham House, there was perhaps only one occasion when I can recall them arriving at the appointed time. I was always the last boy to be collected from the grass island in the middle of the driveway. I even got used to it in the end – it was their calling card and one of the few constants of my childhood.

I later discovered there was a reason for their tardiness. Because they had to get up so early on Sunday to be in Broadstairs by 9 a.m., my mother saved time by always dressing in the car on the way. My father valued his weekend lie-ins almost above anything and this allowed him some more time in bed, even if it was only an extra half an hour. My mother selected a couple of her favourite outfits – she could never decide on one and was prone to changing her mind anyway – two pairs of shoes and whatever else she needed and packed them into the car before setting off. They were invariably running late by this stage as it was. At an appropriate point on the journey, my father would swap over into the driver's seat and my mother would climb into the back seat and proceed to change her clothes. And off they'd go again – my mother attempting to wriggle and squeeze herself into one of her dresses, like the 21-year-old West End chorus girl she once was, my father setting his customary funereal pace behind the wheel, like the ultra-cautious, conservative driver he was and would always be.

Usually by this time, they had attracted a queue of vehicles – one that would continually build until it resembled a small convoy trundling through the Kent countryside – and any number of strange looks from pedestrians. This was almost entirely due to my father's grim refusal to nudge the needle on the speedometer above forty, though it might also have had something to do with my mother's various contortions on the back seat. Sometimes she would manage to get herself dressed in one outfit, only to change her mind at the last minute – nearly pushing my father's patience over the speed limit. When they eventually pulled into the driveway at Hildersham House, the queue had dispersed, my mother was in the front seat, dressed for the occasion, her make-up applied, and no one would have known anything different but for the fact that they were gloriously late.

There was no doubt that my parents' visit set me back – in the end, the confusion over our new long-distance relationship outweighed the sadness I felt – but it was an incident involving Mr Snowden some days later that made me more determined than ever to run away. The incident happened after I left my desk halfway through prep to go to the bogs, as we referred to them. No boy was allowed to leave his desk during prep, but on this occasion, I decided that my need was greater. It was no different at night. If you had the bad luck to need a pee after lights out, you had to brave the corridor with its inbuilt alarm system of creaking, groaning floorboards and pray Mr Snowden didn't catch you. Depending on his mood, he would be quite likely to beat you for it with whatever came to hand – usually your own slipper if you were wearing any. Unfortunately, he had chosen to make his rounds of the classrooms earlier than usual that evening and, discovering my desk was empty, went off in search of me.

The bogs were situated at the end of a flight of stairs leading to our classroom and I immediately heard the sandpaper crunch of his shoes on the stone. The sound was followed by the distinctive complaint of a door being pushed open, and I recognised the rusty whistle of its hinges as it swung shut. I froze... he was inside the bogs. He walked past the urinals towards the aisle of wooden cubicles and halted outside the one locked door, where I sat surrounded by the graffiti I couldn't read. 'Is that you, boy?'

My heart started to hammer on cue. I didn't dare say anything. I thought if I kept quiet and held my breath, he would go away and I would learn my fate later that evening after prep. But then there was a push on the door handle so fierce the cubicle shook and wobbled as though it were about to topple in on itself, and I knew what was coming next. The last time he'd threatened me like this, I had my fox hole in the sheets to dive into for protection, but now I felt horribly and completely exposed, unable to keep my hands and legs from shaking uncontrollably. There was a blow against the door, more violent this time, delivered by the toe of his shoe, and I watched the lock buckle and snap, ripping clean away from the wood, which disintegrated in front of my eyes like rotten cardboard. The door flew open, missing my head by inches, and Mr Snowden's frame filled the space.

'Get off there,' he shouted and clamped his hand around my arm, heaving me off the seat and dragging me out of the cubicle. I realised I hadn't cleaned myself or pulled the chain and frantically tried to wrench my arm free while attempting to gather up my pants and trousers from around my ankles with the other to stop myself from losing balance. But he was too strong for me. I wanted to call him a rude name – the rudest I could think of – but knew I wouldn't dare. My courage always failed me at the last second. I looked down and saw my pants and trousers were wet through. The bogs were awash in running water – they leaked permanently, like a ship that was holed beneath the waterline and slowly sinking. Normally, you had to pick your way past the puddles to get out of the place. Even the walls were wet and slimy to the touch. Perhaps that's why they were called the bogs.

'Boys are not permitted to leave their desks in the middle of prep,' he continued to shout. 'You've been here long enough to know that by now. You do not leave your desk under any circumstances – do I make myself clear?'

'Yes, sir.' I braced myself for the blow I knew was coming.

'Of all the boys here, you're the last person who can afford to waste time during prep. You need to buck up your ideas. Fast. Do you hear?' And with that, he let go of my arm and took several wild swings with his open palm at my backside and the back of my legs, landing a series of stinging blows, the force of which nearly propelled me up the stairs. 'Now get back to your classroom and don't let me catch you away from your desk again.'

I climbed the stairs as swiftly as I could, still grappling with my pants and trousers, which were now clinging wet to my skin. When I reached the top of the stairs, I tucked in my shirt and fastened the elasticated belt we all wore on our trousers, with its S-shaped metal buckle fashioned in the form of a snake, and opened the classroom door. I felt defenceless, humiliated – I didn't yet know the meaning of the word but felt in that moment every ounce of its weight – ashamed, unclean, afraid and, when the fear turned to vapour in my body seconds later, angry. Especially angry.

'That's it for me,' I said to Teague later that evening after telling him what had happened, leaving out no detail. 'We've got to get away from here. It's our only hope.'

'I know,' he nodded, and told me he'd just discovered why Mr Snowden had beaten him so badly that night. 'It's my brother,' he explained. 'He did it. He betrayed me. He told Mr Snowden I had cheeked him and some other prefects – he asked him to teach me a lesson I won't forget. It's all his fault. I hate my brother.'

Teague's brother had stuck in my mind for no other reason than he'd worn a silk dressing gown and a scarf twined extravagantly around his neck when filling our bowls with water on my first morning at Hildersham House – the same scowling boy who pretended not to know his younger brother if he passed him in the corridors. We both had our burning reasons to escape now, and Teague doubly so. We agreed a time and date there and then, a half-day early next week – Teague's suggestion because, as he pointed out, 'half the staff won't be around and that way no one will know we're missing until it's too late'. Our minds were made up at last and there was no turning back. I felt a tremor of anticipation and wondered how I would ever manage to sleep through the next four nights.

'How much money do you have?' he asked suddenly.

I told him my parents had provided me with fifteen shillings of pocket money, but I'd already handed it in to Miss Shepherd to look after. 'I could say I need it back,' I suggested.

He quickly shook his head. 'No, don't do that, you'll get us found out if you do. You know what you're like, you can't hide anything. Just ask her if you can have a shilling and say it's for sweets and comics or something. She'll let you do that. I'll bring the rest of the money. My father slipped me some more over the weekend – he often does that when my brother isn't looking.' And he allowed himself a small grin. 'It's hidden somewhere safe. I'll get it before we go.'

The next few days dragged by so slowly I could almost hear the clink of chains inside my head. Eventually, the time came to go, and we sneaked out through the bushes and trees on the far side of the driveway. Teague warned me that this was one of the riskiest parts of our escape because we'd be visible from the school for about half a minute before we reached the road and anyone could spot us. I was beset by nerves, but he appeared far more adept at disguising his – that is, if he even felt any. We reached the end of the bushes unnoticed and stepped out onto the pavement. It was like stepping onto quicksand. 'We can't run until we're sure we're in the clear,' he said. 'Wait for me to give the signal.'

The desire to run was overpowering – it was the equivalent of oxygen for me, for all of us – and I could barely stop myself from breaking into a trot. 'Slower,' Teague urged, 'walk slower.' I glanced down at my walking shoes, now scuffed and worn, and they seemed to be going at a hundred miles an hour. The same speed as my heart. I kept waiting for Mr Snowden's voice to stop us dead in our tracks but didn't dare look back in case it did. We continued to walk for another minute or two until Teague suddenly shouted 'Now!' And in that exhilarating moment, we were off the leash and running free. He had given himself a head start and led the way for a while, but I lengthened my stride, and we were soon matching each other step for step, our shoes making a slapping, echoing noise on the pavement as if we were running through a tunnel.

We passed the railway station on our left and continued into the bustling high street, which sloped steeply in its eagerness to deliver us to the seafront. We eased off and stopped sprinting after that, and even took time to stare at some of the shop windows. One was a music shop with a selection of record sleeves pasted on the inside of the glass, and I recognised at once some of the singers from TV and knew their names. It reminded me of all the times I had flipped through my mother's record collection, entranced by the shiny covers.

The high street continued to descend before curving sharply to the left and we followed it, pausing outside an arcade close to the seafront to look at the flashing lights, to listen to the whirring, buzzing sound of slot machines and the cascade of jingling coins before moving on again. Although we were dressed in our school uniforms, no one gave us a second glance – too busy with their shopping to pay us any attention. We crossed the road at a brisk pace and walked onto the pier, where we paused to discuss our next move. We didn't have a next move as far as I knew, but that didn't matter because I felt certain Teague would have something up his sleeve – he always did. He just hadn't told me yet. We leaned over the railings at the far end, listening to the rhythmic thump of waves against the side of the pier and watching the fishing boats and yachts bounce and bob below us. Every so often a plume of spray landed with a splash at our feet, catching us by surprise.

'How long do you think it will take to get to America?' I asked.

'About a week, maybe longer,' he replied. 'It's difficult to say.'

I had no idea where America even was, except that it felt about as far away to me as my parents. A long way away, in other words. I left the thought there and we continued to stare out to sea. A silence settled over us after that, and I tried to catch his eye on several occasions in the hope he might say something, but he refused to shift his gaze.

I was anxious to stay on the move and broke the silence. 'What are we going to do?'

'I'm thinking,' he said and furrowed his brow as though the answer to my question lay somewhere out there in the inky depths of the sea.

It was then that I suspected there was no plan – no next move, no last-minute surprise hidden up Teague's sleeve. My earlier suggestion that we stow away on a boat and head for America – the sum total of my contribution to our escape – could not have sounded any sillier in that moment. Perhaps our plan had just been to escape, to run, to make a mad gallop from one end of the town to the other, to take a quick gulp of freedom, to fill our lungs and nothing more. I remained staring out to sea, watching my courage blow away like the spray off the top of the waves, tasting the bitter tang of salt on the tip of my tongue. Had anyone at school noticed we were missing yet, I wondered? What would happen to us when they did? Would they send out a search party? Would they ring our parents or the police? Or both? Should we turn back while we still had the chance?

I turned and looked at Teague again and could tell what he was thinking – he was thinking the same thoughts as me. I knew him well enough to know that. It was just that neither of us wanted to be the first to say it out aloud, to look at each other and see our fear reflected in the other's eyes. Finally, I could stand it no longer. I said, 'Maybe if we leave now, and run as fast as we can, we could still…' I didn't have to finish my sentence because in that split-second he swung around to look at me and, as if a starting gun had fired simultaneously in our heads, we both broke into a sprint.

We bolted past the arcade, back the way we'd come, in a race to beat our fear, not caring any more who saw us. Halfway up the high street I felt my legs buckle and turn to jelly, my strength empty away. 'Keep going,' Teague shouted to me, the gap between us widening. 'Keep going!' Where did he get his strength from?

After the railway station the pavement evened out. I got my second wind and even managed to claw back some of the distance between us. At last, we reached the bushes by the side of the driveway and I slumped behind a tree, my hands on my knees, my head virtually scraping the ground, the muscles in my stomach knotted so tightly that what breath I had felt like it was on fire. Teague still had enough breath in his body to suggest that we split up before going inside. 'We mustn't be seen together, not until we know what's happened,' he said. 'I'll go in first – you wait here and follow me when you're ready. Remember, just act natural.' It was all I could do to nod back at him. I watched him disappear and waited until I could breathe again before following him inside. As usual, my heart was beating outside of my chest like in a cartoon.

The first thing that hit me once indoors was how quiet it was. I had expected the worst, expected to find the place in uproar – a bell ringing, the sound of running feet everywhere – and was surprised to discover it was anything but. I immediately wondered where Teague had got to and decided to head towards our classroom. At that moment a boy appeared at the end of the corridor, walking rapidly in my direction. I stopped and waited for him to say something, bracing myself for the inevitable reaction, but he looked straight through me and carried on. Seconds later, another boy took even less notice of me, much to my confusion. When a third passed by, I said hello to him, but being a senior boy, he didn't take kindly to my jovial welcome – though his reaction at least established I hadn't suddenly become invisible or turned into a ghost.

It wasn't until I started to climb the stairs to our classroom, still puzzling over events, that I heard the first signs of a commotion: a sound of pounding footsteps coming from around one of the many sharp bends. The next thing I saw was the startling sight of Teague hurtling towards me at full throttle. I didn't wait to find out what was happening – whatever it was, it wouldn't be good – and, thinking he was being pursued, turned to run back down the stairs as fast as I could. 'Stop,' he called, then louder, 'Come back, John.' We never normally called ourselves by our Christian names, so I knew it must have been something important. And that was when I looked round and saw the smile on his face. It was a mile wide. 'We did it!' He exclaimed. 'We got away with it. That's what I was coming to tell you. No one knows we've been gone.'

'What? No one?' I asked.

'No one,' he assured me, still unable to keep the smile off his face.

So that was why no one had spoken to me, why they'd just walked by – for the simple reason that there was *nothing* to say.

At no point in our conversation, or at any point afterwards for that matter, did we ever mention the moment on the pier when our courage deserted us. We kept that small fact to ourselves and pretended it had never happened. It was almost as if the things that confronted us within the school walls – the very things that had made us want to run away in the first place – were in some way oddly preferable to the fear of the unknown and what lay out there in the vast spaces beyond.

'I can't believe no one noticed we were missing,' I said wonderingly.

'I know,' he replied. 'They think we've been here all the time.' And with that we started to laugh – an almost delirious, defiant mixture of joy and relief. I realised it was the first time I'd heard Teague laugh since the beating and I didn't want him to stop.

CHAPTER SEVEN

A DIFFERENT WAY
OF THINKING

One afternoon, at the end of lessons, Miss Shepherd asked me if I would stay behind for a few minutes. It was exactly two days before my eighth birthday and almost three weeks before the conclusion of the Easter term. 'There's something I want to talk to you about,' she said in her customary breezy manner. We were often asked to stay behind in class if we had done something wrong or misbehaved, but she immediately gave me a reassuring smile to indicate that all was well. There was the usual clatter of desktops being opened and slammed shut as the rest of the class put away their exercise books, their rulers, pens and pencils and bolted for the door.

When the others had gone, she pulled up a chair and, as was often her way, sat next to me. She told me that she had recently written a letter to my parents and, having received a reply from them, was keen to share the contents of the correspondence with me. 'It is about you, after all,' she continued, weighing her words carefully. 'But before I do, I want you to know that there's absolutely nothing for you to worry about. You haven't done anything wrong – quite the opposite – and I'll tell you why in the next few minutes.'

I knew I could trust her implicitly and unhesitatingly nodded my head in agreement. Curiosity quickly got the better of me, though, and knowing my birthday was just around the corner, I started thinking about presents and a cake with eight candles, and one extra for luck and couldn't resist asking her if it was some kind of surprise. Often, when a thought came into my head, I did not know how to let it go. 'Yes, in a way I suppose it is,' she replied. 'In fact, I'd say it's going to turn out to be quite a good surprise for you.' As she didn't deny that it had something to do with my birthday, I automatically assumed I had guessed correctly.

In that moment, however, I could not have known that what she was about to tell me was bigger than all my birthdays put together. It was a moment that would prove a turning point, a juncture in my young life – one that would change not only how I saw things but how I saw myself. Miss Shepherd had identified something that no one else, no other teacher, had come close to seeing. Something that had been hiding in plain sight all along.

In her letter, she had informed my parents that, despite the recent strides I'd made in my work, it had become increasingly clear that I was suffering from what she described as a 'recognised learning difficulty', one that was affecting my ability to read and write. 'It is nothing to be alarmed by,' she wrote to them. 'And I hope I can put your minds at rest by telling you that I am trained in this field; it is my specialist area, one that is close to my heart, which is why I rec- ognise all the signs in John.' She explained that with the right help and guidance, I could start to make significant improvements in my reading and writing. 'Now that we know what it is that is troubling John, I believe we can make some real progress with him.' She had not raised it with them until now, she added, because she wanted me to be in a position where 'I can start to take him forward, to a point where he can eventually hope to hold his own in class. The encouraging signs I've seen in these past few weeks convince me he has the potential to achieve this. He is on a different path with his learning now. With your permission, therefore, I would like to discuss this with him, so he can gain some understanding of the situation and the specific needs required before we proceed to the next step.' She concluded with the words, 'I know how to help John.'

Although she had pinpointed a 'learning difficulty', she did not use the term when relaying the news to me that day. Indeed, I never heard her mention it once in the many conversations we had or during the innumerable hours we spent together – she always referred to it as 'a different way of thinking', because, as she liked to point out, 'that's what it is when you boil it down'. This alternative way of thinking, she told me, also had a name: it was called dyslexia and anyone who had it was known as dyslexic.

It was not the sort of name I had expected to hear, especially with my thoughts so fixated on my birthday – I expected to hear something more memorable. 'Dyslexia,' she said. On first mention, it sounded like the name of a toothpaste, one of those they were always advertising on television. Or, worse, some particularly foul-smelling cough mixture, which tasted so bad it instantly cured you. It was not the surprise with the nine candles I had anticipated either – although far more concerning for me was the fact that no matter how many times I heard the word, it refused to stay in my head for longer than a couple of seconds. After dispensing with the image of a toothpaste tube and a bottle of cough mixture, I was perplexed to find it had simply vanished from my mind at the speed of light, as if it had never even existed. And I had to ask Miss Shepherd to say it again.

Seconds later, the procedure repeated itself: the word dissolved and disappeared, leaving no trace, no imprint on my mind. I could not make it stick and once it had gone, I had no idea how to track it down. Even when Miss Shepherd reminded me of what it sounded like and asked me to repeat it slowly after her, I invariably mispronounced it or promptly forgot it. It was a long word for me, yet without fail I always succeeded in making it longer by slipping in an extra letter here or there or introducing a new letter, such as 't' or 'o', or occasionally dispensing with the 'x' altogether, pronouncing it in any number of different ways, none of them correctly. Try as I might, I could not remember it. I could not arrange the words into any recognisable, coherent shape or order. It melted into thin air each time I heard it, and it melted my mind.

Sometimes, for no apparent reason other than perhaps to throw me into further confusion, it would mysteriously and unexpectedly appear in my head out of nowhere and allow me to pronounce it perfectly for a day or two. Then, just when I thought I'd cracked it, it would disappear again to wherever it disappeared to and any memory of how it had sounded inside my mind was erased once more. This was not the first time I had been baffled by the pronunciation of a word. When I was very young, I thought disgusting was pronounced 'sergusting' until I learned differently. I remember being disappointed because sergusting sounded so much better to my ears, so much more appealing.

I even tried to remember dyslexia by thinking of a word that rhymed with it, but unsurprisingly, I was unable to come up with any. The only words I could manage were ones I invented myself and they were equally impossible to recall. The fact that I displayed all the classic signs of dyslexia was completely lost on me too. At one point, Miss Shepherd suggested that we split the word into what she called syllables to help me remember it. There were four of them, apparently: dys-lex-i-a. But the letters hung like lead weights on the tail of a kite and still it refused to fly… unless, of course, it was flying straight out of my head and then there was no stopping it.

I found it frustrating and bewildering, and yet somehow oddly fitting, that a word specifically created to describe someone like me should prove so incomprehensible – to the extent that for much of my school life and beyond, I could neither pronounce it, read it, write it, nor spell it, let alone remember it. As a young boy, however, its name was important to me because it meant that I was battling something real, something tangible. I was no longer fighting shadows. It was hardly surprising that I saw it in terms of a battle or an opportunity to go toe to toe with an adversary. After all, every day was a struggle for me and increasingly so at Hildersham House, where it felt as if I was fighting for my very survival. And now, it seemed, I had a battle within a battle just to remember its name. Dyslexia.

Yet for all the guidance and attention Miss Shepherd provided, and for all the progress she told me I was making, I still felt as if I was the only boy in class who didn't get 'it' – whatever 'it' was. Not that she could have done any more to make me feel at home in a classroom – the countless hours she put in on my behalf, often in her spare time, went far beyond the call of duty. Even back then, I knew that I was lucky. She transformed my experience and emboldened me in the process.

Undoubtedly, the best piece of news I received from her was that I was not alone. There were others like me – too many to count, in her words – who struggled to read and write, to make sense of numbers, to concentrate, to sit still, to understand what was written on the blackboard, who didn't get 'it', who thought and learned differently, who saw the letters flit before their eyes. Others who, for all those reasons, remained permanently rooted to the bottom of the class; others who probably couldn't remember the word 'dyslexia' from one day to the next either but were dyslexic, just like me. I felt hopeful, excited, relieved, surprised and curious – especially curious – because I had never encountered anyone remotely like me in a classroom before and would have given anything to have done so, to have had a fellow 'sufferer' for company. Until then, I had not even considered the possibility that such a person existed. How could I when I found myself surrounded by so many brainboxes? I thought I was the odd boy out and always would be.

I learned too that there was nothing to fear about being different and nothing to be ashamed of. It didn't mean I wasn't intelligent or clever – because I was, Miss Shepherd was at pains to explain. It simply meant I thought differently. It was a message she drummed home at every opportunity: 'You might even find it an advantage one day. You wait and see.'

It was a lot of new information for me to take in at once, particularly as it contradicted almost everything that I'd previously been taught at school. But if it meant having to unlearn everything and start again, then I was more than happy to do it. 'There's no rule anywhere that says you're not allowed to think differently,' she told me. 'You must never listen to anyone who tells you otherwise.'

Before too long, I became so infatuated by the idea of thinking differently that I worried if I learned to read, write and spell like the others, I might end up thinking like them. I might lose my powers altogether. When I put this to Miss Shepherd, her eyes instantly sparkled with delight; after all, I had spent so long yearning to be like the others, only to suddenly want to be more like myself. Fortunately, she found humour in much of what I said. 'That won't change. You'll always think differently, that's part of who you are,' she replied, giving me a beaming smile. 'And by the way, it's a question of when, not if. *When* you learn to read and write like the others, you will find you've got the best of both worlds at your fingertips. That will be the difference.'

• • •

Over the next couple of years, Miss Shepherd took me under her wing and started what became the next step: a long, gradual transition for me, in which letters replaced drawings and words, ultimately, usurped pictures. The seven-year-old me would not only have been dumbfounded by such an eventuality, knowing the heavy reliance he placed on pictures and drawings, he would have been dumbstruck by it. How could I possibly have known then that the odd, twisted shapes I saw on the blackboard or in my textbook would eventually transform into something more beautiful and iridescent than I could have ever imagined? As fantastical, perhaps, as the land of Narnia that I had just discovered, a mysterious realm where anything and everything was possible and where I waited with glee to be transported every afternoon – not through the magical portal of a wardrobe, in this case, but through the familiar inflections of Miss Shepherd's voice.

She was halfway through reading *The Lion, the Witch and the Wardrobe* – the first book in The Chronicles of Narnia series – to us, something that always took place during the final lesson of the afternoon. It was almost impossible for me to concentrate on anything else until she had picked up the book, opened it and carefully taken out the bookmark before starting to read. One day, after completing the first sentence, she was interrupted by one of the others, a boy called Knight, who asked her if there were any dogs in Narnia.

There were a few sniggers and snorts and several heads turned in my direction.

'Why do you ask?' she said, keeping a perfectly straight face while knowing exactly what it was he was alluding to.

'Well, you know what Lazenby's like, Miss,' Knight replied, and they all laughed on cue.

Knight's remarks were a reference to the pitiful attempts I'd made to stop crying during the class reading of another book, *Greyfriars Bobby*. The book was written from the point of view of a dog who, following the death of his master, faithfully visits his grave every day for fourteen years. Apparently, it was a true story, which only succeeded in deepening my sadness. I hadn't shed a tear since my first few nights at boarding school but was so overwhelmed by the story that, having abruptly started to cry again, I didn't know how to stop and ended up making a complete spectacle of myself. It was as if I'd stored up enough tears to last me for a whole year, like catching raindrops in a bucket, and they simply gushed out of me. The others found it hilarious and wouldn't let me forget it.

Miss Shepherd ignored them, the phase soon passed and they moved on to something else. Meanwhile, she continued to lead me with a gentle hand – a guiding influence whenever I needed it, which was most of the time. Simultaneously, she encouraged me to write as much as I could on my own, to strike out alone with my pen at every opportunity.

At first, predictably, the letters and words had more command over me than I had of them. They paid no attention to the lines on the page and fell in long curling arcs into the margin, never to reappear. Sometimes they even curved upwards, like a wobbling ladder thrown against a castle wall with letters and words tumbling off it – more reminiscent of my battle-scene drawings than any form of writing. Often, they leaked into each other, intertwined or tied themselves up in knots, crawling over each other as though I had attempted to write them while wearing a blindfold. The size of my handwriting appeared to shrink or expand at will, so small on occasions that it looked like it was trying to hide on the page, so tall on other days that the letters looked like they were walking on stilts. I had yet to accomplish joined-up writing, of course, and would not manage to do so for another three or four years at least. I randomly sprinkled capital letters through my writing too, and although I rarely started a sentence with an upper-case letter, I invariably ended it with one, just to be different.

My early writing was also distinguishable by the sudden, long spaces between words and letters, as if a new train of thought – an express train – had ploughed straight through the middle of my sentence without stopping, scattering everything in its wake. In addition, there was the inevitable assortment of spelling mistakes, coupled with the odd back-to-front word when I slipped back into my old ways. Miss Shepherd was content to let many of those errors go uncorrected, and whether it was in my exercise books or my letters home, encouraged me instead to develop a joy and a rhythm to my writing, as she described it, to explore my imagination. This seemed to please her more than anything. 'I have included John's letter as it is,' she wrote to my parents once. 'I'm not too worried at this stage by his spelling, I just want him to put words on paper. As many as possible. I think you'll agree that his writing is coming on in leaps and bounds.'

Punctuation was non-existent except when, for some reason not even known to me, I would inexplicably insert a full stop halfway through a sentence where it didn't belong. Commas were another lifeform altogether – I had no idea what they were for – and they would remain that way for many years to come. I still sent drawings home, but they became fewer and fewer over the passing weeks and months until eventually they ceased altogether. Because I wrote so slowly, my imagination regularly leaped ahead of me, and I would complete the next line in my head before finishing the one I was writing. But by that time, my head was in such a muddle, I'd clean forgotten what I wanted to say on both counts.

At best, my letters were never more than four or five lines long, but I was making progress – even I could see that. I had also taken to scribbling the occasional word in my exercise book, though they remained heavily outnumbered by the pictures I drew. I would be reminded many times during my early years at school of one thing that Miss Shepherd had said to me: 'Think of letters and words as your friends and they will soon make themselves known to you.' Often during the week, I'd think of something I wanted to write in my letter home to my parents, and I'd keep it mind until Sunday, quietly simmering away in my thoughts. Sometimes, the ideas about what I wanted to write would bank up inside my head to such an extent that Sunday couldn't come fast enough.

Of course, I frequently had to call on Miss Shepherd's help to complete my letters and could never rattle one off like Teague and the others. Their words always seemed to take up to three or four pages of note paper, while mine felt as if they had to be chipped out of tablets of stone. Yet the sense of satisfaction and accomplishment I achieved from finishing my letters home, sealing the envelope, licking the stamp, addressing it correctly (with Miss Shepherd's assistance) and placing it on top of the pile in the school post-box grew, strangely, more irresistible with every passing week, until I couldn't wait to write them. It was like finding my own door to Narnia.

CHAPTER EIGHT

DEAR MUM, DAD, DOW
AND GINA...

None of the letters I wrote home between February 1962 and July 1964 would have been possible without the patience, care and infinite kindness of Miss Shepherd. Left to my own devices, I would have just carried on drawing – I was physically and mentally incapable of writing anything on my own. Initially, she placed her hand on mine and guided it across the page, pausing only to insert the occasional tweak or punctuation mark and thereby add some vague coherence to my letters. If at first our hands looked like dancing partners – she wrote it, mostly, and I spoke it – then it was hers that always led. Yet in this way she taught me the feel and the flow of words, to understand the shape of my journey ahead. Not only that but she helped to untangle my distracted thoughts, to concentrate on one thing at a time, if only for a few minutes, and always encouraged me to write what was in my heart.

Many of those early letters consisted of little more than an endless string of requests or, in some cases, demands – but it was all I could think of to say at the time. I changed comics on an almost weekly basis, swapping *Look and Learn* for *Boys' World*, *Eagle* for *Ranger*,

Lion for *Hotspur*, *Valiant* for *Victor* and so on, until I ran out of options and had no choice but to return to my original selections and the whole process began again. The requests prompted countless visits to the newsagent and were so relentless my parents often failed to keep up with them. Apart from the comics, my requests included everything from toy guns, ammo (as I referred to it and which usually took the form of pellets or dried peas), Airfix or Revel model kits, board games, fountain pens, which I was always losing or breaking, and even books, which I had no idea how to read but ordered nonetheless – perhaps in the lingering hope that one day I might be able to. Sometimes Miss Shepherd found it impossible to suppress her laughter while helping me with my letters home. 'I'm not laughing at you,' she said once. 'It's just that I can't help but imagine your parents' faces when they read this.' I told her that my father didn't read my letters, and she stopped and looked at me for a moment. 'Oh, I'm sure he does,' she smiled. 'Who told you that?' 'My mother,' I replied.

Eventually my letters expanded to include such topics as sport, music, the race to the moon – which had fuelled my imagination ever since I watched my first countdown and lift-off on television – and Bleak House, which was about as far removed from a moon rocket as you could get but remained a limitless source of fascination for me. My undoubted passions were sport and music, though, and the two subjects frequently converged and intertwined in my letters, creating a world in which Tom Jones and Colin Cowdrey, for instance, happily but somewhat improbably rubbed shoulders. The selection of the England cricket, rugby and football teams was always a point of discussion, and there were yet more requests to my parents: I regularly instructed them to provide me with the latest music charts, which they had to cut out of the newspapers and send off that day, so they weren't out of date by the time they reached me.

Music fully entered my bloodstream as early as 1962 – the year the Beatles released their debut single, 'Love Me Do', which peaked at number seventeen in the charts, the Tornados recorded 'Telstar' to become the first British group to reach number one in the US and the Rolling Stones played their first gig at London's Marquee Jazz Club – and has never left it. Those of us who waited with bated breath for the new single by the Beatles, the Rolling Stones, the Who, the Kinks, Manfred Mann, the Animals or the Beach Boys (how fortunate we were to listen to them in real time) were rarely disappointed by what we heard. And for those of us who were shut away in grim, impenetrable places like Hildersham House, that music was an indispensable link to the outside world – backdropping our grey school days with a vivid, vibrant soundtrack.

• • •

11 February 1962, aged seven
I whic I was at hom.
 From john

18 February 1962
Dear Mummy and Daddy and Dow and Gina
 all the boys test me wen we wr dresen bi the way giv my luv to ajax and bill
 from John

In a note beneath my letter, Miss Shepherd had written, 'I feel sure that the other boys are not teasing him – matron assures me of this. He is probably rather shy at undressing in front of others, and I have no doubt he will get over this soon.'

On a separate piece of paper, I had written to Ajax, the dog: AJAX
I WIL CIS YOU I DO LUC ~~YOO~~ YOU

25 February 1962
Dear Mummy and Gina and Duddy and Dow

   I hop you are well I are well I wont granes addres please.

   from John

18 March 1962, aged eight
Dear mummy and Daddy and Dow And Gina

   I hope you are well. We had a lacture on the army, and the
Estern Comando Forces. You must tell the Fish man. I will be
coming back to hom soon. I wish I could see Rawhide again.

   Love from John

16 March 1963, aged nine
Dear mummy and Daddy

   I hope you are well. The school play was very good at the end of
the play the Minister of Foreign Affairs MR So and So came in and
Cronk said to the MR So and So, 'where did you get those lovely
maners from?' and MR So and So said, 'From Hildersham House.'

   Love John

30 May 1963
Dear mummy and Daddy

   I hope you are well when you come over please will you bring
my boat. please will you bag some for batreys. And this time don't
drop it on the floor. please can we go to the Beresford hotle. please
will you send 'Children of the new forest'.

   Love frome John.

22 June 1963

Dear mummy and Daddy

I hope you are well if you can't find the Kit could you get me a frog Kit. It is called Bristol Beaufort I hope Ajax is well. I am going in for everthing in sports exept for the long Jump. DON'T FORget it is a Frog Kit.

Love John.

8 July 1963

Dear Mum and Dad

please could you send me HOTspurs it is a comic. I hope you are well. please could you send me the game Aiation its about aroplanes. Could you please get it cwicly very cwicly

Love John.

20 July 1963

Dear mummy and Daddy

I hope you are well The Eams have finished. Thank you for my EaGle I am glad you have a good drive back I hope Ajax is well. My Eagle comes very late. please could you send it of erlyer.

Love John.

Sep 25, 1963

Dear mum and Dad

I hope you are well please could you send me a fountain pen. I am writiting whith some whone elses pen.

Love John.

Sep 30, 1963

Dear Mum and Dad

I hope you are well Thank you for your pen it was very nise I hope the rabbit is alwright, and Ajax and Bill are alwright. Thank you for my lookandlearn it was very good. I hope I will be home soon. when do I first go out. does Dad ever reed my letters. Dow or ways thinks that thease letters are never hers but they are for us all.

Love John.

Dec 8, 1963

Dear Mum and Dad

I hope you are well. We are having are Exams now and I have don very well in the History, Exam, We have started ruger. I have scored a Try and I would of scored a nother one thow I was pushed in to touch. Just now waddington droped the wooden bilard top on his foot and has probely brocken it. I got 26 for history Exam and it was out of 50. Are form has put chinease lantens up Vickery got us some very nise deackarhons we have made sum paper crackes. and some paper on form door saying HAPPY EXMAS. Vickery did a very good picture of Father Christmas and cut it out and stuck that on door too.

Love John.

Jan 26, 1964

Dear Mum and Dad

I hope you are well. This week I did not come last I came 9th with 66 marks and there was 10 boys in the class. We had a lacture on the Army and they had a peace of History about Rommel in the Desart and Montgommery and they had a great battle in the lacture called Alame and truck. We whent for a walk today and then whent on to the field to play rugger. I am in a senior rugger game and we have the proper rools and we can be of side and you

DEAR MUM, DAD, DOW AND GINA...

have to now your places on the field and I am majely a 3/4 line at rugger. When I was tackling a boy he fell on to my tooth and made it a bit loose I can make it woble with my tung. I hope gina is well and dow and we have got a lucture on february 1st called the Wonders of ancient Egypt by H.H.N perdes.

Love John

PS please do not send Eagle or Valiernt Just boys world. I think I would like a game called Risk and I thing I no how to play it.

Feb 23, 1964

Dear mum and Dad

Thank you for Eagle comic, and my letter I hope you are well. The Stone hous match on Saturday was put of but we will play them on Wednesday I heard that Scotland beat Irland and Spurs beat Arsanal Eagle is really good and they in side a free on how to be a Detective by Roger? Robert Moore who acts the saint on T.V. are next match will be a home match v st peter's court and I am really shore we will beat them this time.

Much love John.

1 March 1964

Dear mum and dad

we went for a walk to day and we whent to bleak house and we had a wonderful win against wellington we beat them 26-0. I do now what I want from dad for my birthday and mum a tin tin book called the secrete of the unicorn. I am glad it is a very short time before my Birthday and before the ent of term the school play is about toud of toud hall and we are reading around the world in eatly days in class and its darn Good.

Much love John.

8 March 1964

Dear mum and dad

I hope you are well thank you for my lovely day, out. we have got a fire in are form because it is so cold today over hear. I cant wate intile geomentry then I can test my new set out.

We had a Wakl to town this Week And I sor bLeAk house peeping out of the placE.

Love John

2 May 1964, aged ten

Dear Mum and Dad

I hope you are well will Dad please send me the test scours please. I arrived safeley at school sitting with Teague, Vickery, Waddington, and me. Carter-Wallace has Mups we are going to drop him out of the camp said Vickery me and Peel and Waddington. I am in the 3rd dorm neerer the Captain help help! I can easily be cort by the Captain, easily and neerer Waddington.

Love John

12 June 1964

Dear Mum and Dad

I hope you are well. and thank you so so so much for the book on Cricket the big green one it was one of the best books I have given in my life it had some wonderful pictures in it of Cricket it really was good and I don't now how to thank you for it. It was called England v Australia and I will try and keep it in nise condition The doctor came today and I will be getting up in a few days time.

Love John.

19 July 1964

Dear Mum and Dad

I hope you are well I have not got my Eagle yet. I saw that Dexter made 123 for Sussex v Austrailer and Griffith 56* and Eric Russell of middlisex got 193* and Parfitt 121 for middlisex v Austrailer at Lords. I thort the term has gone very quikly and I was amazed. In the 3rd IX match was I hit the ball right into the sky and was caught by a bloke called Freeman. Lazenby c Free man b Phillips 0. Those were the actual names of the Players.

Love John.

21 September 1964

Dear Mum and Dad

I hope you are very well indeed I am riting with my new pen. Just to brake it in before lessons torrow. That is Monday. I miss you all very much indeed. I am longing for half term wich won't be long now at leest I hope. and I hope Bill and Ajax are very well indeed. I hope Dad remembers to send me The Cricket tour of South Africa. I hope you like my writing with my new pen. I hope you are all very well and the Animals not forgetting them of cause. I Swear I am going to try this term because I am pretty hiuy on the mark bawd and to please you as much as possible.

every single bit of my love, John.

18 Oct 1964

Dear Mum and Dad

I hope you are well we are in quarnteen for hooping cauf and we did not gow to Church today. I hope Ajax and Bill are well. We play our first 3rd XI match on Monday but I dont think I will play in it now. I was sick last night in bed and had to stay in bed although I whent down for lunch. I'm longing for half term it seems ages since I last sour you. I came 10th in class this week.

all my love John

CHAPTER NINE

THE RECIPIENTS OF
MY LETTERS

My mother always used to joke that she married my father because of the delicious egg and cress sandwiches he brought to their wartime picnics when they were courting. It was on one such picnic, having wooed her with the best that his parents' chickens had to offer, that he plucked up the courage to propose to her. It was March 1945 and they had known each other for barely six weeks. After enduring rationing and the unremitting awfulness of powdered eggs for nearly six years, it was, she remarked, too good an offer to refuse. She might have even mentioned he cut a dashing figure in his Royal Navy uniform. But it was the real thing, in more ways than one.

When their eyes met across a bustling, crowded office on Belfast docks where my mother was stationed towards the end of the war with the Women's Royal Navy Service – or the Wrens as they were more commonly known – there was only ever going to be one outcome. Dad's clean-cut looks and the two half-inch gold braid stripes on the sleeves of his uniform, denoting the rank of lieutenant, did not go unnoticed by her. Equally so for him, her deep blue eyes, dark hair and flawless skin. He noted too how her eyes held his gaze as he walked into the office and how, in the weightlessness of that moment, a small smile played at the corner of her mouth, almost as if she had been expecting him, and to which he responded with one of his own. They were both twenty-seven, born two months apart. And like so many young couples who fell in love and were engaged during the war, they married in a hurry.

My father, Richard, served on corvettes and, latterly, frigates in the North Atlantic and the Mediterranean and fought in what was the longest, continuous military campaign of the Second World War, the 'Battle of the Atlantic' as Winston Churchill dubbed it. It started on 3 September 1939 and ended on 8 May 1945 – a total of 2,074 days. Dad enlisted in the Royal Navy as a rating, where his upper-middle-class tones earned him the nickname of 'Rolls-Royce' from the other men. He trained as a navigator at a newly constructed leisure centre on Hove seafront in Sussex, the Hove Marina complex, which had been requisitioned by the Admiralty and renamed HMS *King Alfred*. The centre had yet to be opened to the public and its underground car park, capable of holding five hundred vehicles, was swiftly transformed into a makeshift battle-ship, complete with guns and a ship-handling simulator. Such was its strategic importance during the war that German propaganda claimed on at least two occasions to have sunk the landbound *King Alfred*, but the bombs fell on the centre of Brighton or on Hove instead. After completing his three-month training in early 1940 and graduating as a navigator, my father joined the crew of HMS *Gardenia*, a Flower-class corvette – so called because the fleet was named after flowers – as a sub-lieutenant before soon rising to the rank of lieutenant.

Corvettes were described as small and squat, not much more

than two hundred feet in length, nearly half the size of a destroyer and below a frigate in the pecking order. With a top speed of only sixteen knots – slower than a U-boat when surfaced – they were not fast. Remarkably for a fighting ship, they were based on the design of a whale catcher and were armed and equipped purely for anti-submarine warfare: an ancient four-inch gun mounted on the bow and racks of depth charges at the stern, leaving them horribly vulnerable to an attack from the air. Their objective was to escort convoys, to provide a lifeline, to keep the shipping lanes to Great Britain and the Soviet Union open, to take the fight to the numerically superior U-boats and, ultimately, defeat them. A Herculean task by any standards – but especially so for a warship tagged somewhat unglamorously as the 'Pekingese of the ocean'.

For the ninety-strong crew of these vessels – many of whom were so green they had never been to sea – it was a brutal existence. Corvettes leaked copiously, water sluiced through open hatches and the living quarters were suffocatingly cramped, uncomfortable, cold and permanently wet. They battled the fury of the North Atlantic, often on little or no sleep, as much as they battled the lurking presence of the U-boats, hiding in their grey wolf-packs beneath the icy waves. The action was constant and ferocious. To make matters worse, corvettes corkscrewed and rolled sickeningly. Unable to slice through the mountainous Atlantic seas with the grace of a destroyer, their bows parting the waves in great curtains of spray, the corvette dipped and twisted perilously on top of the swells, like a novice rider struggling to stay in the saddle of a runaway horse.

My father was sunk twice during his five long years escorting the convoys. On the first occasion, after what felt like several hours in the Mediterranean waters off the coast of Algeria, fighting to stay afloat at night amid the horror and turmoil, he had made up his mind he was going to die. He had no strength left and allowed himself to slip under the waves, to let himself go, to surrender to death. In that moment he was overtaken by a strange sense of peacefulness, a complete calm, and for the first time, the fear and panic that had swamped him on the surface vanished into the depths. It lasted for only a split-second – so powerful he would never forget it – before he felt himself being suddenly hoisted through the dense, dark water back to the surface, as if he were suspended on the end of a hook. He knew he was on the surface because he could feel the stiff breeze on his face again, he could hear voices and confusion all around him and smell and taste the burning fuel oil.

It was not a hook at all, my father soon realised, but the meaty, tattooed arm of a giant British sailor anchoring him in the water – his voice in his ear, shouting something unintelligible in the unmistakable tones of a Geordie accent. He felt as if he had been shaken awake from a deep, restful sleep, and his first instinct was to go under the waves again, where there was no fear, no panic. But the sailor was having none of it – 'No you don't' and 'Not so fast', my father recalled him shouting – and he was hauled back to the surface each time by his collar, coughing and spluttering, his breath coming in short, sharp bursts. My father was not a small man but was made to feel like a bundle of wet clothing or a rag doll in the grasp of this bearded giant. In the end, it was all he could do to cling on while the sailor maintained an incessant volley of words in his ear, only fragments of which he could understand, and never let up until they and others were eventually rescued by another British warship and plucked to safety. After that, Dad knew he would survive the war and death no longer held any fear for him.

On the other occasion he was sunk, he again looked death squarely in the eye but, despite cheating it for a second time, did not escape the fallout. He swallowed mouthfuls of fuel oil, enough to destroy part of the lining to his stomach, leaving him unable to digest anything but the blandest of foods for the rest of his life. His nervous system was in tatters too. The 'wrong' food, which invariably involved something too rich, could make him ill for days afterwards. My mother often had to cook one dinner for him and another for the rest of us. After existing predominantly on tinned corned beef and powdered potatoes, along with every other sailor in the Royal Navy, his stomach was not in good condition as it was. If he had an appetite at all, it was blunted by the twenty or thirty cigarettes he smoked a day for five years, though he gave up after the war because, without the adrenaline rush, they made him sick. As a family, we were used to the measly portions he ate, the way he picked suspiciously at his food or pushed it abruptly to the side of his plate. It was a rare occurrence when he enjoyed a meal – bacon and eggs were a treat for him and so was Sunday roast with the occasional glass of beer, always poured into a foaming tankard. Ice cream was a luxury too, but everything in moderation.

In keeping with so many of the war generation, he rarely talked about his wartime experience or the two occasions he was sunk unless he was prompted, perhaps by me, but he was clearly not comfortable doing so. And even when he did, I suspect he left much unsaid. He preferred instead to relate the more amusing, light-hearted moments he experienced, which, because they were few and far between and afforded him a small ray of light in a sea of darkness, never failed to lose their vividness or humour. I learned, for instance, that for almost the entire war he never received a full cup of cocoa while on the bridge. The galley was situated at the stern and, as corvettes rolled excessively in rough seas, the mug was invariably empty by the time it reached the officer on the bridge, except for a swill of salt water and the dregs of the cocoa powder. The lavatories were particularly susceptible to the great North Atlantic swells too and the pipes, which drained straight into the ocean, frequently filled up with a reverse surge of freezing sea water, flooding the bowl and rinsing the backside of many an unsuspecting sailor. He and my mother would also reminisce endlessly on the first occasion they met or had their first date together, always adding an unexpected new detail here and there, as if they were completing their own jigsaw puzzle.

Surprisingly, considering the severity of his war, Dad's first thought was to stay on in the navy following Germany's surrender. He was a seasoned navigator and a first-rate officer by this time, dependable, capable and methodical. He loved the sea, had passed out among the ten best navigators in the service and promotion and a prominent career in the Royal Navy were his for the taking. But it was not to be. His father was dying of cancer and his last wish was that his eldest son (Dad had a younger brother and an elder sister) should take over the running of the family business, importing and exporting food. His father explained to him that he had inherited the business from his father and it was my dad's turn to continue the line. Being the kind of person he was, Dad was not prepared to refuse the wishes of a dying man and, despite the many reservations he had as to his own suitability for the job, abandoned his ambition to stay in the navy and gave his solemn promise to his father. Within a matter of weeks, before there was time to even catch his breath, he had resigned his wartime commission and started life as a businessman in the city.

Worn down by a war that had emptied his last reserves of strength and resolve, he quickly discovered the business was at a similar ebb. It was barely breaking even. He inherited a tiny staff and a greengrocer's shop around the corner from the office, where he sometimes liked to roll up his sleeves and work behind the counter. Perhaps it offered him a small slice of freedom. For the next thirty-eight years, my father pumped out the bilges and single-handedly attempted to keep the business, groaning at the seams, afloat – to steer it away from the rocks by whatever means he could. He often woke up screaming in the night as the horrors of the war resurfaced, but he was on the train to London and at his desk the next morning without fail – a tweed overcoat in the winter, a rain-coat in the summer, a brown trilby and a briefcase with a handle, which reminded me of a black doctor's bag, but emptier. In fact, his briefcase was a mere appendage and contained little apart from a copy of the *Evening Standard* and the *Evening News*. The news-papers were brought home for Dow, who devoured the crosswords in minutes flat, having earlier disposed of *The Times* crossword. It was not for want of trying that Dad failed to turn the business around, but at least he prevented it from going under, from dashing itself against the rocks. He was still pumping out the bilges on the day he left it behind for good.

He was, by his own admission, a dreadful salesman. He was no more a salesman than I could have been a mathematician or a navi-gator. He always played it straight; he knew no other way. It was the only card he carried all his life, and if that failed, he had nothing else up his sleeve – the feint and counter feint, the easy patter, the manipulation, the bluff and double bluff were not for him. He was all at sea, out of his depth, in a game where no one played by the rules and where the rules were changed at will. My mother often accompanied him on his selling trips, acting as his driver and mo-tivator and attempting to bolster his confidence, galvanising him, feeding him lines to impress prospective clients or delivering the occasional pep talk. She joked that if she could only exchange places with him, she would have no trouble closing the deal. She would, of course, have made a wonderful salesperson and would not have left the room until she'd got what she wanted; she would certainly not have allowed herself to be so casually brushed aside. My father also made regular business trips abroad, sometimes taking my mother with him – he spoke fluent Italian and was conversant in Spanish and French – but always returned home not knowing whether the deal he'd struck would still exist tomorrow. In most cases, it didn't.

During much of my time at school and for a considerable period afterwards, my father was a distant figure to me and it seemed that neither of us could understand, or even want to understand, the other.

He also spent a considerable portion of his life having no comprehension of how unintentionally funny he was – spectacularly so on occasion. In my teenage years, he was easy prey for some of my schoolfriends, one of whom consistently rang him to inform him that the pizza he'd ordered for dinner was ready for collection. Sometimes the prank lasted for as long as five minutes, while my father swore blind that he hadn't ordered a pizza and my friend remained adamant that the order had been made in his name and from his number. In the end, it was my mother who put an abrupt halt to it by snatching the phone from my father's hand and hanging up: 'Do stop it, Richard – you'll give yourself a heart attack.' On another occasion, Dad asked the caller (my friend) whether he was the owner of the business. 'Yes, sir,' he was told. Whereupon my father replied, 'Well, you're a bloody fool. I've never eaten pizza in my life – and I certainly don't intend to eat one from a business as bad as yours.' The cruel irony of the joke, of course, was that my father's stomach would not have withstood one.

It was just his luck too that despite a powerful aversion to pop music, he regularly failed to escape its clutches, no matter how hard he tried. In 1964, my sister and I somehow managed to persuade him to take us to see the Beatles play live in London at the Hammersmith Odeon. The fact that he had no perception of the mayhem he was about to let himself in for undoubtedly worked in our favour. Unfortunately for him, he endured the entire evening being repeatedly hit over the head by a screaming girl brandishing a rolled-up copy of a newspaper, which she wielded like a baton, eventually reducing it to shreds in her hands. Each blow landed in perfect time to the beat – or it would have done had the beat not been totally obscured by the ear-piercing shrieks of some 5,000 hysterical girls, as was my father's plaintive refrain of 'Steady on' to the girl in question. At one point, Paul McCartney took a bite out of an apple and threw it into the crowd, causing a mass stampede of girls who descended on the fruit by clambering over seats or in some cases literally hurling themselves through the air, giving the unnerving impression they were flying. The look on my father's face of utter disbelief and puzzlement during the concert, as girls fainted all around him and were carried out on stretchers, was matched only by his alarmed expression on the train home when, out of the blue, my mother announced that she rather liked the look of George Harrison.

A year or two later, Dad found himself sharing a train compartment with Charlie Watts of the Rolling Stones and fell into a discussion about income tax, of all things. The musician, reportedly concerned that he might lose a sizeable chunk of his fortune to the taxman, asked my father, as a businessman, which party he should vote for at the next general election. When he returned home that evening and mentioned to my sister and me who he had met, we could hardly contain ourselves for embarrassment – the kind of embarrassment you reserve only for your parents. 'He did say the name of his group, but I can't for the life of me remember what it was,' he said.

'Only the Rolling Stones,' I replied, mustering all the awe for them and disdain for him I could cram into one short sentence.

He explained that the man apparently earned more than £1 million a year and, making no attempt to disguise his astonishment, added, 'From playing the drum, I think he said.'

'The *drums*, Dad.'

'Well, naturally enough, I'd never heard of him,' he continued, by which time I almost had my hands over my ears. 'Anyway, he asked for my advice, so I gave it to him in no uncertain terms: if he wanted to keep his money, I told him, there was only one party he should vote for and that was the Conservative Party.'

While my father made no apologies for his unabashed efforts to try to convert a member of the Rolling Stones to Toryism (the political implications were entirely lost on me at that young age), he resolutely refused to impose his will on me or to deny me the right to do whatever I wanted with my life. 'I had to do what my father wanted, and I would never wish that on you,' he once told me. 'God forbid that you should ever have to follow me into the business.' A lesser man might have taken the view that, because he had suffered all his life in a job he'd never wanted to do, I should have to endure the same fate in the natural order of things – 'I had no say in the matter and nor should you.' But that was not my father's way, to repeat the damage, or prolong the pain. 'I don't care what you do as long as you're happy and you're doing what you want.' In many ways it was a bold call for a man of his generation and upbringing, and it was the greatest legacy he could have left me.

By the 1970s, having already sold the grocery shop, my father closed the London office and relocated the business to a smaller premises in Sevenoaks, Kent, making the fifty-mile journey from his front door to work each day by car. He had at least retained a few loyal clients who'd stuck faithfully by him, but it was hardly a new start – rather a position from where he could go through the motions, gently running down the clock until retirement. But it did not work out like that and the business continued to exert a heavy toll on his health. Something had to break and in the summer of 1975, thirty years since taking over the firm, it did.

He was driving back from work one evening when he failed to spot a Road Closed sign and some bollards and suddenly found himself marooned on a stretch of road that was being tarmacked. Within seconds, he was confronted by the sight of a steamroller and a crew of angry workers bearing down on him. Some of the men rocked and shook the car while he remained at the wheel, the windows wound up, his beloved James Last Orchestra on the cassette player, the steamroller stationary in front of him, primed like a battering ram, its engine grunting. For a moment he thought it might shunt him off the road or the men might drag him out of the car. He turned up the music as loud as it would go, so he didn't have to hear them swearing at him, abusing him; one of them gobbed on the window and he watched it dribble slowly down the glass. He could smell the burning fuel oil again, hear the screaming and shouting and feel the terror, the tug of the waves pulling him down. When he eventually got home, he sat at the kitchen table and without saying a thing, put his head in his hands and sobbed uncontrollably – a conflagration of thirty years of trauma and responsibility flaring deep inside him.

He took the next five weeks off – my mother wanted him to take longer, but there were only so many visits to the doctor he could stand, only so many times he could mow the lawn, sit in front of the Test match on the television or walk round the garden with the same thoughts repeating in his head before he realised there was no other choice than to return to work. He had given his word. It was what he did.

• • •

My mother was two months shy of her thirty-seventh birthday when she finally gave birth to me. I say finally because my parents had been hoping to start a family for nine years and had already passed the point where they accepted it might never happen.

In a ward of young mothers-to-be, she soon lost count of the number of times she heard the term 'geriatric pregnancy' directed at her by the hospital staff – the term used to describe women of that time who were thirty-five or older at their estimated delivery date – or 'geriatric mother', as she was also routinely referred to. She lost count too of the number of doctors, young and old, who came to gawp at her, as she put it, and who never failed to warn her of the many risks involved in giving birth at her advanced age. Being pregnant for the first time at thirty-six was still considered a rarity in the 1950s. However, my mother was not the sort to fret about such things – she didn't have a moment's doubt that her 'geriatric' body was up to the task, and she was quick to correct any doctor who dared suggest otherwise. She even joked about it with the other women in the ward. As it turned out, she was right and my birth could not have been any more straightforward. It was only my timing, as ever, that proved haphazard – having taken the best part of a decade to make my grand entrance.

And yet it was also typical of my mother. She was a free spirit who rarely conformed to the conventional way of doing things. Her strength of will, her capacity for the unorthodox and the unusual, her delight in bucking the tide, her determination to take on and beat the odds shaped so much of her life. Mum was unvanquishable: she had beaten polio as a child, danced as a West End chorus girl and given birth to my sister, Gina, twenty-two months after me. The list does not end there.

The genetic link between Mum and me was never more evident than during her early school days when she struggled hopelessly with maths – a subject that had such a disastrous effect on her brain it sometimes felt as if it could shut it down entirely. I have met only one person in life who was worse at maths than me and that was my mother. My ability to work with numbers, to carry out almost any mathematical task, big or small, has always amounted to the square root of nothing. She was the same.

Unfortunately, she had a particularly severe maths teacher, a woman in her late fifties with threadbare patience and a combustible temper. Her name was one Mum could remember decades later: Miss Cooper. The more she scribbled on the blackboard, invariably snapping the chalk into pieces in her impetuosity, the more unfathomable and indecipherable the numbers became to my mother. She once described them to me as resembling a swarm of bees, each one indistinguishable from the other. Every time the teacher asked her to provide the answer to some fraction or equation, she would make a hurried, panicky guess – usually the first number to come into her head – and blurt it out. It was so wide of the mark, it instantly reduced the class to laughter. Whenever that happened, she knew what was coming next: the blackboard eraser, a sturdy wooden object like the head of a broom, which Miss Cooper kept permanently lodged in her right hand to hurl in my mother's direction at a moment's notice. Luckily for Mum, her aim proved so wayward it was often the other pupils who came off worse. Except for one occasion, when the teacher finally succeeded in scoring a direct hit on my mother's head. She had taken her eye off the ball for no more than a moment and although she managed to turn away at the last second, the projectile caught her a jarring blow on the temple.

When she returned home, her mother took one look at the dark blemish on the side of her head and demanded to know what had happened. At first, she pretended it was nothing, but her mother warned her that if she didn't tell the truth, she would march down to the school and find out for herself. Reluctantly, Mum explained how the teacher had hurled the eraser at her, whereupon her mother marched down to the school anyway. She was a curious mix, her mother: dreamy and vague at times, her dressing gown pockets stuffed with bills she intended to pay but never did, stubborn, forthright and formidable at other times, especially when it came to defending her daughters. After that, the teacher never threw another eraser at anyone again – though, it must be said, my mother's maths never improved either.

She made up for it with her reading and writing, and it was there that our neurodivergent paths seemed to separate. She excelled in English and regularly finished among the top pupils in class. She had learned to read and write at an early age and was rarely without a book in her hand growing up, sometimes devouring them in a single sitting. She loved words and remained a voracious reader until the end, her bedside table always stacked with a teetering pile of books. As a child, she was frequently told to slow down when talking and to think carefully before opening her mouth. Often, the words were out of her mouth before she could catch them. 'Count to five', her father advised her, 'and think about what you're going to say before you blurt something you might regret.' It was a trick she never mastered. Nonetheless, for all her life, she could hold a conversation with anybody and had that wonderful knack of being able to treat everybody the same.

Virgina Mary Rose was born in 1917, the second daughter of the England and Kent cricketer Jack Mason and his wife Mary Mason (née Powell), an international golfer for Wales. Sara, their eldest daughter was born two years earlier and Daphne three years later in 1920. An all-rounder, Jack Mason played in five Test matches for England and captained Kent for five seasons from 1898–1902. 'Mason always returns to the memory from the opening years of the century as one of the most accomplished of amateur cricketers and one of the most attractive of men. There was some indefinable atmosphere of class about him,' *The Times* wrote in his obituary. Undoubtedly, there would have been more opportunities with England, perhaps even the captaincy, had his father not decided to expedite his retirement from the game to pursue his career as a solicitor in the family firm. 'You've had a good run,' he was told. 'It's high time you earned a proper living.' By all accounts, his father was a fearsome, domineering man who chose the professions of each of his seven sons and expected his wishes to be carried out – though not before he placed a pile of crisp new five-pound notes on the table first. 'You either take up the profession I've chosen for you or you take the money. Which is it to be?' Jack Mason was twenty-eight at the time and at the pinnacle of his powers as a cricketer. As *Wisden* observed, 'If comparatively brief, his career was brilliant.' But the business had to come first.

Mary Mason represented Wales against Scotland, Ireland and

England in the Women's Home International Amateur Championship, which was established in 1905. As well as being an active sportswoman, she was a talented amateur musician, composer and singer. She wrote poems too, which came to her in a flash and which she often kept on scraps of paper in her dressing gown pockets, along with the unpaid bills. Her piano playing and singing every evening at their home in Beckenham, Kent, regularly drew a captive audience of frogs from the garden, where they formed an orderly queue on the sitting-room windowsill and refused to disperse until she had finished. Some of her compositions were written especially for them. My mother inherited her singing voice, her stubborn streak, her refusal to play by the rules and Dow her imagination and flair for the piano.

Singing was without a doubt the great love of my mother's life and nothing surpassed it, not even books. Yet there might have been a very different tale to tell had she not overcome an excruciating experience after participating in a talent show aged fourteen. She had chosen to sing 'Lady of Spain', a popular song of the time recorded by the likes of Bing Crosby, but a combination of the romantic lyrics and her operatic-style rendition of it sent one member of the audience into a spasm of such unrestrained laughter that he succeeded in setting off others in the room. By the time she reached the last verse and chorus, she could not hear her own voice for laughter. Somehow, her mother managed to convince her that the audience were laughing at the man and not at her.

Undeterred, she auditioned for a place as a singer at the Royal Academy of Music on leaving school and to her immense delight, she was accepted. Her heart was soon set on appearing in a West End musical and after graduating from the academy two years later, she auditioned for any London show that was hiring. Usually at some point during these auditions, the director would ask to see her legs – a request she dreaded above all others. The polio she contracted as a child had left her with a right leg that permanently splayed out at an awkward angle (my sister and I could always pick her out in a crowd because of it). Her plan for this was to distract the director by standing her full height – she was five feet eight inches tall – fix him with her most dazzling smile and twinkling blue eyes and hope he failed to spot her polio leg, as she called it. It must have worked because she landed a part in the chorus of the *White Horse Inn*, a musical comedy, and continued to perform in musicals until the outbreak of war in 1939, when London's theatres were temporarily plunged into darkness. As much as she loved show business, she wanted to do her bit for the war effort and joined the Wrens instead. But she never stopped singing.

I grew up listening to the sound of her singing to herself, her voice, crystal clear, ringing out from every corner of the house. 'Ticket to Ride' by the Beatles, George Harrison's 'My Sweet Lord', the Frank Sinatra classic 'That Old Black Magic' or the wartime favourites 'Every Time We Say Goodbye' or 'A Nightingale Sang in Berkeley Square'. She had a vast and eclectic taste in music and could rattle off songs with the rapidity of a jukebox. But because she was unable to break the shackles of her musical training or her vocal technique, 'Ticket to Ride' and 'A Nightingale Sang in Berkeley Square' always sounded, hilariously, as though they had come out of the same era – the 1930s and '40s. Once a song was inside her head, it was impossible to shift.

In May 1970, she even attended a rock festival with me – a two-day event held at Plumpton Racecourse, just down the road from our house, so close we could hear the music from our back garden. I must have been at home on a half-term break but was told I was too young to go to the festival on my own. As I recall, my parents gave me two choices: miss out on it altogether, which I had no intention of doing, or be accompanied by my mother. I chose the latter – although the prospect of being seen with her was so embarrassing I insisted she had to wear some kind of disguise. As usual, she entered into the fun of it and dressed up in my father's old brown herring-bone overcoat – which he used for gardening during the winter and had more holes in it than our shared knowledge of trigonometry – a crushed green trilby, which looked as if it had been run over by a tractor and which she pulled down over her face, and a pair of mud-encrusted Wellington boots. 'There, will that do?' she asked. I had to admit even I was taken aback. Fortified by two glasses of gin and Dubonnet, and with a packet of Du Maurier thrust into the pocket of the overcoat, she set off on foot for the racecourse with me in tow.

What I hadn't bargained on was her dancing. It started barely ten minutes into the set of the festival's headlining act, Ginger Baker's Air Force, and didn't let up for what felt like another couple of hours. Roy Harper, the penultimate act, had failed to appear and Ginger Baker agreed to play an extended set, which resulted in a series of interminable jams and drum solos and a torrent of abuse aimed at Harper. The band employed three drummers, including Ginger Baker himself, two percussionists and a conga player, and featured Steve Winwood, Denny Laine, Ric Grech and Graham Bond amid a twenty-strong line-up that might have earned them 'supergroup' status. At one point there seemed to be so many musicians on stage they were in danger of falling over each other. But the longer they played, the more my mother loved it and the more my frequent and increasingly frenzied efforts to stop her dancing went unheeded.

'We're here now,' she said, 'so we might as well enjoy ourselves.' It should have been my line.

Richie Havens, King Crimson, Julie Driscoll, Black Sabbath and Chicken Shack were all on the bill that day, but I have no recollection of seeing them. As the night wore on and the scent of cannabis swirled about us, my mother's dancing became wilder and more exaggerated until, in her torn coat and crushed hat, she resembled some kind of deranged farmer's wife. She finally stopped when the band, having played way beyond their allotted time, had the plug pulled on them by the organisers, like a needle jumping off a record, and the lights were extinguished. My last memory was of seeing Ginger Baker, midway through another colossal drum solo, being hauled off his kit by a team of security men, while the crowd, including my mother, shouted for more.

One way or another, Mum always managed to make the school holidays memorable for Gina and me. She went out of her way to organise outings, shopping expeditions, meals out and no end of trips to Brighton, to the beach, the pier, the cinema. Her flair for the unusual and her love for discovering anything new, whether it was music or films, meant that she enjoyed it as much as, if not more than, we did. The only downside was that she made it infinitely harder for me to go back to school again when the time came, especially when I was very young.

It was typical of her that on the day I returned to Hildersham House for the start of a new term, we always paid a visit to the cinema at Victoria Station where it perched, like a small ocean liner, on the corner of platform nineteen. I was eight by this time and travelled to Broadstairs on the school train. I used to spend the entire journey from Haywards Heath to London pleading with her not to have to go back. Sometimes even her wonderful smile faltered under the weight of my misery, but whatever she felt inside, she never wavered. 'Yes, I'm afraid you do have to go back,' she replied and valiantly attempted to change the subject.

The cinema mainly showed cartoons and newsreels, but it provided a small diversion, somewhere to hide my sadness and delay the inevitable for another hour. Often, we were the only ones there and I allowed myself a quiet blub in the darkness while the cartoon voices screeched and hollered, as only they could, and the sound effects pinballed inside my head. Anything was better than taking tea at the station's Grosvenor Hotel, where Mr Snowden held court, greeting parents with a diabolically short haircut, a fixed smile and cold eyes. There was usually time for a couple of cartoons or a newsreel before we had to go. Then it was out into the tumult. We hurried across the crowded concourse to the other side of the station where the school train awaited – the booming announcements, shrill whistles and sound of slamming doors sucking the breath out of me. My father joined us at the last minute, hotfoot from the office with his overcoat, trilby and empty briefcase, just in time to shake my hand before the train departed. Occasionally, if my friends had saved a seat for me, I'd board the train early and forget all about my heartache for a moment. The hardest part, though, was trying not to meet my parents' eyes when the train pulled out of the station and I would do anything to avoid them. How could I not? I was returning to the spectre that haunted my holidays and they were going back to everything I loved and held dear.

My mother's desire to do everything within her powers to make the school holidays special faltered on only one occasion, when she hired a maths teacher to come to the house to provide me with some extra tuition. I would have been no more than nine or ten and regarded it as a form of betrayal; selfishly, I even accused her of ruining my holidays. But at least she quickly made amends when it all went wrong. I had to take only one look at Mr Imrie, my new maths teacher, to know it would.

Mr Imrie looked like every schoolmaster I had ever known. He wore a heavy tweed jacket with the texture of a wire-haired terrier that crackled like static on the radio every time he moved; there were leather trimmings on its sleeves and patches at the elbows. A knitted green tie and the ubiquitous grey flannels completed the look. I drifted restlessly in and out of his lessons or looked longingly into the garden, unable to concentrate or to pull myself out of the torpor of having to learn maths during the holidays. In fact, the only time I attempted any maths was when I counted the number of grey hairs – five from memory – he plastered from ear to ear, without any discernible parting, across the top of his head. The rest of my time was spent puzzling over how someone with such sparse hair could have a permanent dusting of dandruff on his shoulders and eyebrows, while trying not to wince whenever he exhaled in my face – his breath smelled horrendously of iron filings – or sighed, with regularity, at my mathematical stupidity. I won't deny that he intrigued me – principally because he was so repellent.

The lessons continued in much the same vein until one morning, after failing to answer another of his questions correctly, he snaked out his right hand and, using surprising speed and force, struck me across the side of the head. There was no indicator of the abrupt change in mood and I never saw it coming. 'Wake up,' he hissed. 'And stop wasting my time.' I suppose I should have been better prepared for it. After all, I was used to Mr Snowden pulling my hair in lessons, so hard that scraps of it often fell out over my exercise book, or kidney-punching us when he lost control, which was often. But I never mentioned Mr Imrie's actions to my parents – in the same way I never mentioned the more horrific bouts of violence that were inflicted on us at Hildersham House. It was as if we were bound by some code of silence that forbade us from blabbing about it: never tell anyone, especially not your parents. So I kept quiet. But what shocked me most about it was that Mr Imrie had chosen to hit me in my own home, during the holidays, as if it was a perfectly acceptable thing for him to do – that and the sly glint of pleasure I detected in his eyes afterwards. Having broken the ice, as it were, he then proceeded to hit me two or three times every lesson for the next week, darting his hand out and catching me just behind the ear whenever he felt like it, each blow landing with a crackle of static and a hot gust of iron filings.

Occasionally while this was happening, I heard the creak of a floorboard in my parents' bedroom above my head but didn't take too much notice of it. Because the house was old, the timbers regularly creaked and groaned of their own accord. We were coming to the end of a lesson one day – Mr Imrie had been in a particularly foul-tempered mood and had delivered his third or fourth blow to the side of my head – when the creaking became more distinct and I recognised my mother's footfall.

Her bedroom door flew open and I heard her walk down the stairs into the sitting room, where we were seated at a table by the window. She had never interrupted our lessons before, so I knew something was about to happen – I just wasn't prepared for what followed. She marched straight over to the table and lifted Mr Imrie out of his seat by the collar of his jacket. I knew that look on my mother's face only too well – when she was in a temper, which was rare, it was advisable to stand back. 'That's it,' she said. 'The lesson's over.' For a moment, Mr Imrie dangled in front of me, twisting helplessly like a parachutist snagged on a branch. My mother's strength had acquired an almost legendary reputation in our house and it was always her that Gina and I took bottle tops or jars to if they needed opening, never my father. Part of the fun was to watch the terrifying faces she pulled while she grappled with the lid until it came off in her hands, as it always did, with a satisfying pop. But this was an impressive show of strength, even by her standards.

In her grasp, Mr Imrie now resembled a man trapped inside his own jacket. 'Mrs Lazenby... Mrs Lazenby,' he repeated. His voice had a strained, high-pitched quality to it, his eyes bulging, his face an odd puce colour. He attempted to scrabble his papers back into his briefcase, just managing to do so before he was dragged towards the door. His trousers gave the impression they were walking in a straight line by themselves, while his body went in another direction. 'Mrs Lazenby,' he tried again. 'What are you doing?'

She was steering him through the sitting-room door by this time. 'What do you think I'm doing?' she replied, opening the front door with her other hand and thrusting him forcibly through it. 'I'm throwing you out of my house, that's what I'm doing. And not before time.'

Desperate to see what happened next, I followed them across the garden, keeping a safe distance. They looked like two people locked in some weird embrace or a dance where they made up the steps as they went along. I stopped by a gap in the hedge next to the drive and watched her bundle him into his car. She leaned in and said something to him and he looked at her, his hands clamped to the wheel. I saw the face of a man who had been rumbled, who knew his game was up. I would never forget it. Whatever it was she said, it had the desired effect because he turned on the ignition and immediately flung the car into reverse, the engine revving, the wheels spinning furiously in the gravel. For a few seconds, the car sat in the middle of the road while he fumbled with the gearstick, his humiliation complete. Then, there was a loud crunching noise and it suddenly lurched forward, taking off up the road at a similar speed to the skyrocket I'd once recklessly launched. My mother stood and watched him disappear out of sight. It was payback time for her too, of course. And before turning to go back inside, she briefly clapped her hands together, no more than twice, as if she was wiping the dust – or was it the dandruff? – from them.

· · ·

My mother's sister came to live with us in 1960, after the death of their father, Jack Mason, at the age of eighty-four in October 1958. She had stayed on at Kismet – the house where they'd lived together on the edge of Cooden Beach in Bexhill, East Sussex – for almost two years, organising its sale, overseeing the estate, auctioning off much of the furniture and tidying up the obligatory loose ends. But the hardest part of all was having to say her goodbyes over and over to what had been the family home since 1939, when she was eighteen. Before then, Kismet had been their holiday house by the sea, where they spent every August without fail. It was a huge departure for her in more ways than one: she was closing the book on one chapter of her life and opening another, exchanging a golden past for what would have felt like a decidedly uncertain future. Knowing her as I do, it was an undertaking that would have tested her to the full, living there on her own with the rooms emptying out all around her and the memories crowding in.

It was during those summer holidays at Kismet that Jack Mason taught his three daughters to catch, throw and hit a tennis ball to a standard of which he approved. Not surprisingly, given their sporting pedigree, they were all naturals and needed little encouragement. This became so ingrained in them, in fact, that if they were ever in two minds about a boyfriend – not that there was ever any shortage – their favourite game was to take him into the garden and throw a ball to him. If he caught it, he remained in the game, but if he dropped it or couldn't throw it properly or wasn't in any way sporty, he was out – out of luck and out of the running. My grandfather was often an amused spectator during these 'trials' in the garden; on other occasions he would join in, the passing years having done nothing to diminish the speed of his reflexes. He had been one of the greatest slip fielders of his generation and it was said his reactions were so fast he could snaffle a catch and produce it from his pocket seconds later, to the wonderment of the crowd.

In my mind, Kismet was a house that always brimmed with light, laughter, music and the constant shuffle of the ocean, but there was a time when its walls echoed with a deep and resounding sadness. Mum's elder sister Sara had not been married long when, at the age of thirty-one, she was diagnosed with Nephrotic syndrome – a type of kidney disease for which there was no known cure at that point. She spent the last few months of her life at Kismet planning constantly for the future before passing away in 1948, almost two years since the diagnosis, the family having decided to keep from her the inevitability of her impending death. Mary Mason never recovered from the grief of losing her eldest daughter so young and died two years later, aged sixty-five, after suffering a stroke while working in the garden. She would often work long into the evening, ignoring the pleas from her family to take a rest, carrying rocks from one side of the lawn to the other in her efforts to build another rockery, as though she were in a race against time.

Jack Mason's death eight years later came as a massive shock to family and friends alike, and none more so than Dow, who bore the full force of it. His aura of indestructibility was as genuine as the famous modesty and charm for which he was known and celebrated. He had caught a bad cold, according to his doctor, who prescribed some medicine and a few days' rest in bed. No one thought anything of it – he was fit and healthy, a practising solicitor still, commuting daily to his office in High Holborn, walking the ten minutes from Kismet to Cooden station and back, regularly taking dips in the ocean during the summer. When he appeared to get no better, my mother went to visit him. 'I think I'm on a bit of a sticky wicket,' he said. A cricketer to the last. She repeated what everyone else had told him: you'll be up and about in no time. Within days, the infection had spread to his chest and affected his heart and lungs – so quickly that no one considered the possibility he might be dying, or even mentioned the thought, until it was too late.

Before he died, Jack Mason had one last request: he asked my father to look after his youngest daughter should anything happen to him. He wanted Daphne to have the support and security of a loving family, to be safe and cared for. Above all, she had stayed faithfully by his side following her mother's death and he wanted to make sure she was not left alone when he too was gone. My father, of course, gave his word. He and Virginia would see to it, he promised, thereby sealing the second of two pledges he had made to men on their deathbeds.

And so, at the start of a new decade and having just turned forty herself, Dow came to live with us. I looked forward to her arrival and often wandered over to her end of the house where everything was ready for her to move in. I imagined her living with us and wanted her to be happy in her new home. Yet at the same time I was sad there would be no more holidays at Cooden Beach. I spent several weeks a year at Cooden and loved nothing more than staying with Dow and my grandfather; the rich aroma of furniture wax warmed by the sun, my grandfather's pipe tobacco and the salt air was intoxicating. My mother always swore that I barely slept for the first four years of my life, but at Kismet, I had only to hear the rumble of waves at bedtime, the crunch and gurgle of pebbles snagged in the foaming backwash, and I was out like a light. Like Dow, I never wanted to leave.

She brought as many of Kismet's treasures as she could feasibly squeeze into her new surroundings and appeared to have no trouble settling in. She swiftly acquired a companion too. One evening, our fox terrier Ajax took a long look at us while we were watching television, as if he were somehow appraising us all, and without so much as a backward glance, trotted off to her end of the house, never to return. From that moment on, he rarely let Dow out of his sight, guarding her with a jealousy that bordered on fanaticism. She kept her sitting-room door permanently open, like a standing invitation, so I regularly stepped in to visit her and Ajax. It was only a short distance from our end of the house to hers, the merest touch of the radio dial, but it was enough to transport me to another world: the world of racing results and racing commentaries, the sports news, the football pools, football coupons, spot-the-ball competitions, county cricket scores, betting odds, betting slips scattered like ticker tape, *The Times* crossword and the shipping forecast, which she ritually listened to because she loved the resonance of the place names and because it reminded her of Kismet. I waited eagerly for the Scottish football results in her sitting room every Saturday for the same reason. I loved the unforgettable names: Hamilton Academical, Dumbarton, Third Lanark, Heart of Midlothian, Partick

Thistle, Greenock Morton, Stenhousemuir, St Johnstone, Cove Rangers, Bonnyrigg Rose and more. For a while, it was a close-run thing between Hamilton Academical and St Johnstone as to which was my favourite, but St Johnstone won out and became the first football club I supported.

There was, however, one golden rule that had to be observed whenever you entered Dow's part of the house: you never talked during the racing results. Anyone unfortunate or foolhardy enough to do so – and usually it was the blurters, Mum and me – was met with a *shush* of such glacial severity that the atmosphere in the room didn't thaw for at least another twenty minutes.

I cannot recall a day when Dow didn't have a flutter on the horses, though obviously there must have been times when she resisted the impulse. To help fund her betting, she gave piano lessons at home in her sitting room. Unfortunately, her students never stayed longer than a dogwatch, in her words – which was an interesting way of putting it because Ajax instilled the fear of God into them. If they managed to get past him into the room without getting their ankles attacked, they then found themselves bailed up by the piano stool and unable to leave once the lesson was over. It probably didn't help that Dow sometimes halted lessons to listen to the racing results.

Eventually, she took a job playing the piano at women's keep fit classes – a role that required her to learn some of the current songs in the hit parade. Her 'homework', as she called it. She often came home with an amusing story or two – most of which involved some unfortunate person letting out an uncontrollable fart in the middle of an exercise. 'The ladies were at it again, I'm afraid,' she'd report on her return. 'Of course, that means everyone stops for about five minutes while we all have a jolly good laugh and get it out of our systems before starting again. And then – would you believe – someone lets off another one.'

If betting on the horses was Dow's lifeblood, then words were undeniably her signature tune. She loved the sound of them and had an inexhaustible fund of her own expressions and sayings at her disposal, which she subtlety slipped into a conversation usually when you least expected it. Hers was a talent for marrying words that, in the natural order of things, should never have fitted or belonged together, like malfunctioning pieces in a puzzle, yet somehow did. 'It looked like fried ice,' she once said of a friend's new hairstyle. The words were like music to my ears, although as a small boy, I had no idea why or what fried ice even meant or looked like. I still don't. The truth was that she fired my imagination with her words; she used them in a way that I had never heard before. She brought them to life, she played with them as if she were tuning a piano, she made them luminous and gave them meaning so that whatever she described sounded new, fresh, funny and exciting. Dow didn't just teach me the power of words – she taught me to love them before I could even read or write them.

As the years ticked on, she became gloriously more eccentric and complicated. In 1981, my parents decided to put the house on the market and started looking for somewhere smaller. The decision rankled with her, reawakening old fears of her departure from Kismet, despite my parents' insistence that she could come with them wherever they went. An appointment had been made for a late evening viewing, which in normal circumstances would have been carried out by the owners. But my mother was unavailable, so Dow stepped in. An elderly couple arrived at the front door and she proceeded to show them round in the fading light. When the man innocently turned on a light and made the mistake of announcing, 'There, that's better, we can all see where we're going now,' Dow bristled and instantly switched it off. 'No, I'm very sorry,' she said – how often those words were the prelude to a full-blown row, the delivery of a stern lecture or a withering dressing-down. 'But we don't do that sort of thing. We don't just walk into someone else's house and decide to switch on their lights. Thank you very much.' The rest of the viewing was conducted in semi-darkness and silence, until the man tripped over a stool in my parents' sitting room and sprawled full-length into a side table, hitting his head and destroying a lamp. Not surprisingly, she was never asked to show anyone round again. The house sold later that year, though not to the man with the head injury, and another chapter in our lives was closed.

Dow always entered wholeheartedly into family life. No one could have made the school run to St Peter's Court more fun, bumping along in the back of her grey Morris Minor van, sitting on the rear-wheel hub and pulling faces at the drivers in the cars behind until, in desperation, they overtook us. She showed an interest in everything Gina and I did, teasing us mercilessly when we got things wrong or made fools of ourselves. It wasn't always perfect between us, and she wasn't always the easiest, and I probably received the I'm-very-sorry-but treatment with more regularity than most. But she also took it upon herself to keep every letter, every drawing, every meaningless scrap of paper I sent home during eleven years at boarding school. Nothing was discarded, nothing treated as inconsequential. Like a curator, she collected them into bundles in chronological order, neatly folded in their envelopes after they'd been read, carefully tied them with ribbon and placed them in a drawer, where they stayed in her safekeeping for nearly fifty years.

She faithfully wrote to me every week I was at school too, although she didn't have to.

It would never have occurred to me to have done the same with her letters – I kept only a couple, no more – but if anyone's letters were worth saving, they were surely hers. I would give anything to read them again and blame myself for being too casual with what were clearly precious time capsules. I asked her once why she had preserved all my letters so beautifully. 'Oh, I don't know,' she said, giving a gentle shrug of her shoulders. 'I just thought they might be of interest to someone one day, that's all.'

CHAPTER TEN

KEEP SEEING THE PICTURES

When I returned to school after the summer holidays in 1964, it was to discover that I had lost my lifeline at Hildersham House. Miss Shepherd – the one teacher who understood me, the one person who understood me better than I knew myself – had left.

The announcement was made by Mr Snowden at assembly and I felt my hopes, along with my heart, instantly plummet. She had gone to South Africa to start a new life, a new venture. He didn't say what – almost as if it were a mystery. 'And I know you will all join me in wishing her well in her future endeavours.' I heard a rustle of movement around me as some boys nodded their heads and a low murmur of agreement came from the staff on the stage in front of me, but I couldn't bring myself to join in. It was a blow I had not seen coming, and for a moment I was so shocked I wondered whether I'd heard it correctly. But the chair where she always sat during assembly – positioned at a slight but nonetheless noticeable distance from the others – had been pulled into line and was now occupied by another woman, whose name I couldn't even take in. A part of me wanted to stand up and shout, 'Why?' Why had no one thought to tell me about this? Or more to the point, why hadn't she told me herself? Surely, she must have known it would matter to me. I couldn't control my thoughts, I couldn't sit still – all I wanted to do was run outside, to try to make some sense of it all. But Mr Snowden had already moved briskly on to the next topic and in the space of barely a minute, Miss Shepherd was consigned to the past.

I had progressed to the fourth form at the start of the summer term in 1964, when I was ten. And although I was no longer in her class and therefore no longer being taught by her, Miss Shepherd kept an eye out for me, still took an interest in my work, especially my written work, still occasionally pulled up a chair to sit next to me to help me with my reading, my letters home or whatever it was I was doing. She had never given me any indication that she was leaving. Perhaps she hadn't known she was at that time. Or perhaps she didn't want to make a fuss but to just quietly slip away – that would have been typical of her. Perhaps she had seen enough to know I could manage on my own without her, that I could get by. The last words she had said to me at the end of that term had been, 'Keep seeing the pictures.' The more I thought about those words, the more they took on a special relevance, and because I had nothing else to go on and was unlikely to learn the truth or ever see her again, I decided to create my own version of events and to stick to it. Anything to help me through the next few days and weeks. *Keep seeing the pictures.* It was her way of saying goodbye to me, I told myself.

For the next three years, I lagged so badly behind my friends and contemporaries that I was usually a form or two in the rear, always fourteenth out of fourteen boys as it stated on my report. Unsurprisingly, I was always the oldest in my class – a status that on this occasion carried no distinction, like a forlorn badge of honour. I gradually climbed to the second form but stayed there for the rest of my time at Hildersham House, constantly held back to repeat another year, never to touch the rarefied heights of the first form. My friends surged so far ahead of me that I felt like one of those runners who gets lapped by the rest of the field, who is still competing while the winner is celebrating his victory in the distance and the others are engaged in their own sprint for the line.

What made it worse was that by the time I was twelve, many of the eleven-year-olds in the second form had already overtaken me and some of the ten-year-olds in the third form were already at my shoulder or snapping at my heels, poised to do the same. Sometimes it felt as if I was going backwards not forwards, such was the regularity with which the others left me in their dust. Some even took delight in pointing it out to me. One week when I finished thirteenth out of fourteen, it was as astonishing to me as if I had won an Olympic medal. Hamer, the boy who'd broken the mould by finishing beneath me, was informed that 'even Lazenby has beaten you' and reminded of the fact on a weekly basis. It must have been the insult to end all insults because he made immediate amends, moving three places above me before the term was out to secure his place in the first form.

After Miss Shepherd left, none of the other teachers mentioned the word dyslexia to me again. Perhaps, like me, they'd never heard of it before and didn't know what it meant either. It was as though she had taken it to South Africa with her, where it now belonged. Sometimes I felt as if it no longer existed or had any meaning. Its absence made me long for her – it was my strongest link to her, after all – and I wondered whether I would ever hear the word again. I still thought of myself as being dyslexic, however, and told anyone who cared to listen... if I could only remember how to pronounce it correctly. As usual, the letters slipped through my hands like sand. Mostly, to save myself from embarrassment, I told people that I thought differently instead and left it at that. 'Oh, we know you're different all right,' Mr Foden told me once in the middle of a geography lesson, encompassing the whole class, his audience, in the sweep of his hand. 'You don't need to remind us of that fact.'

Although my writing had improved slightly by the age of ten, my reading had still not progressed sufficiently enough for me to read a book from cover to cover. And that was usually because I couldn't get past those covers: the artwork was always more enthralling than the words inside. I wouldn't manage to read a book, any book, in its entirety until I was thirteen or fourteen, and even then I would have to fight my way to the end of every sentence as if I was hacking my way through a jungle. It always felt more like hard work than enjoyment. I could never understand those boys who walked around school with a well-thumbed paperback sticking out of their jacket pocket, who pulled it out to read whenever they got a spare moment. Once I tried to slog my way through a paperback in the dormitory before lights out but hardly got beyond the opening line, having to repeatedly return to the beginning. Mr Snowden walked in, took one look at me and scoffed, 'What are you doing with that, boy? You can't even read.' I remember the laughter. For a long time after that, I always made sure I was on my own or no one was looking when I attempted to read a book.

Unfortunately, maths was already a lost cause, and the teacher would often address me first before explaining what he wanted the rest of the class to do, thus saving himself the trouble of having to decode it a hundred times over for me. 'Lazenby, I don't expect you to understand this...' Which was my cue to switch off, if I hadn't already.

Like every other boy, I remained terrified of Mr Snowden and hated his French and Latin lessons with a passion – with a fear and loathing so deep and layered that most of us would be affected by it for years to come or for the rest of our lives in some cases. For me, it went even deeper: how could anybody seriously believe me capable of learning French or Latin when I was still struggling to read or write English, the language I'd spoken all my life? But no one escaped Mr Snowden's wrath, no one was immune. We were all victims. Occasionally, some of us were exceptions to that rule and to my great surprise, I even counted myself among that lucky few but only for a brief interlude. Even the brainiest of boys, who appeared to know the answer to every question, who got everything right, slipped up sometimes and, like the rest of us, paid the price. Once the red mist descended, we all looked the same to Mr Snowden in his fog of anger.

On those days when there was a French or Latin lesson, my nerves kicked in the minute the bell for morning prayers sounded – the signal for me to begin my familiar, plaintive refrain. 'Please, God, please put Mr Snowden in a good mood today.' Often that was not enough to quell my fear. 'And if he isn't in a good mood,' I pleaded – not even God had power over Mr Snowden all the time – 'please don't let me be the one who gets into trouble.' I made sure I included my family, and Ajax and Bill, in my prayers and finished on an optimistic note, as if he had already taken care of it and ticked it off his substantial list. 'Thank you, God.' My prayers were hardly elegant and rarely effective, but I never gave up on them and repeated the mantra over and over, clasping my hands together and squeezing my eyes so tightly shut that I couldn't see how he could fail to ignore me.

Occasionally, if my prayers were answered and the lesson passed off without any eruptions, the excitement and relief were so pronounced I forgot to thank God – until the next time. 'Thank you, God, for putting him in a good mood the other day. I'm sorry for not thanking you earlier. I know it's a lot to ask of you, but please could you make sure you put him in a good mood again this morning.' I was not the only boy who turned to God in case he could bring some divine influence to bear on Mr Snowden – we all did, though few of us admitted to it. The two or three minutes before the start of the lesson was when you could really smell our fear – the air in the classroom was laden with the gas of fourteen nervous, fidgeting boys, waiting for the glass-crunching noise of Mr Snowden's shoes in the corridor. It was as if we had amassed one unholy collective fart and unwittingly unleashed it on the whole school.

We always knew what mood he was in the second he walked into the classroom. The jut of his jaw, the curve of that loose strand of hair over one eye, the sound of his shoes, the tone of his voice gave us an early flavour of what was in store – even his moustache appeared more pointed and clipped than usual when he was in a bad mood. Sometimes I made a point of not looking, because if he was in one of his tempers, you knew it instantly and there was nothing you could do about it anyway.

The first thing he did on entering the room, after he had thrown open all the windows and dispersed our gaseous emissions, was to mark the previous night's prep. The rest of the lesson was dependant on how well or how badly we had performed with our prep – if it was the latter, the lesson rapidly followed a predictably ugly course. I watched him work his way down the rows of desks, our exercise books opened in front of us at the relevant page. You could tell by the flourish of his wrist, the little embellishment he applied to it, who received the ticks, who got the questions right. Equally, you knew by the sound of his pen nib on paper, the manic thrust of his elbow, when he was striking lines through someone's work. He had this habit of standing behind you and leaning over your shoulder while making his marks, so if he punched you, using a short-arm jab into your kidneys, or violently pulled your hair, jerking your head back with the force of it, you never saw it coming – although you were already flinching in preparation for it, for his temper to go off in your face like a firecracker. I knew it was coming because every time he put scalding red lines through my exercise book, his rage reached such a pitch that his pen tore a hole in the paper and pierced the next page.

Sometimes he kept his fists to himself and just bellowed at us for no other reason than we were there to be bellowed at – so loud, it was said his voice could be heard booming out from halfway up St Peter-in-Thanet high street. He could have bellowed for Kent, had such a thing existed. One of our classrooms looked out over the school driveway and during the summer term when the windows were wide open, a passer-by would often stop outside the entrance to listen to him fume and rage. 'Du, de la, des, boy!' he'd scream in frustration, as if hurling French partitives out into the street. 'Do think.' There was even a kind of symmetry to it. Occasionally, a small knot of people would gather outside – a woman with a shopping basket, someone walking their dog, someone who had nipped out to post a letter – and stare at us in bemused silence as if they were watching some strange spectator sport, or they would exchange words with each other or gesticulate or motion in our direction. But no one ever intervened or walked up the drive to complain or check on our safety; it wasn't any of their business and they soon moved on. To them, we were probably just those poor boys of Hildersham House. And what could we possibly have done to deserve it?

It seemed that French lessons were one of the few occasions when the others were glad to have me in the class with them. My inability to concentrate, my inclination to blurt out the wrong answer or to jiggle my legs and shuffle around in my seat – it was like trying to sit still in a hurricane – meant that for much of the lesson I was the sole focus of his anger. I may have been a moving target, but I was an easy one, and it allowed the others to keep their heads down, to breathe a little easier, as if I was some kind of human decoy, a safe shield for them to hide behind. I had my uses, I suppose. But I couldn't please them all the time and inevitably had the knack for making things worse than they already were. 'Why did you have to say that?' one of them moaned at me after I'd given a particularly clumsy answer to a question. 'He wasn't in that much of a mood until you had to go and open your mouth and then we all got it in the neck. Typical.'

But I wasn't the only one who brought out the worst in Mr Snowden. A boy called Andrew Stimpson, who sat two desks away from mine and suffered badly from asthma attacks during French and Latin lessons, rarely escaped intact. He often started the lesson gently wheezing away to himself, with a pen in one hand and an inhaler in the other, but once Mr Snowden was in full steam, his breathing quickly deteriorated. At his worst, he sounded like someone out of breath trying to play the trumpet, or more alarmingly, he made a noise like a set of bagpipes between notes. 'Oh, do use your inhaler, boy!' Mr Snowden shouted at him. Stimpson couldn't keep his legs still either, causing his desk to tremble and shake loudly as if there was an engine inside it and it might drive off without any warning, taking him with it. Sometimes the fountain-pen ink jumped out of the well and slopped over his exercise book.

Throughout, the pair of us kept up a silent, running dialogue by regularly catching the other's eye and exchanging glances. It wasn't something we planned – it was something that evolved, that we carried on between us to ease the pressure, the tension. His huge eyes, magnified by fear, conveyed an emotion like no one I had met, more clearly than words ever could, while mirroring the exact thoughts that raced through my head. There was a common bond between us and we always understood what the other meant. I won't lie, there was also a part of me that was relieved to know there was somebody worse off than me, but I regularly looked out for him and wouldn't let anything happen to him. Whenever Mr Snowden picked on him, as he couldn't resist doing, I made sure I said something incredibly stupid so he would concentrate his ire on me instead; as I was always saying incredibly stupid things, no one suspected, certainly not Mr Snowden. Without fail, Stimpson gave me a look to assure me that he understood and that he would thank me for it later, when he had mustered enough breath. It wasn't until the bell rang at the end of the lesson that we both relaxed and gave each other a look in a way that said *We did it – we got through it unscathed.*

Except, of course, we weren't unscathed.

• • •

There was one area at Hildersham House where I excelled more than any other boy: I had a rare talent for getting beaten. Not just occasionally, as in two or three times a month, but twelve times a term sometimes, which roughly translated into once every week. Obviously, I was a natural candidate for it, with my lack of concentration and self-control, my inclination to blurt out nonsense, to seek out trouble wherever I could find it – or, as I preferred to explain it, trouble always found me.

I was beaten for any number of reasons – a list of offences that veered wildly from the mundane to the spectacular. They included spilling milk (I hated drinking the cream at the top of the bottle), losing my exercise books, talking after lights out, talking too much before lights out, standing on my bed and opera singing 'Edelweiss' to the rest of the dormitory, calling the assistant matron 'Memphis Honey' after a character I'd seen in a western, loosening the screws in the teacher's classroom chair or placing drawing pins on its seat, dangling my hand out of a miniature train window and smacking passers-by on the head during a school outing to Dungeness, stealing the flowers from another boy's garden and transplanting them in my own – something I am not proud of – or fronting a one-boy crusade against the awfulness of the school food – something I am. And they were just the ones I was unlucky enough to be caught doing. It was a talent that knew no bounds.

The incident with the food was typical of how I always managed to insert myself into trouble. About six of us had decided to make a stand against the quality of it, the lack of it, the fact that it was often served cold, with the bread invariably stale. We agreed the time had come to make our displeasure known; on a given signal, which Teague announced he would make, we'd jump to our feet during supper and spout our piece in front of Mr Snowden and the whole school. Our slogan was *We deserve better food*, though I preferred my version: *Food, food, disgusting food.*

We prepared a few words to say and waited for the right moment. I was already counting down the seconds, itching to make my move, when Teague gave the signal – somewhat half-heartedly, I noticed

– and I leaped to my feet. I had hardly pushed back my chair and the slogan was out of my mouth. I even threw in a word of my own, unedible – later, I learned the word was inedible – before realising I was the only boy on his feet. My co-conspirators had remained steadfastly in their seats, as if glued to them. I felt the heat of some seventy pairs of eyes on me – apart from Teague, who was staring at his plate – and the cavernous silence that greeted my outburst. The others could not have looked any more horrified than if I'd stood before them stark naked. I turned to face Mr Snowden and sensed seventy heads shift in the same direction. He was standing in front of me, a scowl hewn out of rock. 'My study now, boy,' was all he said.

Moments later he was selecting a cane from the rack, testing it for its pliability with some vigorous swishes through the air, when there was a knock on the door and Teague and four others shuffled uncomfortably into the study. Teague explained that although none of them had got to their feet or uttered a word, they were each as guilty as I was, if not more so. It was their idea, he admitted: they had planned it and they agreed with everything I'd said. 'Although we regret it now, of course, sir,' he added sheepishly. I knew Teague wouldn't let me down when it mattered, but I didn't expect it to make much difference to the outcome.

'Good,' Mr Snowden replied. 'In that case, I'll cane the lot of you.' And he grabbed the collar of my shirt before bending me over the arm of his chair. 'Starting with you, boy.'

The food, at least, was a worthy enough cause. However, even I had no answers for an impetuous act of vandalism that would haunt me for years to come. Everybody knew about Talbot's garden – it was as much a part of school life as football or cricket, or letters home or walks to the sea front. If one of his flowers died, we all heard about it. His garden shone; it was a thing of wonder and it put the rest of ours to shame. Mine, which had the misfortune to border his, was a wilderness, a tangle of overgrown grass, weeds and rocks. Thankfully, the other boys' efforts were not much better. If we had our comics, our 'swappets', our model aeroplanes and tanks, then Talbot had his gardening gloves, his packets of seeds, his rake, his shears, his watering can. Indeed, so beautiful was his garden that some of the staff often wandered down to the bottom of the playing fields to sit on its bench, to admire it in full bloom – its beds of red and white roses, its purple, blue and yellow lupins standing proudly to attention like soldiers. 'Talbot's garden of England', as Mr Foden named it.

It was on the morning of sports day during my first summer term at boarding school that I sneaked down to the gardens with a pair of nail scissors and a plan in my back pocket. The plan, if you can call it that, was to cut off Talbot's lupins at the stems to transplant them to my garden, to push them down into the soil as deep as they would go and hope they stayed upright. Parents had been invited to visit the area later that morning, when the gardens would be put on display, and my father had declared an interest in seeing mine, despite my best efforts to dissuade him. Consequently, some of the other boys had attempted to smarten up their gardens, and I was determined not to be left behind, determined not to finish bottom of the class again, fourteenth out of fourteen. This time I wanted to steal the show or at the very least to surprise my parents – the trouble was, I had no idea quite how much of a surprise it would turn out to be for them. Or me, for that matter.

I soon learned that cutting flowers with a pair of nail scissors was anything but easy. The stems were stronger than I thought, and because the scissors completed only part of the job, I had to snap or tear them off at the base with my hands. By the time I had finished, the ground was pockmarked with rows of mangled, jagged stalks – the beheaded remnants of Talbot's lupins. Trying to stick them into the earth once I had transferred them from his garden into mine was not exactly straightforward either. The soil crumbled like dust, and the only way to prevent them from toppling over every few seconds was to build a mound of earth around the base and pack it in as tightly as I could. It never occurred to me to pull up the weeds in my garden. When I was done, I returned to the main building and awaited the arrival of my parents. They had spent the night in Broadstairs, and it was one of the very rare occasions that I can remember them turning up on time. After the usual bout of handshaking, we made our way down to the gardens where a small group of people had already gathered. There was no sign of Talbot yet. I pointed out my garden to my parents while trying to keep my excitement in check, adding, 'The one with the lupins.' They both looked at it for several seconds.

'The ground looks very dry to me, John,' my mother remarked. It was not the reaction I'd been expecting. 'And your lupins seem to be rather leaning over, unless it's just me.'

I explained that lupins always did that. 'That's the thing with lupins – that's why they're so difficult to grow. They always look like they're leaning over.'

'That one in particular,' she said, gesturing to a yellow lupin that had almost buried its head into the soil while continuing to peer at them in a slightly quizzical, bemused fashion. 'They most definitely need some water, John.'

At this point, my father entered the conversation. 'I think your mother's right – a little bit of water might help to revive them.'

'They're certainly colourful, though, I'll say that for them,' my mother added hurriedly.

It was at that moment my attention was drawn by the sight of Talbot, flanked by his parents, striding purposefully towards the gardens. He reminded me of a king about to address his subjects. His mother, I couldn't help noticing, was dressed from head to foot in an identical yellow to his lupins – or my lupins, as they were now. Even her hat bristled with yellow flowers. My mother, however, refused to let the matter of the lupins rest. I wished at times like these that she had an off switch you could press and all would be well, all would be quiet again. 'When did you say you planted them, John?' I never replied because no sooner were the words out of her mouth than there was a blood-curdling scream and I turned around to see Talbot pointing at me, his face contorted in a grimace of pain and anger.

'What have you done?' he shouted. 'You've ruined my garden.' His voice started to break. 'You've wrecked it. Why would you do that?'

For a split second, I thought he was going to make a lunge at me and braced myself, but his anger subsided as rapidly as it flared and he started to whimper instead. His parents each placed a comforting arm around him, while staring pointedly at me over the head of their sobbing son. A few people gasped and I joined them in looking from his ransacked garden to my tilting lupins – which were now fading fast, as if in sympathy with Talbot – and back again. No one said anything, until my mother spoke. 'How could you do such a thing, John?' At least I'd left his roses intact. My father, meanwhile, wore the expression of a man who had just witnessed an unidentified object whirring silently towards him but could not quite bring himself to believe it. For an awful moment, I thought he was going to bend down and pick up one of the fallen lupins and hand it back to Talbot, but it was just the position of his body, I realised. He was actively trying to make himself appear smaller, as if attempting to disappear in front of our eyes, to submerge himself beneath the soil, to disconnect himself from my presence.

Talbot was eventually led away by his parents, still sobbing, and the others quickly followed. One mother even hissed at me as she walked past – not once but twice. Another called me a 'nasty little boy', so close to my ear that only I could hear it. My parents and I remained staring down at my garden; we stayed there without speaking a word for what felt to me like an eternity. As if on cue, the last lupin standing keeled over and joined the others on the ground.

I consoled myself that the sports events were still to come, but there was no redemption there either. I even failed to finish in the egg-and-spoon race. Like everything else that day, even the gentlest of races turned to dust in my hands. By the time I finally managed to coax the egg onto my spoon, the winner was breasting the tape at the far end of the track. I could tell by the burst of applause that someone's race was already run, followed by a runner-up and what sounded like a possible tie for third place while mine was just beginning, amid much laughter. Finally, I set off, the egg wobbling from side to side on my spoon, my concentration so intense I feared I might trip over my own feet. So much so that the inevitable happened: the egg dropped to the floor halfway down the track. Not only that, but it bounced backwards in the direction it had just come. Perhaps it had something to do with the fact that I was left-handed because whenever my spoon came within touching distance of the egg, it rolled further away from me each time, as if it had a life of its own or the metal was somehow mysteriously propelling it back to the starting line. 'Throw him a shovel,' someone shouted, and the laughter redoubled. It was at this point that Mr Snowden strode onto the track, calmly pocketed the egg and walked off, much to the delight of the spectators and the relief, no doubt, of my parents – though I suspected they were both facing in the opposite direction by this stage.

I spent the rest of the day being ignored by people – the egg-and-spoon race apart, where I had made such a fool of myself it was impossible to ignore me. No one talked or engaged with me, not my friends, not my parents, especially not my parents. People talked to me only if they absolutely had to, as in the case of Mr Snowden, who told me that I was to report to his study later that evening – I knew exactly what that meant – and that I was to hang my head in shame and consider the consequences of my actions until then. The only time my parents spoke to me was when I explained that all I had wanted was for them to like my garden. 'That's why I did what I did. I just wanted you to like it.'

My mother could barely bring herself to look at me. 'We would have preferred it if the flowers had been your own,' she replied, before resuming the silent treatment.

Later, during prize-giving, Talbot was presented with the award for the best-kept garden – a popular victory, judging by the cheers that greeted it – for his 'glorious roses'. And the smile returned to his face. The following day, Mr Mosten, the master in charge of gardens, took me aside and informed me that I was 'no longer welcome in the gardening community'. Furthermore, he would be offering my garden to Talbot. 'I don't think you can have any complaints on that score,' he said.

Happily, people soon forgot about it – though not Talbot. He neither forgot nor forgave me for the damage I waged on his garden. Things returned to normal again for me… well, as normal as they could be. Until my next act of impulsivity, in a long line of such acts that I simply could not explain, led to my next offence or my next beating.

The most disconcerting thing about being beaten so regularly was not the fact that it was usually done last thing at night, when you were in your pyjamas, or that you had to walk down three darkened flights of winding stairs to Mr Snowden's study, then race up the stairs as fast as you could go when it was over in an attempt to outrun the burning pain. Sometimes it burned so intensely you felt your backside was ahead of you going up the stairs, before you returned to the full glare of the dormitory and waited, in agonising pain, for Mr Snowden to come and switch off the lights. No, the most disconcerting thing about it for me, was that there was always a member of my family present.

Every time I placed my hands on the well-worn arm of the leather club chair in Mr Snowden's study, bent over and braced my legs in preparation for the first stroke from the slipper or the cane, the first face I saw was my grandfather's, in profile, on the wall directly in front of me. Jack Mason was dressed in his cricketing whites, crouching at first slip, his hands cupped, his fingers outstretched in anticipation of a flying edge from the bat. If he was looking at me, he was looking at me only out of the corner of his eye. But the image – sealed behind glass – was enough for me to remember the man I had known, albeit briefly, as a small boy.

I knew the painting by heart – Kent versus Lancashire at Canterbury in 1906 – because for many years a print of it hung at home in the corridor between our end of the house and Dow's, like an unbreakable link between us. Jack Mason was a full-time solicitor and only a part-time cricketer when the artwork was created; he closed the office every August and used his holiday to turn out for

Kent in the county championship. At the age of twelve, I knew most of the names of the players from both teams by heart too – not that that surprising fact would have saved me from a beating. It was painted by a man called Albert Chevallier Tayler, in celebration of Kent's first county championship triumph that year. The batsman was Lancashire's Johnny Tyldesley, the bowler Colin Blythe. Behind the arc of Blythe's left arm stood the pavilion, and to its left, in the background, were lime trees, cream tents, fluttering flags and the distant shape of Canterbury Cathedral and the tower of Bell Harry.

I always imagined that it was close to tea-time (in fact, the scene was fixed in the moments before lunch on the second day of the match) and I could hear the murmur of conversation from the crowd, several thousand deep, drift across the pitch to where my grandfather was fielding in the foreground of the picture. And then I closed my eyes and counted each stroke, each blow, of which there were usually eight or nine; Mr Snowden always stopped short of ten for some reason known only to him. I always counted because I knew the first question the others would ask me was 'How many strokes?' It didn't really matter that much as I'd usually exaggerate the number anyway.

When I opened my eyes again, my grandfather remained sealed behind the glass – his concentration on the game unbroken by my torment below, his hands still outstretched, still waiting for the ball to leave Blythe's left hand, to tickle the outside edge of Tyldesley's bat like a feather. How I wished in those agonising moments while I waited to be beaten, before I closed my eyes, that he had stepped out from behind the glass or, even more magically perhaps, that I had stepped inside to join him. I often wondered what he might have said to me, what piece of advice or words of encouragement he might have imparted, what memory he might have shared with me from our days together at Cooden. In the end I comforted myself that, if nothing else, he would surely have mentioned my progress on the cricket field.

In a complete reversal of my fortunes in the classroom, I had been selected to play for the school first XI aged eleven years and two months and became the youngest boy in the team by some distance. I finally realised I was reasonably good at something other than setting records for the number of times I got beaten – and, against all expectations, life took a turn for the better. Not only that but Mr Snowden refused to touch a hair on my head during French lessons if there was a school match later in the afternoon. It was only a brief respite, and all hell could break loose on any other occasion, but just not on matchdays. I discovered too that sporting prowess won you new friends and boys who wouldn't normally give you the time of day suddenly showed an inclination to do so. Even teachers viewed you differently. However hopeless I was at maths, French or Latin, or wherever I finished up in class, didn't seem to matter much any more as long as I took five wickets or knocked off a rapid twenty or thirty runs to win the match.

But with the highs, inevitably, came the lows. We were sometimes beaten by Mr Snowden if we bowled more than two balls an over down the legside, even in practice games – or, worse, we failed to hit a ball wide of leg stump to the boundary when batting. 'There's no excuse in cricket for missing a ball bowled down the legside,' he would shout. 'Any ball pitched there should be summarily dispatched to the boundary.' Whereupon he would snatch the bat from your hands, bend you over and demonstrate the shot on your backside. 'Like so – that's how you hit a bad ball to the boundary. Four every time.'

He would also frequently berate us from the boundary as a

spectator, or in his capacity as an umpire, during school matches. 'That's the longest run in China, boy,' he would scream from his position at square-leg if one of us failed to take an easy single. 'Every run counts.' Often, the opposition were so stunned by this outburst of bias that they forgot to throw the ball back to the wicketkeeper and you could complete the run anyway. On another occasion, after I had decided to mimic the Test batsmen I had seen on television and studiously prod the wicket with my bat before facing my first delivery, he barked at me, 'That's not your wicket to ruin, boy.' I was promptly bowled first ball. In one of my earliest games for the team, during the tea interval, I quickly scoffed the last cake when I thought no one was looking and was beaten for not having the manners to offer it to the opposition first.

Mr Snowden was not the only one who ruled us with a fist of iron. The first XI captain, Robert Pugh, regularly took matters into his own hands too. Pugh was held personally responsible by Mr Snowden for every defeat inflicted on us. Fortunately, they were few and far between, but the fallout was severe enough for him to take his frustrations out on us – or, more precisely, on me, as the youngest and smallest boy in the team. His preferred method of punishment was to don a batting glove, an old-fashioned one adorned with rows of protective rubber spikes on the fingers, and punch me with it. He seemed to take as much satisfaction from slipping it on, flexing and wriggling his fingers inside it, moving the spikes up and down like some malevolent caterpillar was crawling along his hand, as he did from slamming it into my head or body. He maintained that it was good practice for me because it helped to sharpen my reflexes. 'Don't let me down on Saturday,' he would say, almost apologetically, after he'd landed his final punch. 'We have to win this one.' However, by summer 1967, in my final term at Hildersham House and now a senior member of the first XI, I'd managed to secure a status I would otherwise not have attained.

• • •

If my love of cricket might have been easily predicted, then my fascination for bookshops – or the Albion Bookshop in Broadstairs, to be exact – came as much of a surprise to me as it did to everyone else. It would be fair to say that, up to that point in my life, I had no interest in bookshops at all. I couldn't even tell you if I had been in one, unlike cinemas or record shops – worlds into which I had no trouble entering and where almost every detail was rubber-stamped on my mind. But everything changed one rainy Saturday afternoon when I was about twelve. My parents were down for the weekend and we had decided to take a brisk walk to the seafront, just as a squally rain blew in. We were passing the Albion Bookshop – a shop I had never noticed before, despite having walked past hundreds of times. I glanced inside; the lights shone invitingly bright and several people, made blurry by the rain-streaked window, were intently browsing the shelves. It was no more than a pebble's throw from the seafront but looked warm and snug and offered some convenient shelter from the rain, which had started to drum loudly against the pavement. We opened the door and went in. I'm glad we did because the alchemy was instant and completely unexpected.

What struck me straight away was the smell. It was leathery and inky, gluey even – the scent, I later learned, of crisp new pages and fresh print, of books waiting to be opened. On this occasion, it had merged with the whiff of tobacco and still-damp gabardine raincoats to form a powerful, unforgettable concoction. I quickly discovered that I loved the smell as much as I loved the dust jackets and the covers. The shelves were laden with books of all shapes and sizes, some stacked so high they scraped the ceiling and needed a ladder to reach them. There were paperbacks too, their spines packed so tightly in rows it was difficult sometimes just to pull one out, to gaze at its cover. Much to my surprise, I lost myself in them, in the feel and weight of them, as if I was trying to measure the excitement that lay within – pausing only to listen to the rain clatter on the roof or watch the world outside the window disappear, reduced to splashes of colour like paint running down the glass. I loved the noise a book made when I snapped it open or let its pages ripple back and forth; I felt that if I did this for long enough, or breathed in its unique smell, something might rub off on me.

I managed to persuade my father to buy me a book that afternoon – a paperback I'd chosen called *The Blue Ice*, by the prolific thriller writer Hammond Innes. I had seen the other boys with Hammond Innes books and knew he was a popular read, along with Ian Fleming and Alistair MacLean. My father was worried that I might not understand it but was pleased at least that I wanted to improve my reading. I told him that I would set myself a target and try to read a page every day until it was finished. In fact, I had yet to finish a book, despite having started more than I could count. Usually, I set off with the best of intentions but then lost concentration or interest or switched off a few chapters in and had to return to the start and reread pages to remind myself of some of the characters. I concentrated so hard on the reading that the plot became super-fluous. In the end, it was often easier to give up. Sometimes I lost the will to live before the end of page one. On other occasions, it was enough for me just to own a book or to give the impression to everyone that I *was* reading it – thoughtfully turning a page every minute or so – though they must have known I wasn't. But that was no longer enough for me now. I wanted more. I wanted to read a book all the way to the end, to discover everything inside it. And, in case I needed reminding of that fact, I carried *The Blue Ice* in my jacket pocket everywhere I went, copying some of the other boys I'd seen. I had another ambition too: I wanted to become an author, like Hammond Innes.

Typically, I thought nothing of wanting to be an author before I could read or write properly – before I'd even ascertained whether I could pass my own test of managing to finish an entire book. Only I could get so gloriously ahead of myself that I would seriously entertain such thoughts. I even talked about getting a book *a-published*. I thought that was how you pronounced it, much to everyone's amusement. *Do you think my book will be a-published?* No wonder they all laughed. And yet it felt strangely normal to me. Invariably, for most of my young life, I never allowed the obvious to hold me back.

When my parents visited me after that, we always made a point of calling in at the Albion Bookshop and I rarely left without a book in my hands. By then, it was impossible for me to pass by without going inside. During my last couple of terms at Hildersham House, while the other boys bunked off to play the slot machines in the arcade, I went to the bookshop and browsed the shelves. Whenever we sneaked out of school without anyone knowing or didn't want anyone to recognise us in town, we always put our caps in our pockets and turned up the collars on our raincoats and called ourselves by made-up names, especially if we went into a shop to buy cigarettes – not that we would have fooled anybody. If anything, the more mysterious we tried to look, the more contrived and conspicuous we became, like boys playing at being spies. Perhaps the owner of the bookshop suspected who I was or, at the very least, recognised me from my visits with my parents; after all, we spent enough time there. But he never let on. If we caught each other's eye, he'd give me a quiet smile and look away, not wanting to put me off, content to let me carry on poring over the books.

One of my favourite games was to hold a book in my hands – one I'd specially selected – thumb through its pages and try to imagine it was my name on the cover. Sometimes I lost all track of time and was alerted only to the fact by the sight of the others thundering past the window on their way back to school from the arcade. I'd swiftly join them. Halfway up the high street, we'd put our caps back on and run hell for leather. If the others thought it odd that I preferred the bookshop to the arcade, they didn't remark on it – maybe they just assumed I was practising my reading.

• • • •

During the summer of 1967, in pursuit of my new-found ambition, I wrote my first book, inspired by a family holiday near Dartmouth and a trip on a pleasure cruiser along the River Dart to Totnes. It was entitled *Murder on the River Dart*. The hero was called Pete Entwistle, an amalgam of the names Pete Townshend and John Entwistle of the Who. Entwistle was a chief inspector in the Devon constabulary, with a yearning to join Scotland Yard in the 'big black smoke'. I called his sergeant, Roger Moon, after Keith Moon and Roger Daltrey – that way, I'd name-checked all four members of the band. I was more than a little impressed by the Who. Sergeant Moon had just endured a spell back in uniform after driving a police car into the River Dart but was destined to follow in his boss's footsteps to London. They made a formidable pair. *Murder on the River Dart* was the start of what I hoped would be a sequence of adventures involving the duo, culminating in their arrival at Scotland Yard, which would set in motion another chain of escapades.

A day or two after I started writing it – a collection of misspelled words in scrawled longhand – my parents presented me with a gift from the heavens: a shiny new, black Remington typewriter, complete with its own case. I was so excited by the thought of owning one – and more than a little daunted by their unexpected show of faith in me – that I sat and looked at it for some twenty minutes before daring to touch one of the keys. I typed murderontheriverdart on one line and byjohnlazenby on the next, with two fingers, and sat staring at it for another twenty minutes. I don't think I left my room for the rest of that day. I was so entranced by the clickety-clack, the distinctive ding of the bell at the end of each line, the flow of the ink stamping its imprint through the ruffling ribbon onto the page.

I stopped only when I lost feeling in my two fingers and decided to read what I had written. It turned out to be nothing more than a collection of jumbled letters, most of them joined together in long, tangled lines of gibberish, which added a new dimension to my dyslexia. That was when I learned what the space key was for – not to mention the little white bottle, labelled Tippex. I also learned that it was quicker and far more satisfying, when I made a mistake, just to rip the pages off the roller and start again, crunching them into a ball and throwing them into a pile of rejection slips on the floor. I selected a handful of paperbacks from my parents' bookcases and placed them on the edge of my desk for inspiration, perched like a set of building blocks. 'You're a real writer now,' my mother said after pausing in my bedroom doorway to watch me hammer out another sentence. All I lacked was an ashtray on my desk, with the smoke from a lit cigarette curling upwards – but I couldn't tell her that.

Entwistle and Moon – appropriately enough, they were the engine room of the Who – weren't my first fictional creations. That accolade belonged to a character I invented called Nanny Baston. Her job was to save the world on at least three or four occasions a week, when I regaled the dormitory with stories of her crime-fighting exploits after lights out. As I could barely read or write a word of the story, being no more than ten or eleven, I carried it all around inside my head or just made it up as I went along. Nanny Baston was a little, grey-haired old lady with a pair of spectacles resting on the tip of her nose who, when she wasn't shaking a baby's rattle, pushing a pram or cooing sweet lullabies, could defuse bombs, drive racing cars and throw a left hook with the explosiveness of Henry Cooper. Equally adept at firing a machine gun or a bazooka, she could pull the pin from a grenade with her teeth like taking a bite from one of her favourite cucumber sandwiches. Naturally, her services were required by everyone from British intelligence, the government, Scotland Yard and Interpol to even the England football, rugby and cricket teams.

The only problem was that I struggled to keep up with the others' requests for more stories and worried whether I wouldn't exhaust all my ideas. I needed Nanny Baston's superpowers to refuel my imagination if I was to meet their demands. Fortunately, I didn't run out of stories and was so surprised by what I found in my head that I wondered how some of the thoughts got there without me knowing or whether they were even my own. Sometimes the ideas for new stories came so fast that, like a starburst, they were gone before I could catch them, and I learned that if I didn't make use of them there and then, they'd be lost for ever.

I invented an arch-nemesis for Nanny Baston, none other than Mr Snowden, whose attempts at world domination were foiled on an almost nightly basis – something that was always guaranteed a cheap laugh. I experienced the strange (for me) but delightful sensation of having people laugh with you instead of at you, of being able to hold forth without being interrupted, of having people hang on to my every word. I especially liked it if they laughed out loud, though I had to be vigilant, of course, because Mr Snowden had a habit of listening outside the dormitory door. Their pin-drop silence when I nearly killed off Nanny Baston one night was just as pleasing. Above all, I hated being laughed at in the classroom – no matter how many times it happened, I never got used to it – and my storytelling, I was thrilled to discover, more than made up for it.

Once I had finished typing *Murder on the River Dart*, I couldn't wait to try it out on anyone who came to the house, to gauge their opinions or badger them if needs be. No one got off scot-free. Most were happy to listen to a chapter or two and some were kind enough to offer the advice and encouragement I desperately sought. Then they had to negotiate the burning question of 'Do you think it will be a-published?' without disappointing me. There was, however, one person who had no intention of letting me read my book to her and that was a friend of my parents' with the memorable name of Lettuce Tuckett. 'Not now,' she'd say, batting my book away with her hand whenever I asked if she'd like to hear a chapter – which, as she was staying with us, was at least two or three times a day. I was nothing if not persistent and finally persuaded her to relent. Perhaps it was because I'd caught her on the hop when she was half-asleep after an afternoon nap and hadn't had time to marshal her defences. 'Oh, if you must,' she sighed irritably. 'It's not long, I hope.'

I explained it was no more than three chapters but failed to mention I regularly added new twists or ideas into the plot, which occurred to me while I was attempting to read it. I was also prone to introducing new characters and including reams of additional dialogue, which I made up on the spot and which, coupled with the slowness of my reading (though, to be fair, I could recite most of it from memory), helped stretch it out further. To make it more entertaining and to incorporate what I hoped was a touch of authenticity, I impersonated the Devonian accents of Entwistle and Moon, adding the unmistakable burr whenever the opportunity arose. Eventually she could take no more and jumped to her feet. 'Is your mother in the kitchen?'

'But don't you want to know who the murderer is?' I asked urgently to no response. 'You're going to miss the best bit.'

Indeed, she was. The identity of the murderer was about to be revealed after a frantic foot race through the streets of Totnes, with Entwistle and Moon in hot pursuit of their man. Halfway through the chase, the murderer made a last-ditch effort to evade their clutches, ducking unseen into a second-hand clothes shop where he hid behind a rack of overcoats, before running out disguised in a stolen coat and hat. He was finally apprehended by Entwistle and Moon on the quayside while attempting to board the boat back to Dartmouth, still wearing the stolen items and trying to pass himself off as a tourist.

'You're nabbed,' Entwistle told him, placing a firm hand on his shoulder. 'The game's up – you're under arrest for murder.'

'You've got the wrong man,' the murderer insisted. 'I'm innocent.'

The last word in the book belonged to Moon. 'Like hell you are!' he said and eagerly applied the handcuffs. My mother provided the exclamation mark.

• • •

By the time I left Hildersham House in July 1967, I had known for a year or two that the name of my next school was Shiplake College and that I would be exchanging Broadstairs and the English Channel for Henley and the River Thames. It hadn't always been planned that way. In the ultimate act of optimism, my father had enrolled me at Marlborough College, his old school, when I was seven and still happily writing my name backwards. Clearly, that was never going to be an option for me. For one thing, I would have to achieve a Common Entrance Exam pass mark of 50 per cent or more in each subject – and there was as much chance of that happening as Britain suddenly joining the space race and beating the US and Russia to the moon.

Although I had made undeniable progress with my reading and writing – to the extent that I scored a mark of forty-one in my Common Entrance English exam and a score of sixty-nine in history, surpassing all my expectations – maths remained an insurmountable barrier to me, a frontier hopelessly beyond my reach. I managed a grand total of twenty-nine across the subject's three papers, which, in all honesty, was twenty-nine more than I expected: eight in general maths, seven in geometry, fourteen in algebra. And three of those marks, my maths teacher could not resist pointing out, were because I'd spelled my name correctly at the start of each paper. A pass mark of fifty in French, however, remains a mystery to me to this day. The look of utter astonishment on Mr Snowden's face was almost worth the six years of pain and misery he doled out to me in the classroom.

Of course, my overall Common Entrance score of 37 per cent hardly bore scrutiny with the marks achieved by the likes of Teague and some of my other friends, for whom failure was never a part of the syllabus; some even attained scholarships to their next schools. But I did not let that worry me unduly. I had gone from being thrown out of my first school for being unteachable to being accepted, six years later, as a new student at Shiplake College, having completed an examination whose reputation filled me with the utmost dread. And that was good enough for me.

It was true that the past couple of years had been more bearable for me, though that had more to do with the arrival of a glamorous, young assistant matron, Miss Forbes, than my improved ability to read and write. 'Have you seen the new assistant matron?' we asked each other during her first week. The question was invariably followed by a long exhaling sound, as if the thought was too hard to contain in one breath. It was a stupid question because you had to be blind or half-dead not to notice her, but we asked it anyway. She certainly made an instant impression on the senior boys, of which I was now one, and whenever our paths crossed, I discovered a spring to my step, walked a little taller and tried desperately to catch her eye. Caroline Forbes – even the name had a special ring to it – achieved something that until then I would never have dreamed possible at Hildersham House. She took our drab days and breathed sunshine into them.

Admittedly, we hadn't got off to the best of starts, especially after I called her Memphis Honey, but it seemed I was soon forgiven. We shared an interest in music, particularly the hit parade, and I'd often find her in the music room listening to a new single she'd bought. She liked Georgie Fame and the Blue Flames, the Walker Brothers or Eric Burdon and the Animals. The sound always drew me in, and on one occasion I opened the door to discover her dancing, the room filled with cigarette smoke, the volume on the record player turned up. I felt embarrassed and was about to close the door and walk away in the hope she hadn't noticed me, when she swung around and smiled. 'Are you swooning, Laz?' She always called me that. I had no idea what swooning meant, though I suspected that whatever it was, my face was probably screaming yes.

I had to wait another week or two, until my parents next came to visit, before I learned what it meant. In the meantime, Miss Forbes often repeated the question whenever we bumped into each other. I had to fight to keep the surprise off my face when my mother explained its meaning, but not before she'd asked me why I wanted to know. 'It seems a strange word for you to ask about,' she said. I told her, as matter-of-factly as I could, that I'd heard it in a film we'd seen at school and wondered what it meant, that's all. Fortunately, she didn't ask me the name of the film. One afternoon, not long after that, I'd gone upstairs to the dormitory to collect a book off my bed when Miss Forbes strolled in. The dormitories were out of bounds during the day and normally you had to have matron's permission or, at the very least, a cast-iron reason to be there – and, as usual, I had neither. I could tell by her smile, however, that I wasn't in trouble.

'I hope you've got permission, Laz.'

'I was just picking this up,' I grinned and showed her the book.

'I don't know if that's a good enough reason,' she said, still smiling, and pushed me onto the bed. 'I think I might have to confiscate all your clothes if you can't come up with a better excuse than that.' I was too surprised to say anything and tried to jump to my feet, but she pushed me down again. 'This can come off for a start.' And she loosened my tie, laughing in my ear as she did so, pulling it halfway down my shirt before lifting it over my head and discarding it on the floor.

Usually, I was unfazed by most things that happened to me at school and was always being egged on by the others to do something daring or foolhardy, to flout the rules whenever possible. Yet in that moment – despite it appearing to be nothing more than a game – my nerve deserted me and I found myself behaving in a way I could not have predicted. As fast as she unbuttoned my shirt and untucked it, I buttoned it up again and tucked it in; when she tried to pull off my shoes and socks or undo the clasp on my belt, I fought to keep them on as if my life depended on it. For the most part I was successful in repelling her efforts, though one of my shoes ended up flying across the dormitory like a missile, along with my socks. Finally, she gave up the struggle and stared at my dishevelled state, her hands on her hips, a despairing look on her face. 'Oh, you're no fun, Laz,' she said, and walked off, leaving me to hunt for the various bits of clothing I'd lost in the struggle.

I managed to avoid her for a while after that, to give myself time to recover from my embarrassment. But a few weeks before the end of term, she stopped me one afternoon after games and invited me to her room to watch *Top of the Pops* with her. I didn't have to think twice. I knew it would be a perilous climb into the eaves, that I'd have my heart in my mouth the whole way, but nothing was going to stop me. Dressed in my pyjamas, dressing gown and slippers, I crossed three floors that night, two of the longest, darkest corridors in the school, with their in-built orchestra of sound effects, before reaching my final hurdle – a narrow spiral staircase that led to her room. Halfway up, I heard her television and breathed a deep sigh of relief. I knocked quietly on her door, and she let me in. 'You're just in time,' she said.

She sat in the one armchair, with an ashtray in her lap, while I perched on the end of the bed. Jeff Beck had just launched into 'Hi Ho Silver Lining'. After a minute or two, she lit a cigarette and offered me another from a blue and white Rothmans packet. I immediately blew a cloud of smoke across the room and heard the familiar sound of her laughter. 'That's not how you smoke a cigarette,' she said. I wasn't aware there was any other way to smoke a cigarette and stared at the one smouldering away in my hand as if it had mysteriously taken on some new life form. It looked like every other cigarette I'd ever smoked. 'You're supposed to inhale the smoke, not puff it out like that – that's a waste of a cigarette.' So I'd been doing it wrong for the past few months and no one had told me. 'Look – watch me.' And I watched her draw the smoke deep into her lungs, hold it there for a couple of seconds and then emit a thin, blueish jet of smoke from between her lips. 'You try it.'

I took a tentative drag, but the smoke instantly stung the back of my throat, causing me to cough and splutter and my eyes to water. I cursed myself under my breath. 'Don't stop – keep going,' she urged. I tried again but blew out more smoke than I inhaled; some of the smoke went up my nose before I could prevent it and the same thing happened. 'You'll get used to it, don't worry. I used to cough at first,' she reassured me. For the next twenty minutes we sat there smoking, discussing the music, her voice growing huskier by the minute, mine more high-pitched, until the haunting tones of 'A Whiter Shade of Pale' by Procol Harum signalled the end of the programme. By this time, we were leaning against her headboard side by side on the bed.

Procol Harum's hit was in the middle of a six-week run at number one that would dominate much of the summer – its mystifying lyrics already unshakeably wedged inside my head. 'Waterloo Sunset' by the Kinks was at number three, 'The Wind Cries Mary' by Jimi Hendrix at six, and my favourite, the Who's 'Pictures of Lily' – appropriately enough, about a boy who couldn't sleep at night

– was number ten. When *Top of the Pops* finished, we listened to Radio Luxembourg for a while before, all too soon, the time came to make my long descent to the dormitory.

Strangely, it held no fears for me on the way back – the floorboards could shriek and caterwaul or go off like a car horn all they liked when I trod on them. It didn't matter. It was as if I was walking on air. The back of my throat was hot and stinging and I could smell tobacco on my fingers and the collar and sleeves of my pyjamas. I climbed into bed, pulled out my radio from under the pillow and switched on Radio Luxembourg knowing she was listening to it too. I kept the volume low until I eventually fell asleep, cradling it in my hands.

I didn't receive another invitation to watch *Top of the Pops* with Miss Forbes because she left unexpectedly a week later and never returned. No mention was made of her departure, there was no official announcement, and no one talked about it except the boys. Some said there had been a row with matron and she'd walked out – one claimed to have overheard it but couldn't tell us what the row was about. Another insisted she had been fired but failed to provide a reason, though we all agreed on one thing: whatever it was, it must have been serious for her not to see out the last few days of term. Either way she was gone, and with her departure, a light was extinguished. I even wondered if it wasn't something to do with me, that in some way I was the determining factor in why everyone left without saying goodbye. It hurt not knowing why and every time I walked down a corridor or turned a corner, I wished more than anything to see her standing there or to catch a trace of her perfume. But another *Top of the Pops* came and went, and my final days narrowed and limped disappointingly towards the finishing line.

Nothing, though, could have prepared me for the inexplicable feeling that overwhelmed me on the day I left Hildersham House – the baffling realisation that I was about to miss something I'd always told myself I hated. It was an experience I couldn't come to terms with, as if I was somehow curiously at odds with myself, with who I was. I'd put so much of my energy into hating the place, only to have a part of me feel sad suddenly at the prospect of leaving it behind, to emerge dazed and confused into the summer holidays instead of overjoyed. How could that possibly be?

On the morning school broke up, I stood on the island in the middle of the drive awaiting the arrival of my parents' car, standing beneath the shadow of the old building one last time. I didn't need to stare at it to know how formidable it looked, how sure of itself, how indestructible – I could feel its presence in my every bone. It must have been there for a hundred years or more, and I had no doubt it would be there for another hundred and another after that – its ocean of ivy still sprawling over its red and brown bricks, rippling in the breeze, making a noise like the backwash. If I had known the fate that was about to befall it, however, I would have taken a little more notice. I would have paid it more attention than just the cursory glance I gave it. But I didn't. I climbed into my parents' car and didn't look back.

CHAPTER ELEVEN

'I AM IN THE SENIOR WEADING CLASS'

7 March 1965

Dear Mum and Dad

I hope you are well. Whe have just been on a walk, and some teds threw some snow balls at some off us and were hit. Then Mr Black Man ran after them and they ran away. Thank you very much indeed for taking me out it was very kind of you. I enjoyed it very much. My yoyo is going well, I hope Gina's is going well. Please could you send me the latest scors between W.Indies and the Aussies. I am going to write a letter to Gran now. Sorry it is short.

Much love John.

9 May 1965, aged eleven

Dear Mum and Dad

I am writing with my new pen, I hope you like my writing. I am in the senior weading class. And in the big game, at cricket. I am aloud to use the school's slip catching machine. I hope Sussex do well against Yorkshire. Vickery has got the Manfred Man's record

O! no not my Baby. We have got 11 new boys. Mr Snowden said I showed propise at bowling.

Much love John.

16 May 1965

Dear Mum and Dad

I hope you are all very well. Thank-you all for yours letters, And top 30. On wednesday June 30th we will visit the County Police head-quarters. I came last only by a few marks wich I thought was quite good. I have got my ear pluck on and the Walkers Brother's are on.

Much love John.

10 Oct 1965

Dear Mum and Dad,

I hope you are well. We have got a very good first IX this term, at football Penn is a very good goalkeeper and made some very good saves althought the staf one 2-1 but they were playing flat out. Colin Cowdrey was in church to-day and I got a very good look at him. I will not play for the 3rd IX on thursday. in a prac-tise match Mr Snowden called me some very rood words and has rather taken a hating about me. I have played jolly well in the game at football and many boys think that I ough to be in the 2nd IX. I will tell you what he called me when you take me out. please write and tell me when you are going to take me out. See you when you come and take me out.

Much love, John.

24 Oct 1965

Dear Mum and Dad

I hope you are well. The school now owns a cinema, we had 3

films on saturday they were called 'Our Native Country', 'Controlled Landing', and Micky the Mouse film. Mr Snowden has ordered some more films. The funny little boy you met in the Castle Keep hotel has got his-self into the 3rd IX. Looking forward to seeing you at half Term.

Much love John.

29 Nov 1965
Dear Mum and Dad,

I hope you are well. I am looking forward to seeing you on December the 4th. Vickery is in the sick-bay at the moment but will be up on Monday all being well, I hope. We had 6 film shows on Saturday. A boy had a splinter stuck up his bottom during an English lesson. The Doctor came and pulled it out and he had an injection. We have got a 3rd IX, match on Monday against Stone House. How are the terapins? And Ajax and Bill? On Monday it began to snow heavely al through the evening until everything was covered in snow. I hope that Dow and Gina are well.

Love John.

Following the death of one of our rabbits, the animal menagerie at home had been swelled by the introduction of two baby terrapins.

6 June 1965
Dear Mum and Dad,

I hope you are well. I came one but bottom. I played against Wellington and Stone H for the first IX. Which Mr Snowden said I bowled very well. We have started swimming already. The other day Mr Macaulay blowed a blackbird's egg. And out of the egg came the vanes of the baby bird and the eyes which were just forming. When you blow an egg you get a little glass tube and make a little hole in the egg, and blow threw the tube, all the yuck seeps out. Thank-you for your letters and top 30. From Russia with love is going to be very good now.

Much love, John.

11 June 1965

Dear Mum and Dad

I hope you are well. Thank you for your top 50. from the Record Mirror. Crisp has called our Dorm Captain, this morning a B.F and other words which can't be menshoned in a letter. I came 10= this week. If the top 30 is not in the paper on thursday, it might be in on tuesday, or could you try please the other paper. Much love John.

20 June 1965

Dear Mum and Dad

I hope you are all very well. Once more this week I come bottom but I got 138 marks. the camp has been caught with are food. And we are going to get the stick to-night, I think. Please don't worry. All our Ian Fleming books are going to be convescated there are 47 in the school. There is now perants race this sports and no tug of war.

Much love, John.

P.S. On monday there are 5 more weeks.

Of the forty-seven Ian Fleming thrillers that were handed in during Mr Snowden's crackdown, I was personally responsible for seven of them. In addressing the school, Mr Snowden stated that it was, in his opinion, forty-seven too many. 'One boy who shall remain nameless contributed seven to that number alone,' he announced. Not that I'd read any of them, of course. I started all seven but found them impossible to follow and gave up a few pages in. As usual, it was the Pan paperback covers I treasured. Naturally, I loved the James Bond films – *Dr. No* (1962), *From Russia with Love* (1963), *Goldfinger* (1964) and *Thunderball*, which opened four days after Christmas 1965 – and they more than made up for my inability to read the books. To my mind, Sean Connery was the personification of Bond – the by-now iconic film score perfectly fitting his every movement and mannerism. He had made the mould and I couldn't picture anyone else playing him. Imagine my surprise, therefore, when he retired his Walther PPK and relinquished the role after *You Only Live Twice* in 1967, to be replaced by an unknown actor with the name of George Lazenby.

21 Nov 1965

Dear Mum and Dad,

I hope you are well. I have sold my stamp album to Vickery for some very rear queen Victoria stamps and he will give me 5/- at the end of term. The lecture on the Navy it was very good. I asked two questions they were; Are Sea plans still used, he said no. and what is the bigest fighter aircraft in the fleet Airarme? I hope Dow and Gina are well and Ajax and Bill. Also in the lecture he asked who was going to be in the Navy and I was some boys who put his hand up.

Love John.

24 Jan 1966

Dear Mum and Dad,

I hope you are well. We arrived saftly at school to find three, new members, of the staff. I am in the top Dorm. I have settled down very well. Please could you try very hard to send me a Sekedem Gun they shoot dry peas please could you try very hard for me if they do not have one please could you get a small gun that fires peas or little pelites you will find 2/6d in my purse and if you do get one please could you buy a few packets of amo. not a cap gun. if you can't find one in Sussex ask Dad to have a go in London. Ajax and Bill and the terapins are well i trust. And how are Dow and Gina? Did Dow get any think on the pools? Did you remember to send of the approvals and the 5/1d Postal order? Did you also ask Mr Connford to stop Victour and Valiant? When you send my Sekedem Gun please could you send it in a box with some stamps in it as well you will find some in a big, tall tin in my carboaurd. To see you in 3 weeks.

Love John.

26 Jan 1966

Please Mum do not send the gun to school. Give it me when I go out. Love John.

6 Feb 1966

Dear Mum and Dad,

I hope you are well. I came 9th this week out of 14 boys. Please could you send Ranger to school for me please. We will probably have a really good 1st 15 this term. The scrum will be jolly heavy. It has rained nearly all to-day, so we went for two walks. Thank-you for your letters you sent me this week. Please could you keep on sending the football results.

Mr Macaulay has been ill with shingles, so we have got a new master called Mr Balchin he is horrible No-one likes him, he is just like a escaped convict. Worst of all he takes us for maths. In my paper it had some jolly good pictures on close up of the Moon from luna-9. I am glad Wales beat Scotland 8-3. Bad test news. Mr Snowden said that he thinks Australia will win the 5th test match. When you buy my gun please could you also buy some ammunition for it.

Much love John

On 3 February, Russia's unmanned Luna 9 became the first spacecraft to make a soft landing on the surface of the moon and transmit photographic data back to earth. Some had predicted that the probe would sink beneath the thick layers of lunar dust, but its successful landing allayed any such fears and paved the way for America's Surveyor 1 to accomplish the same feat four months later.

6 Nov 1966, aged twelve
Dear Mum, and Dad,

I hope you are well. Thank-you for taking me home at half-term, I enjoyed my-self very much. On saturday we played Wellesly House, and I was selected at left half for the 1st IX, but just tipical, the match was rained of. We had three films on saturday, plus the schools fire-work display, £10 worth. There are a few matches that are going to be played in the next few weeks and the rest are mostly away or home, if you come down again this term, you can watch a match, because one is bound to be played. Love John

20 Nov 1966
Dear Mum and Dad,

I hope you are well. On Wednesday we had a sort of criss-cross quiz. I answered all my questions right except for 2, my questions that I got right were, 'Who is the England football Managure, who won the Gillete Cup this summer, who sings Semi-detached Suburban Mr James, Who sings Girl don't come, who is a left handed guitarist who sings, and I got rong what is a red duster and why is an oak of the egg white. I have just completed my first oil painting, and Mr Catterall, said it is worth at least 15/- it is a waterfall. Love John.

4 Dec 1966

Dear Mum and Dad,

I hope you are well. I came top in the history exam. I have made a list of some of the presents, I might want for Christmas, Manfred Mann's latest L.P, the new Stanly Gibbons, the Guiness book of recoords, one or two descent novels such as 'H.M.S. Ulysees', or the Cloister, and the Harth, and Star Soccer annual. I hope that list is some help to you. I must say I do like Tom Jone's latest record, and the Beach Boys also. We have got a lecture tonight on Rain deer by a Mr Evatts. Love John.

22 Jan 1967

Dear Mum and Dad,

I hope you are well. I have a part in the play, I have quite a big part, I am the Black Dog, who is a nasty pirate. Gina should of read about him in Treasure Island. We had four film shows on Saturday:-

1. Storm at Sea 2. Monte Carlo (formula racing) 3. King of the Bath, an Abbot and Costelo film 4. Rock of Gibralter. When you wright to Mrs Blackman could you ask her if I could have my cake for the 13th of March, not the 10th, because in tea, the people in

the play, are having make-up put on. I shall explain it to you in detail when I go out. Sorry that I forgot Gina's birthday, I meant to send a card to her. What does Gina think of the Stone's latest? We started rugger this term, I play in the second row of the Scrum. Well done Ireland! beating Austraila 15-8. Is Gina enjoying King Soloman's Mines?

Love John.

5 March 1967

Dear Mum, and Dad,

I hope you are well. We did not play a match this week because there is a bug in the school. There is a dress rehearsal on Wednesday, we have all been fitted out for the play now, in the way of clothes. I think the play starts at 5.30, but arrive a bit early to be safe. I have been thinking of a birthday preasant, but nothing has come into my mind yet. I hope Ajax and Bill are well, and Dow and Gina. Well done Dow! winning £73 18 shillings 0d in the pools, Dad must have frozen stiff when he heard. I would be interested to see the England XV, for the Calcutta Cup, against Scotland. I would be tempted, to drop Hansen, and Jennings, Hiller, and Webb, are possibilities with McFadyean moved into the centre, to add some punch there. After the play you will go into the hall probably, and have drinks, and talk to the other parents, and chat up people, or congratulate Miss Beal, and her helpers. The Actors will be having a feast and a lot of rejoicing in the kitchen. Gina will probably be a bit bored, but there will be other sisters there probably. Looking forward to see you on Saturday, and Sunday, you can come to church if you want, at 10.0, be there by a quarter two, if you want to come, but you'll probably want a lie in – see you.

Love John.

7 March 1967

Dear Mum and Dad,

I hope you are well. The play has been switched to the 19th of March. as you have seen, we have got a bad illness. Please could you not__ send my birthday presents to school. I shall order my cake on the 10th of March with Mrs Blackman. I don't think theres any need to right to her about it. Oh by the way I have just received my School Rugger 1st VX colours. So I shall be in the Rugger XV till the end of term, I can't be dropped now I have my colours. I t also means I shall be in the 1st XV photograph. Will you be coming down to take me out this coming Saturday-Sunday or not at all. I don't mind, but it is so near the end of term I don't think it is much point. Please, the only present to sent to school is my Conan Doyle Stories. But a bit after the 10th, so it arrives on the 11th, 10th or 12th. Thank you.

Much love John.

30 April 1967, aged thirteen

Dear Mum, and Dad,

I hope you are well. I am. I had a safe journey back to school. Could you send me my pen, wich I left on my desk, it is attached to some paper. And my mixture for my wharts. There is trouble about Radios, we have to have a lisence. 14/-, so I shall need a lisence. If I am Going to continue with my radio. I am looking forward to the start of the season. But have not practised my batting mutch, yet. Please right soon.

Love John

To own a radio at school, you had to obtain permission from Mr Snowden at the start of term – a task that appeared on the face of it to be relatively straightforward, yet proved, for me at least, anything but. I was nine when I decided to take my radio with me to Hildersham House. Mr Snowden was seated at his desk when I knocked on the door and entered his study, clutching my transistor.

'May I please have a radio this term, sir?'

'What's a radio?' he asked, making no attempt to look up from his desk where he was earnestly sifting through some papers.

Confused, I showed him my radio. 'This, sir,' I said, but he refused to look in my direction.

'Don't you understand English, boy? I've just asked you – what's a radio?'

I decided to give it its full name. 'It's a transistor radio, sir.'

'What's that?'

'My radio, sir. I can prove it's a radio.' And I immediately switched it on so that he could hear it.

'Turn that thing off,' he shouted. 'That's not a radio – that's a wireless. What is it?'

'Is it a wireless, sir?'

'Of course, it's a wireless – I've just told you.'

I was still confused. 'Is that the same as a radio, sir?'

This time he stopped what he was doing and looked at me. 'What is?'

'A wireless, sir – is it the same as a radio?'

'Don't be so stupid, boy. I've just spent five minutes explaining to you that's it not a radio, it's a wireless. Don't you listen to a thing anybody tells you? I'm trying to help you here, do you understand?'

I nodded. 'So what is it you're holding in your hand?'

'A wireless, sir.'

'Finally. So you want permission to listen to a wireless this term, is that right?'

'Yes, sir.'

'I do wish you'd think.'

And he quickly ran through the rules for me, explaining that wire-lesses were allowed to be played only on half-days and holidays, that they were not allowed in the dormitories or outside of the school grounds and must always be kept in our desks. Boys were permitted to listen to them on Sunday afternoons outside in the grounds, but under no circumstances should they be played loudly. The volume on a wireless should never be turned beyond the halfway mark, he in-sisted. 'Wirelesses are not meant to be played loudly – not the racket you people listen to anyway. If I hear yours, I will confiscate it and you won't see it again until the end of term. Do I make myself clear?'

'Yes, sir.'

Sometimes I wondered whether people didn't go out of their way to make life as difficult as they could for me. Regardless, I spent the rest of the term listening to my wireless, though secretly, I knew it was really a radio.

4 June 1967

Dear Mum, and Dad,

I hope you are well. I am. Work is going well, I am glad to say. I took 8 wickets for 3 runs against St Peter's Court in the 1st IX, I have got my colours now, and on Saturday I took 3 wickets out of 8 wickets. I have taken 11 wickets in the last two games. I have signed my name on the bat. Sorry the letter is so short but I'm very busy. I shall write later in the week possilby.

Love John.

18 June 1967

Dear Mum, and Dad,

I hope you are well, I am. To-morrow being Monday is the Common Entrance. I hope I pass, I think I shall. So far this season I have taken 18 wkts in 6 matches. I scored 0 not out in the Welles-ly Match without facing a ball! We had a swim this after-noon. When I first got in, by the means of a belly flop, I found it very, very cold. I have just finished my painting in extra art, it was, or at least to my mind, and Mr Catterall's quite good. Please write soon, I hope I shall pass, looking forward to our next matches. I hope we win, we shall be expected too. Love John.

16 July 1967

Dear Mum and Dad,

I hope you are well. I am. We have finished cricket, in 12 match-es I took 39 wickets, Knight took 36. I'm not to sure but someone has not taken that amount for a very, very long time now. I hope that Ajax, and Bill are well, and Dow. I am looking forward to seeing you on Thursday, I am really rather sorry to leave.

Love John.

25 June 1967

Dear Mum, and Dad.

I have just received my C.E.E results.

Marks:- *good +bad

English 41 *

History 69 ***

Geography 44 *

French 50 ***

Scripture 48 **

Maths 8 +

Algebra 14 +

Geometry 7+

but I have passed. Mr Snowden was very pleased. Everyone was amazed at my: Scripture, French, and History marks. If my maths would have been round about 40% I would have gained at least 58%.

Love John

P.S. The papers were quite hard, I shall show them to you when I come out.

CHAPTER TWELVE

WRITE 500 WORDS ABOUT THE INSIDE OF A PING-PONG BALL

The first golf ball crunched into the metal locker behind my head with such force that it left an immediate dent and a ringing, reverberating sound in my ears. The second golf ball was already on its way, a split second behind the first, travelling just as fast in its slipstream, on an almost identical trajectory, and I had to swerve my head three or four inches to the right in the opposite direction to avoid it striking me between the eyes. Another one slammed into the locker door, which was swinging free with the same terrifying momentum, and ricocheted off it. The boys who were throwing the golf balls – there were eight of them and eight of us – were standing in the middle of the room some twenty yards or so in front of us, about the length of a cricket pitch perhaps. Maybe they were a bit closer, judging by the velocity at which the balls were hurtling towards us, or maybe they were a yard or two further away. It was difficult to tell and I wasn't too clever at calculating distances at the best of times. All I knew was that we – the new boys, that is – were under attack, lined up like a row of ducks in a shooting gallery, dodging and weaving as if our lives depended on it. Which at that very moment, they did.

A couple of minutes earlier we had been ordered by the eight senior boys, five of whom were house prefects, to stand by our lockers in the junior common room and await further instructions. There appeared to be nothing particularly suspicious about the command; we had spent the first two days of term doing much the same thing, waiting around for something to happen, for lessons to start, not sure what to do with ourselves, getting to know one another and our new surroundings. The common room housed a scruffy sofa, a pair of armchairs frayed at the seams, a television, a kettle, a toaster, a bottle of milk that had already curdled, an assortment of wooden chairs and tables and a bank of lockers, where we stored our exercise books, our radios and the few possessions we had brought with us from home.

The senior boys were relaxed and smiling at us when they entered the room – little did I know they were merely getting their ducks in a row. One of them was carrying a white cardboard box, which he proceeded to place with almost exaggerated care on a table in front of him while the other seven gathered round. For a moment it crossed my mind that the box might contain a cake – perhaps a welcome-to-Shiplake cake, or some sticky buns, or it might be someone's birthday. Only I could come up with a thought that stupid. We all looked at each other, standing shoulder to shoulder by our lockers, wondering what would happen next. One of the boys lifted the lid off the box and I saw him reach inside and help himself to what I now realised was a fistful of golf balls. The others did the same and, still smiling, loaded them purposefully into their hands, as though they were trying to scrum as many chocolates into them as they could. I'd like to think it was at this point that I had an inkling, a prickling sense of danger or detected a ripple of alarm, a warning voice in my ear, just loud enough to alert me that something was wrong. But the first golf ball was already in motion, landing like a scream through a letterbox before I came to with a sickening jolt. It wasn't cake I was going to be eating but golf balls.

It was all over in a minute or so – the time it took for them to run out of ammunition. One of them scooped up the golf balls, some of which had travelled to the far end of the room, and returned them to the box while we tensed our bodies, flinching at their every movement, waiting for round two, for the next barrage or the off-chance that one of them might attempt a sneaky parting shot at the last moment. Having been caught with our guard down once, we weren't about to let it happen a second time. But they'd had their fun; the boy who'd collected the balls put the lid back on the box and, without addressing a word to us or even looking in our direction, they departed, talking and laughing among themselves as if they were just walking to class. The door slammed shut behind them.

I untensed my body and looked around at the others. One or two of them were rubbing their bruised arms or legs, one was holding the side of his head where an ugly red lump was about to sprout. A couple were picking themselves off the floor, having sprawled there after taking a hit or flinging themselves down for protection, curled into a ball in the hope that their assailants might take pity on them. One of them was crying quietly to himself. I could see that I had got off lightly in comparison, apart from a screaming elbow which I'd used to successfully fend off a golf ball. Our lockers looked as if someone had taken a sledgehammer to them – for no other reason than the senior boys wanted to have a bit of fun. No one spoke, none of us knew what to say to each other; we were still virtually strangers. It was as though our minds had temporarily shut down and we were waiting for them to switch back on again.

As initiations go, it was casually brutal – amplified by the ease with which the violence had been unleashed on us. It was men against boys, adults against children: eighteen-year-olds, who looked twenty and in some cases were almost a foot taller than us, against thirteen-year-olds, some of whom might even have passed for younger (I included myself in that category). It was a frightening mismatch in which we hadn't stood a chance, hadn't known what hit us until it was too late.

And there wasn't a thing any of us could do about it either – as we would quickly discover.

• • •

For at least my first two years at Shiplake College, the house prefects and senior boys were the equivalent of our masters and they did everything but teach us in class. The duty prefect took us for prep, made sure we were in bed at the appointed time, switched out the dormitory lights and, along with the other senior boys, administered house discipline. Any slip-ups or misdemeanours were routinely, and often cruelly, punished. The majority enjoyed the power they wielded over us and didn't hesitate to take full advantage of it. Clearly, they had been treated in the same manner when they were juniors and were simply passing it on in the only way they knew how, perpetuating the cycle of fear. I never felt truly safe during my first two years there – none of us did – and we lived in permanent dread of another bruising rite of passage, a repeat of the shooting-gallery incident or something similarly scarring.

On arrival at college, new boys were assigned to one of four houses. Mine was Skipwith House, based in the main school building of Shiplake Court, which was an imposing, red and grey brick Victorian structure overlooking the river, two miles upstream from Henley-on-Thames. Hildersham House, which had always appeared so vast to my young eyes, would have fitted into it several times over and there would still have been room to spare. The main building included the oak-panelled Great Hall, where school meals were held, the library, a medical wing, the kitchens, the house dormitories with the usual iron beds and cold wooden floors (some things never changed) and the house prefects' single bedrooms. The other three houses, Burr, Everett and Welsh, were situated at various points in the school grounds; all houses contained between fifty and sixty boarders and in most cases the house master lived under the same roof as the boys. However, it felt as if Skipwith, despite its central location, was a separate state, hived off from the others and operating under its own authority with its own rules and rulers.

Some of the senior boys even owned knuckledusters and threatened to take us to the basement and use them on us if we were disobedient or stepped out of line. Knuckledusters were banned throughout the school and boys caught in possession of them faced instant expulsion, but that didn't stop several from brazenly wearing theirs in the house for all to see like a tattoo, a symbol of who they were and the menace they posed. Primarily, they were worn to frighten and intimidate yet I can distinctly recall one of them – a boy called Welbeck – using his on at least a couple of occasions, though never on me. The look he gave me sometimes, when we passed in the corridor or on the stairs, suggested it was only a matter of time before he did.

Welbeck was a pockmarked, sandy-haired boy who was no more than fifteen or sixteen but, because of his size and height, appeared appreciably older. He was obsessed with the Kray Twins, the leaders of a fearsome London gang known as the Firm, and various other East End gangsters, whose names meant nothing to us but whose exploits played inside his head like an ever-revolving reel of horror film. He was one of the few people I've met whose presence could abruptly change the atmosphere in a room, injecting the chill of ice into it. When he left school suddenly and never returned, the sigh of relief among the juniors was palpable. It never occurred to me for a minute that I would catch a glimpse of him again a few years later. I was walking to a cafe in Soho and he was working as a doorman for a strip joint. I would have recognised him a mile away. He was looking in the opposite direction, fortunately, and never saw me. No doubt he was still wearing his knuckledusters.

Another of the seniors used to aim his air rifle out of the upstairs window of his single room and train his telescopic sights on us for his own amusement, just to watch the terror on our faces. There was even one occasion when we had to run for cover. Many of them were troubled boys, but just how troubled I didn't realise at the time, having nothing else at that age to measure it against: I thought, simply, that was how life went. After all, weren't we all troubled boys? Wasn't that part of the reason we were at Shiplake College in the first place? What made it infinitely scarier for me, however, was that some of the masters were troubled too, and in some cases, more troubled than the boys they were supposed to be teaching.

As new boys at Shiplake in September 1967, we were made aware at every turn that we were the lowest form of school life and as such were despised for it. To make things worse, boys who were no more than a couple of years older took it out on us too despite also being classed as juniors, trapping us in a downward spiral of pressure, like a ceiling slowly crushing us. It would be another three years before we felt we had any semblance of control or order over our lives, having finally climbed the pecking order – a greasy pole if ever there was one. In addition, many of our tormentors had left by that time and were making their way in the world, where they had already no doubt found others to terrify, and we could breathe a little easier.

If nothing else, I quickly learned that I possessed the requirements to survive and there were occasions when my perpetual motion, my heightened reactions and my reflexes served me well – though, as ever, they did not preclude me from getting into trouble. My experiences at Hildersham House had for the most part prepared me, like tenderised steak, for much of what lay in store during those first years at Shiplake. However, that did not mean you could switch off, relax or dare to take your eye off the ball (the golf ball) for a second. The stone-cold reality was that no one had our backs, no one was in our corner and no one cared about our welfare… most definitely not our housemaster, Mr Faber.

Mr Faber was a distant, indeterminate figure, who appeared in our lives from time to time, like a ship drifting on the horizon, and then disappeared again from view. He was not a bad man or even an uncaring one, but because of his inattention, forgetfulness and the negligence of his duties as a housemaster, he made our days considerably harder and more frightening than they should have been. He lived in the school grounds, at the end of a mazy, meandering path, with his wife and young son. He walked the path to school every day through its corridor of trees and overgrown wildflowers, distractedly swinging his briefcase, a thatch of greying fair hair fluttering in the breeze, his black gown with a long tear at the back trailing out behind him (all masters wore gowns, though not generally in such a state of dishevelment). It was as if the walk accentuated in some way his predominantly dreamy, vague state of mind, clouding his thoughts and adding another layer of mist to his absent-mindedness. You could almost hear the birds singing inside his head when he passed by. A former oarsman and celebrated rowing coach, his muscled, finely tuned body was both unexpected and surprising, looking as if it should have belonged on someone else.

He devolved the day-to-day running of Skipwith House to his prefects and the care of two live-in masters, who maintained only a token presence at best, and one of whom – Mr Soper, the music teacher – we were more in need of protection from. Mr Faber frequently forgot he had a house of boys to look after, or indeed which boys were in his house or which class he was supposed to be teaching at any given time. He had simply no idea of the levels of violence to which his prefects were prepared to stoop. 'The best-behaved boys in the school belong to Skipwith House,' he would often point out to no one in particular.

I had been at Shiplake for barely a week when Mr Faber took it upon himself to instruct the juniors in how to shut a door by making the least noise possible. 'It's something I insist on all you boys learning from an early age,' he explained. 'Don't forget I have to sit in an office directly above the junior common room and I've already lost count of how many times a day I hear one of you slam it.' The demonstration was performed at least four or five times for our benefit: repeatedly, he walked over to the door and with the meticulous care of a mime artist, gently twisted the handle, opened the door slowly and widely before quietly closing it again with the faintest of clicks, removing his hand from the handle as if he'd just touched a flame. 'Who heard the click?' he asked. We all heard it but looked at each other unsure whether we should tell him we had. 'No one? Well, that's how softly I want you to shut the door from now on. No slamming, no banging, no crashing, just the gentlest of clicks, like squeezing a trigger.' And he demonstrated it again. 'Like the kiss – no more – of a billiard ball against another.' I think we were too surprised to laugh. 'That's so much more satisfying, wouldn't you agree?' And we all nodded.

One by one we were called forward to take our turn at shutting a door as softly as we could while he sat in a chair and watched us. Only one boy showed a little too much force, as he put it (surprisingly, it was not me) and had to have several more attempts at it. Eventually, he was satisfied that we had all mastered the trick. 'From now on I expect you to always close a door that quietly – is that understood? Good.' Whereupon he walked out, slamming the door behind him so loudly that half of the lockers flew open and the entire room hummed and vibrated like a tuning fork for almost a minute afterwards. We could not control ourselves any longer and, in response, an instantaneous roar of laughter followed him down the corridor and back to his office – a roar that encapsulated perfectly the way we viewed Mr Faber for the rest of our days at Shiplake.

The only other time we encountered him was when we did something serious – a transgression that could be dealt with only by the housemaster or, worse, the headmaster – or we incurred the wrath of another teacher, or a senior, who reported us to him in the hope we'd receive a punishment to fit the crime, one that 'teaches you a lesson'. And sure enough, it wasn't long before I found myself standing in Mr Faber's office for just such an offence. In this case, I was guilty of badly cheeking a senior by the name of Collister, who also happened to be the most unpopular boy in the house, possibly the school, and therefore posed no threat – or so I thought. He had an enormous round face that reminded me of a balloon with glasses on it – the type of balloon face where the glasses are always too small. I'd heard his fellow seniors call him Piggy or far worse more times than I could remember; I'd seen them punch and kick him and thought just because they insulted him, so could I.

My ability to attract trouble or unwanted attention remained as acute as ever and hadn't magically disappeared overnight simply because I'd changed schools or found myself in a new environment. It was a part of who I was and impossible to dial back: I could not resist pushing my luck, seeing how far I could go. The moment I saw 'Piggy' Collister lumbering towards me on the stairs, I knew I wouldn't be able to stop myself from saying something to him.

'Excuse me, Collister.' He stopped and looked hard at me, as if to say *What do you think you're doing talking to me? You're a junior.* I pulled my most concerned expression. 'Is your face hurting you?' Instinctively, he went to put his hand to his face but paused and held it there in mid-air.

'No, why?' he answered. I could feel temptation building like a wave and dived in.

'Because it's *killing* me.'

I paid no attention to the spray of angry threats that followed me down the stairs – he was always shouting at other boys who offended him, usually aiming it at them after they'd walked off, an excess of hot air that blew back on itself. I carried on, rather chuffed with myself, eager to tell the others how easy it had been to insult him. And then later that day I received the call to report to Mr Faber's office 'this minute'.

'What makes you think you can get away with talking to a senior boy like that?' he asked me.

'I don't know, sir.'

He thought about that for several seconds, frowning deeply as

224

though I'd said something profound, while I looked around at the small, cluttered office, taking in the mountain of papers in his tray, most of which had spilled onto the desk like someone had emptied the contents of a post bag across its surface. I imagined him picking up a piece of paper, glancing at it and randomly replacing it in the ever-burgeoning pile.

'We pride ourselves on how we respect our elders and seniors here at Skipwith House,' he said at last. 'It's a house tradition.' And he made a loud sniff, more of a snort, which he was prone to doing, particularly if he wasn't enjoying the conversation. 'You know what this means, don't you?' I shook my head. 'It means that I'm going to have to beat you, unfortunately.' The last word was tagged on at the end of the sentence, almost as though it were an afterthought. Unfortunately for him or me? I couldn't be sure. 'You do understand that don't you?'

'Yes, sir,' I replied.

'Have you ever been beaten before?'

'No, never, sir.' I thought if I told him that he might think twice or take pity on me.

He didn't respond but rose slowly to his feet and pulled out a long bamboo shoot from behind a dusty tower of books stacked in the corner of the office. The bamboo shoot was almost as tall as me. I couldn't seriously believe he was going to beat me with it. It looked more like a makeshift fishing rod than a cane – if indeed a cane was what it was intended to be.

'Follow me,' he said, taking the bamboo shoot with him, and set off down the corridor to my dormitory. 'Which is your bed?' I pointed to it. 'Bend over the end of it.' I did as I was told while he took off his gown with its long gash at the back, followed by his jacket. He folded them over the next-door bed and unbuttoned his right sleeve, rolling it halfway up his arm. It wouldn't go any further, I noticed, because of the size of his bicep; the left sleeve remained buttoned down. I stared at the muscle on his arm and at the length of the bamboo shoot. 'Face the wall,' he ordered. I turned around and closed my eyes.

The first stroke caught me just above the knee, but I hardly felt a thing and waited for the next swish. The second landed fair and square on my backside, but again I scarcely felt it. The third hit me across the small of my back, with considerably more force than the first two blows. Whether it was the additional power I don't know, but as it connected with my spine there was a sudden tearing, snapping sound, like a Christmas cracker being pulled, and the bamboo shoot disintegrated – exploded might be a more accurate description – scattering a shower of fragments from one end of the dormitory to the other. When I turned my head, Mr Faber was standing there holding what looked like the remains of a cigar butt in his hand. We both stared at it for several seconds in astonishment. I waited for him to say something, but he continued to look at the object in his hand, like a man who had just carelessly dropped and smashed a precious heirloom on the floor.

'May I go now, sir?' I asked finally. I couldn't stand it any more – I was still bending over the end of the bed, waiting for him to speak, to move, to unlock the moment in which we were both temporarily frozen. A part of me wanted to laugh, but I didn't want to aggravate the situation any further.

'Yes, that's it,' he said, as if what had happened was a perfectly routine occurrence, nothing out of the ordinary. 'Consider yourself beaten.' And he tossed the cigar butt onto the floor along with the rest of the debris. 'Oh, before you go, fetch a dustpan and brush from somewhere and clean up this mess, will you.'

If Mr Faber was a bemusing, often frustrating presence, Mr Soper, whose rooms were next door to our dormitory, was an altogether creepier proposition. His pronounced, egg-shaped head, his unnaturally dark hair, which fitted around it like a tea cosy, and long, thin face gave him an almost ghoulish appearance – especially if you woke with a start at night to find him standing in the middle of the room watching you while you were sleeping. We had been warned about him by the other boys and were only too aware of what to expect. We laughed openly at his attempts to coax us out of our pyjamas to lie on top of our sheets in the summer when it was too hot to sleep but knew that there was also a point beyond which we dared not cross. He kept an Eton cane on permanent display in his sitting-room and reached for it at any opportunity, particularly if we made some egg-shaped innuendo – as the boy who asked him in class whether he'd been 'shelled' in the war learned to his bitter cost. Mr Soper brandished his cane like a master swordsman, flexing and fizzing it with zeal, zipping it through the air, landing each blow on the same spot, drawing blood or leaving welts on your backside so it looked like you'd been burned by a hot iron. Not for him the ham-fisted efforts of Mr Faber. He was also known, after administering a beating, to hand you the cane and say, 'Your turn.' As far as I know, no one ever took him up on the offer, usually because we were in too much pain to oblige.

He also inflicted on me the strangest punishment I received during my time at school. I forget what I'd done to annoy him on this occasion, but he commanded me to sit at the front of the class and, as it had been raining heavily, proceeded to rub his dripping umbrella through my hair until it was soaking wet and the water was trickling in rivulets down my face and neck.

Of the glut of punishments that came my way during my first two years at Shiplake, easily the most inventive – though nonetheless taxing – were devised by a house prefect called Ronnollson. Less intimidating than the others but hardly friendly to us all the same, Ronnollson was an unathletic, slightly lugubrious-looking boy who wore a pair of glasses with shiny black frames like Michael Caine. His were always slipping down his nose and appeared in permanent need of sticking plasters to stay in one piece. Instead of taking us to the basement to beat the crap out of us, as the other prefects phrased it, or ordering us to polish his shoes until we could see our faces in them, Ronnollson delighted in delivering a more cerebral form of punishment.

I managed to get on the wrong side of him one night after prep while we were watching an episode of *Sherlock Holmes* – the 1960s incarnation, starring Peter Cushing as Holmes and Nigel Stock as Dr Watson. From that moment on, he had me pegged as a trouble-maker. The television in the junior common room was the only one in the house, so the seniors regularly came down to watch it, sometimes flicking over the channel without asking us if there was something they particularly wanted to see. On this occasion, Ronnollson had wandered in on his own and stood watching it for a minute or two before asking, 'What's this?' There was a hint of an-ticipation in his voice, as if he'd just stumbled on something special.

'It's a television, Ronnollson,' I told him.

Some of the others laughed, which didn't help my cause any. Ronnollson was one of those boys who hated being laughed at – and being a prefect, not to mention one of the more academically inclined boys in the school, he especially hated it. 'You can write me 500 words about the inside of a ping-pong ball for that,' he fired back, barely missing a beat. In the time it took to switch TV chan-nels, the others had turned their laughter on to me.

At first, I thought he was joking. 'Five hundred words about the inside of a ping-pong ball,' I repeated.

'Count yourself lucky it's not one thousand.'

'But there's nothing inside a ping-pong ball.'

'Not my problem,' he said and settled down on the sofa to watch the rest of the episode. 'And I want it by tomorrow morning, first thing before lessons. Failure to deliver or write enough words will mean another five hundred on top of what you've already written. Don't try any tricks either, like repeating the same paragraph over and over, because I'll be reading every word. If I were you, I'd start work on it now.' And he looked at his watch as if to emphasise the point.

I'd never written 500 words on anything before to my knowledge, certainly not in one sitting, and I wondered how on earth I was going to manage it. It was true I'd written more words while completing *Murder on the River Dart*, though that was under very different circumstances: I had written it on a typewriter, without the punishing deadline, for my own enjoyment and on a subject matter that hadn't left me dazed just thinking about it. I started by laboriously writing fifty words but soon exhausted every thought I could muster regarding the inside of a ping-pong ball. I would have been there all night and the next day still writing it, but for the intervention of one boy – Dean Mordell, a Canadian, who was the only person to respond to my anguished plea of 'What in the hell am I going to write?' Mordell had introduced me to the first Leonard Cohen album, his prized possession, which he played on a small portable record player in the junior common room. The rest of us had never heard of Leonard Cohen before. Perhaps Mordell reasoned he owed me a favour because I was one of a handful of boys who'd taken time to listen to it with him and professed a liking for it.

His advice to me was simple but effective, so much so that I wondered why I hadn't thought of it myself. The gist of it was to use my imagination, to write anything I liked and say it happened inside a ping-pong ball. 'It doesn't have to be a normal sized ping-pong ball, does it?' he explained.

'Like the Tardis,' I said, suddenly sitting up and taking notice.

He looked confused for a few seconds but carried on. 'Just don't write about what's really inside a ping-pong ball – that's impossible and that's what he's expecting you to do. Instead, write about anything you like, anything you're interested in, and imagine it taking place inside a ping-pong ball.'

'So I can write about a game of football or a rugby match,' I suggested, warming to the task.

'Anything you want.'

I wrote frantically that night, not even bothering to read my customarily misspelled and unpunctuated collection of words. I finished it under my sheets by torchlight in the dormitory while the others slept. In the end, I wrote more than 500 words on the topic of a rugby international played inside a ping-pong ball. I handed it in to Ronnollson the following morning before the start of lessons, trying not to smile at my sense of accomplishment or the look of surprise on his face.

When I next fell foul of Ronnollson, as I was bound to, it was to discover he had changed tactics. This time, he told me to write 500 words on any subject I liked. There was a catch, of course: it had to contain eight words, hand-picked by him, all of which I'd never heard of before and which I had to weave through the essay. They were long words too, such as intangible, dilapidate, malcontent, incongruous or oxymoron – words I would normally have no idea how to spell. These words had to be used correctly, he stipulated, they had to be spelled properly and I had to demonstrate that I fully understood their meaning.

'But how will I know what they mean?' I asked.

'What do you normally do when you want to learn the meaning of a word?' he replied. I looked at him blankly. 'You look it up in a dictionary, idiot. That's the whole point of the essay.' And he banged his hand on his head as if to indicate I had a screw loose.

Ironically, being such a stickler for accuracy – any missing full stops, spelling mistakes or grammatical errors were ruthlessly seized on – Ronnollson did me more of a favour than he will ever know. He certainly improved my vocabulary immeasurably with his eight special words in every essay. He sharpened my imagination too and, thanks to his command of the language and attention to detail, he probably taught me as much as any of the English teachers I came across during my time at school... with the notable exception of Miss Shepherd, of course.

● ● ●

It was at Shiplake College that my wish to be in a class of fellow dyslexics and strugglers was finally granted and for the first time, I experienced a sense of safety in numbers.

There were any number of firsts. I didn't have to worry about being laughed at in class any more – sometimes if we failed to understand something said to us by our teachers, we laughed at it collectively as if we were expressing our unity, our sympathy, our relief at our new-found freedom. I was equally relieved to find I was no longer bottom of the class, no longer fourteenth out of fourteen. I was holding my own, occupying a safe space somewhere in the middle ground, in unfamiliar but welcome territory. I had never felt comfortable in class before, but this was unquestionably the closest I'd come to it – the closest to feeling that I fitted in, I belonged. For the first time, I no longer felt alone.

At least half of the boys in my form were dyslexic. Most of them were there because, like me, they had failed their exams and run out of choices. Shiplake was one of the few places that would accept us – or, for some, it was the last resort, the only alternative. We each had a similar story to tell, a common link that bound us. The tale of the tape was that we knew how it felt to be a square peg, a misfit, the odd boy out; we knew what it was like to trail miles behind the others in class, to be blamed for obstructing their learning progress, for wasting the teachers' time with our disability and our distractibility, to be picked on for our own lack of learning progress.

The policy at Shiplake was to allow us to work at our own speed, to encourage us to flourish in a more streamlined environment. We would receive help and extra tuition in the subjects where we floundered and specialise in those we excelled at. That was the theory, anyway. As I had already identified history and art as my favourite subjects, this all made perfect sense to me – until it came to maths, where I had only one gear and one direction. Permanent reverse.

My introduction to college-level maths was comical to say the least, and an incident during my first lesson set the tone for much of what followed. Our teacher was a flamboyant character called Mr Barbour, who sported a colourful collection of striped bowties and wore a monocle in class. When at one point the monocle fell from his eye, a boy in the front row suddenly launched himself over the desk, flinging himself onto the floor to try to catch it in his outstretched hand before it struck the ground. Unsurprisingly, the boy came up clutching thin air, only to see the circular lens dangling tantalisingly above him on a red cord. Mr Barbour looked suitably startled and even more startled to discover that the boy, called Charteris, had no clue what a monocle was.

Mr Barbour turned out to be the most thoughtful of maths teachers I had encountered and appeared genuinely concerned with and intrigued by my utter uselessness in the subject. He informed me that he had never met anyone with such a blind spot for numbers but insisted on more than one occasion that 'it doesn't mean we should just give up on you – quite the contrary'. But in the end, even he had to accept defeat, silently conceding that, unlike his monocle, the penny was never going to drop for me. The moment of truth arrived when he caught me drawing a cartoon of him, complete with monocle, in the back of my exercise book. Instead of punishing me, as any other teacher would have done, he was so taken by the likeness of the sketch that he set me the task of completing a cartoon of everyone in the form. 'We'll pin them up on the class noticeboard at the end of term and have some fun awarding a mark for the best one,' he said. 'That way, we'll stop wasting each other's time – I can get on with teaching the rest of the form and you can finally put your talents to good use.' It was a throwback to my days at St Peter's Court, where I was often separated from the others in class, but as I had already given up on maths and it on me, it provided the perfect solution to my problem and kept me occupied.

By this time, maths had a rival for the confusion it sowed inside my head and that subject was physics. The teacher, Mr Voce, was an earnest man, tall and angular with wavy hair the colour of chalk dust and a matching moustache. He hardly ever ventured outside the confines of his subject in class, except for the time he described how, as a colonel in the army, he had designed and built the first gallows used by the British military in the Second World War. This revelation prompted such a torrent of questions from us – how long did it take to build? Was it used? When was it used? How many times was it used? Where was it used? Did you have to operate it yourself, sir? – that he was forced to threaten the next questioner with a week's detention if we didn't desist immediately. His lessons rarely concluded without the sound of an explosion and the splintering glass of a test tube above a Bunsen burner flame on full bore. The conversation between Mr Voce and the boy responsible seldom varied either.

'What's happened this time?'

'The test tube just exploded, sir.' A reply that simmered with innocence.

'Test tubes don't just explode by themselves.' Mr Voce repeated those words so many times they might have served as an epitaph for him.

'This one did, sir.'

'Nonsense.'

On another occasion, he ordered me out of class to comb my hair, with instructions not to return until I had managed to make myself look presentable. I took the opportunity to skip the rest of the lesson, hoping he would forget all about me. When he finally tracked me down later that day, he asked me why I had failed to return to class as requested. 'I tried, sir,' I said. 'But I just couldn't get my hair right.'

My hopelessness at the subject eventually persuaded me to strike a deal with another boy: I would help him with his history if he agreed to provide the answers to my physics prep. The arrangement worked well and Mr Voce registered no surprise at the sudden and inexplicable improvement in my work. But then came the end-of-term exams at the conclusion of my first academic year at college. Without anyone to supply the correct answers for me, I had no other choice than to try to imagine what they might be – unfortunately, my imagination didn't extend very far when it came to the raw elements of physics. A few days later Mr Voce returned our examination papers, and I was slightly perplexed to find that mine was unmarked and ungraded. Instead, he had written just one word, in stark capital letters: FOOL.

I absorbed the insult in much the same way I absorbed all the others, having long ago resigned myself to the fact that this was my academic fate. I was far more taken aback to discover that against all expectations, I had finally been sorted to the top of the pile in one specific subject: I'd been awarded the junior English essay prize. I was fourteen and so shocked to hear my name read out that I thought it must have been a mistake or a joke – a part of me even expected everyone to laugh. I still didn't understand the concept of paragraphs, grammar or punctuation, and my spelling continued to bedevil my written work to the point where it often altered the intended meaning of it. Indeed, after submitting my entry I hadn't given it another thought, I had so little confidence in my chances. After all, people like me weren't supposed to win academic prizes. It took days for the award to sink in, but finally, the shock gave way to elation and pride.

The topic of the essay had been 'My Dream House', though weirdly, when I started writing, I had no notion what it would look like. I hoped that through the process of writing it, the building would simply take shape around me. The pictures soon came to me – but the only problem with this was that I couldn't give a name to what I was seeing. I could describe the interiors, the features, even the style of the house, but didn't know what they were called. Fortunately, I knew a boy who did. Gordon Milne was the same age as me but resembled a kind of wandering encyclopaedia, dispensing facts wherever he went; he loved nothing better than showing off his expertise, luxuriating in his vast repertoire of knowledge, and took no time in reeling off the answers for me.

'That's called a ceiling rose,' he said, as I ran through my extensive list. 'And that sounds to me like Rococo flooring.' He even spelled it for me. When I started to describe the red tiles on the roof and the window shutters, he didn't wait for me to finish. 'That's Italianate,' he interjected.

'What is?' I asked, momentarily confused.

'What you've just described,' he smiled. I had my house.

I received copies of *David Copperfield* and Jack London's *The Call of the Wild* for my prize – both of which, I'm ashamed to say, I've never read to this day. I was still in my Hammond Innes and Alistair MacLean phase at the time. Many of the Alistair MacLeans I'd ticked off my list had, in fact, been read to me. Our English teacher, Major Blatchley-Hannah, regularly set aside two lessons a week when he did no more than read to us. He always read Alistair MacLean thrillers: *The Guns of Navarone, When Eight Bells Toll, Where Eagles Dare, HMS Ulysses*. It was the way he narrated these tales that made his lessons so memorable for me. There was a fascinating quality about him that suggested he might have stepped out of the pages of one of Alistair MacLean's novels or that he had successfully carried out himself some of the missions he described so enthrallingly. Before reading to us, he indulged in a small ritual: he carefully took out an ashtray from his briefcase, a packet of cigarettes and a lighter from his pocket and put them on the desk. It wouldn't have surprised me had he produced a handgun and placed that in front of him too, such was the stamp of the man, with his swept-back dark hair and matching military moustache.

It was not unusual for teachers to smoke in class in those days and Major Blatchley-Hannah would pause only to draw slowly on his cigarette, light another one or tap ash into the tray while he read to us. Another English teacher at Hildersham House, Mr Blackman, smoked so heavily that at times he appeared to be teaching the class through a sea fret. He used to start the lesson with cigarettes – menthol-flavoured ones because he was trying to give up – before lighting up his pipe so he could remove the taste of menthol. Aside from being the most debonair smoker I'd seen, Major Blatchley-Hannah had a voice like the comforting hum of a radio by a fireside and it continued to play inside my head long after the lesson ended. I rarely left one of his classes without the burning desire to write something and it was his influence as much as anything that inspired me to enter the junior essay competition. It was like being read Alistair MacLean by Alistair MacLean himself.

Buoyed by my success, I began studying for my O-levels – or GCSEs, as they are known today – in the winter term of 1969. But there was an unwelcome surprise waiting for me when I returned to school after the summer holidays – one that punctured the fragile balloon that held all my hopes and instantly filled me with dismay. Instead of specialising in history and English, as I'd been led to believe I would, I was to spend the rest of the term concentrating on maths and physics, with one teacher who'd already washed his hands of me and another who regarded me as little better than a FOOL. I had to read the noticeboard three times, just to make sure I hadn't misread it. If that wasn't bad enough, I would receive a daily dose of biology and chemistry as well – subjects that made me feel equally inadequate. I wondered what I'd done to deserve this and why the two biggest academic achievements of my life so far – finishing top of my form in the end-of-term history exam and winning the junior essay prize – had counted for nothing.

When I told Mr Faber that I'd been put in the wrong class, he snorted loudly. 'The school's not in the habit of making mistakes of that sort.'

'But everyone knows I'm no good at maths and science, sir,' I continued.

'Perhaps that's why you've been put in those classes – to get you up to the mark in those subjects.'

'I really want to specialise in history and English – how will I manage that if I'm doing maths and science all the time?'

'Look,' he said, quickly cutting me off. 'If you feel that strongly about it, I suggest you take it up with your form teacher or your housemaster, one or the other.'

'But you are my housemaster, sir.'

Typically, it seemed that no sooner had I started to make progress or find some impetus in the classroom, I was knocked back to the bottom again – or, on this occasion, taken in completely the opposite direction to the one I was supposed to be going. The cycle of underachievement seemed doomed to continue. So I did something I'd never done before: I told my parents. I felt embarrassed telling them, but my father explained that making a fuss was the right thing to do; it showed I cared. 'Of course, they've got it wrong,' he reassured me down the phone. He promised he would drive to the school and speak to the headmaster and my housemaster as soon as he could make an appointment. For the first time in my life, I realised, I felt angry about my treatment in a classroom – or it might have been more accurate to say that for the first time in my life, I actually cared about my education.

A week later, my father visited the headmaster, Mr Buxton, who confirmed he would personally investigate the matter and report back when he had an answer. He suspected that a mistake had been made in my case and admitted that the school's failure to acknowledge the strides I'd made in history and English had been an oversight. 'One that hopefully we will endeavour to put right.' My father's meeting with Mr Faber did not go so well. At one point, Mr Faber announced he was more concerned by the possibility I might be on drugs (despite being barely fifteen years old) than whether I was placed in the right class or not. Several seniors had been caught in possession of drugs at the end of last term and subsequently expelled – a scandal that gripped the school and caused further embarrassment after it made its way into a Sunday newspaper. The fact that Mr Faber thought I was on drugs was news to me, although it was just as likely, knowing him, that he had mixed me up with someone else. Ironically, I had never felt the need to seek out a drug high – usually my brain went off on such spectacular tangents that I rarely craved the need for extra stimulus. My father could not contain his anger, however. 'That's the most preposterous thing I've ever heard,' he said, thrusting back his chair. 'If anyone's on drugs here, it's you, Mr Faber.' And he walked out.

The question of which class I should be in was satisfactorily resolved and, in the summer of 1970, I achieved something I'd have considered unthinkable when I had arrived at Shiplake three years earlier: I gained three O-levels in English language (scraping home with the lowest grade), English literature and history. Maths was ungraded, as usual. It felt like a vindication of sorts and the first person I wanted to tell was Miss Shepherd. Although I had no way of knowing where she was or what she was doing with her life, she remained an essential part of me, the first person to understand me, a presence, a voice inside my head, always urging me on, urging me to play to my strengths. So much of who I was began with her. I knew she would be pleased for me but perhaps not surprised, because much of what she predicted for me had already happened.

In a strange quirk of timing, my O-level results coincided with the news that Hildersham House was closing. Far from being the indestructible edifice I had always imagined, it turned out that its walls were no more than paper thin. It had existed on borrowed time since the mid-1960s and none of us knew. I'd often wondered why Hildersham House had never got rid of me, washing its hands of me like St Peter's Court – the truth was, it couldn't afford to jettison pupils. It needed every penny it could get. At the start of 1970, the roll had dropped below fifty and with no hope of reversing the decline, Mr Snowden was forced to sell up. The school was eventually replaced by a housing estate, Hildersham Close. In the interim, it stood empty and boarded up, harbouring its ghosts – a playground for local kids to sneak in and spook each other down its darkened, creaking corridors. Until the demolition men finally arrived to reduce it to a welter of splintered brick and rubble and eighty years went up in a plume of dust.*

• • •

I was halfway through my second term studying History and English at A-level, safe in the knowledge I would never have to attend another maths lesson again, when I sensed something wasn't right. I had already lost count of the flurry of Bs or B-pluses, interspersed with the occasional A or A-minus, that I'd racked up in my history essays and had started to question the validity of the marking. The

---

* Hildersham House was built in 1890, so it wasn't even 100 years old or more as I had always assumed it to be.

grades had sat uneasily with me from the moment I received my first B-plus; it wasn't just that I didn't think of myself as B-plus material, or an A-level student for that matter, or that I felt like an imposter. It was because I could tell there were times when my grades were clearly not merited, when my thought process was so muddled that my writing made no sense even to me. Yet there it was almost every time, staring back at me from the top of the page: another B-plus.

The consensus among my fellow pupils was that the head of the history department, Mr Faber, did not read our essays or if he did, he merely skim-read them or marked them on a whim from impressions he had formed of us as individuals, which, once they took root in his head, were impossible to dislodge. Some pupils went so far as to suggest that if you were in Skipwith House, you were rewarded with a high mark regardless. Worryingly, those who were patently more adept at writing history essays than me, and knew it, were having to make do with Cs and the odd C-minus.

So I concluded it was time to put our suspicions to the test. My plan was to insert several paragraphs of gobbledygook in my essay – or something so wildly off-topic it couldn't have been further removed from the Napoleonic Wars, the period we were studying. I informed the others. If he fails to spot it, I told them, our suspicions will be confirmed. 'That's the last time you'll get a B-plus if he does,' someone pointed out.

After giving it some more thought, I decided to write a fictitious football report. I had become an avid reader of the sports pages and often amused myself by writing my own accounts of football or rugby matches I'd seen on television. I chose two teams – Tottenham and West Bromwich Albion – and built my report around a duel between England's two titan centre-forwards, Martin Chivers and Jeff Astle. I sprinkled in names like Cyril Knowles, Alan

Mullery, Martin Peters and Asa Hartford and embedded it in the middle of the next essay: 'Was France's invasion of Russia, and the subsequent retreat from Moscow in 1812, the beginning of the end for Napoleon? Discuss.'

I waited until Napoleon's retreat from Moscow on 19 October before abruptly switching subjects:

The first snowstorm of the Russian winter engulfed the Grand Armée on 6 November and their campfires quickly burned out in the plunging temperatures that night... *Bobby Gould opened the scoring for West Bromwich after fifteen minutes, engineering a clever one-two with Len Cantello on the edge of the Tottenham area to drill a low right-footed shot past Pat Jennings...* Napoleon hurried ahead to Paris on 5 December, where there were rumours of an attempted coup, leaving the army in tatters and in the command of a cavalry officer, Joachim Murat... *as Peters, Ralph Coates and Steve Perryman fought to wrest back control in midfield for Spurs.*

I was now building to the conclusion of my essay, namely that Napoleon's invasion of Russia was a spectacular own goal.

With Murat vainly trying to rally his troops in the face of marauding Cossacks... *and the scores locked 2–2 at The Hawthorns. Peters slipped his marker and floated the ball to the far post, where Chivers headed a thunderous 89th-minute winner past the despairing Jim Cumbes.*

As I suspected, victory was also in my sights. A couple of days later, my essay was returned with the obligatory B-plus and no comment about my future as a football writer. We had our answer.

When Mr Faber wasn't randomly generating grades for us, he was often late for class or even failed to turn up at all. Sometimes he would wander aimlessly into view, his gown trailing along the ground behind him like a ghost walking on his heels, and stop outside the classroom door where we were waiting. 'You boys should be in class, not standing around here talking.' We looked at him, trying hard not to laugh. 'Who's supposed to be teaching you?'

'You are, sir,' we told him, our voices echoing in unison. Once, before the start of a lesson, he opened his briefcase, pulled out a toaster, plugged it in and proceeded to warm his hands over the grill. In fairness to him, the history department was always draughty as hell.

Mr Priestley, who taught A-level English, was a different proposition altogether – a B-plus from him, let alone a B, was rarer than gold dust and he repeatedly undermarked us. That way he kept us hungry, forcing us to up our game. An impassive Yorkshireman, he didn't say much but weighed his words carefully and deliberately for maximum effect, bluntly at times. Should we have had any doubts about what he thought of us, he communicated it through the roles he chose for us whenever we read a play aloud in class. Mostly we read Shakespeare – we were studying *Othello* and *The Tempest* for A-level – George Bernard Shaw, Christopher Marlowe and Ben Jonson. The more basic the part he assigned you, the lower his opinion was of you or, as in the case of some unfortunate boys, the greater his contempt. His delivery, the mocking tone of his voice when he announced the cast list, said it all: 'Bonham-Carter... clown; Rimmer... handmaiden; Fottrell... peasant; Harmeson... first crone.' He left no nuance unturned.

Some of these pupils never graduated from the ranks of playing clowns, messengers or crones during the entire two years we spent studying English. For once, I wasn't included among the usual suspects, but I never felt at ease reading aloud in class and my mispronunciations provoked the odd bout of laughter. Sometimes I struggled to keep up, lost my place in the text and missed my cue. Milne, my friend the wandering encyclopaedia, was one of the more accomplished readers but, for some reason known only to Mr Priestley, was always handed the female roles. He was Ftatateeta, Cleopatra's nurse, in Shaw's *Caesar and Cleopatra* – we never failed to laugh at that – and Desdemona in *Othello*, a part he alternated with Emilia, Desdemona's handmaiden. What made it hilarious was that Milne was built like an ox, with a deep, booming voice, and a more unlikely Desdemona would have been hard to find.

Occasionally, Mr Priestley would offer me a rare word of encouragement, noting a slight improvement in my written work, though it still earned a C-minus or D. I had started to try my hand at poetry by this time, often rattling off one poem a week, and took it as my opportunity to ask if he would read some of my work and give me his considered opinion. He duly agreed to do so, told me to pick four examples of my best offerings and leave them on his office desk. A day later he called me into his office to collect them. I was somewhat surprised by the speed of his response but excited, nonetheless. He was busily writing when I knocked and, without speaking, waved me inside, indicating the poems on the corner of his desk. I didn't want to leave without hearing his opinion – that was the whole point of the exercise – and plucked up the courage to ask him what he thought.

'Prosaic, lad,' he replied without looking up, hooking a finger over his cigarette and drawing heavily on it.

His voice betrayed no hint of what the word might have meant but, being an eternal optimist, I presumed it to be a positive affirmation.

'Thank you, sir,' I said. He glanced up, gave me a curious look and carried on writing. The first thing I did after leaving his office was to consult a dictionary. It took me several attempts to find the word. I had no idea how to spell it and tried several permutations, eventually finding it by a process of elimination. I nearly dropped the dictionary in disappointment when I read the definition. Prosaic: unimaginative, uninspired, lifeless, dull, humdrum, ordinary, pedestrian, plodding. You name it, that's what my poetry was. The list of explanations was endless – I didn't need to read them all, to keep rubbing my face in my embarrassment, and hurled the dictionary against the wall. Afterwards, I even thought I might write a poem about it called simply 'Prosaic'. But I soon abandoned the idea and didn't write another for weeks.

To be fair, one of the poems I'd selected for Mr Priestley was called 'Old man in a Wheelchair at a Football Match' and it contained the immortal line (immortal in its awfulness) 'All his Guineveres long threshed to tears of stone'. It was wrong on just about every level, quite apart from the fact it didn't make sense; one of those overblown lines you get out of your system when you're sixteen or seventeen, hopefully, and recoil at in embarrassment years later. In the end I didn't write another poem for the rest of term. Each time I tried, the word prosaic crept up and mugged it of any meaning and hope.

The episode captured exactly how I felt about everything at that point, including how I saw myself. A part of me was disillusioned with the education system, especially with those who taught within it. Another part felt enveloped by a creeping indifference. It was as if, having worked so hard to get to where I was, I no longer had the heart or enthusiasm to do it all again, to set myself targets, to keep improving. I knew I was falling further behind in class, that I had lost myself somehow, but had no idea how to arrest the slide.

Before too long, it seeped into everything. I gave up on my art and even turned down the chance of a county cricket trial with Oxfordshire – something I would have jumped at two years earlier – slipping out of school to go to a rock concert instead. (The band was Lindisfarne and their album *Fog on the Tyne* rolled into the charts in the spring of 1972 and stayed there for an astonishing fifty-six weeks.) In the process, I used up what little patience Mr Buxton had left for me. A former Oxford Blue who had played county cricket for Derbyshire, the headmaster was visibly disappointed by my decision to pass up the chance to play for Oxfordshire: 'I would have thought at the very least it was worth a shot, Lazenby.' Although I appeared nonchalantly casual about it on the surface, a hidden part of me had reached the conclusion that if I didn't try, I couldn't fail.

Not long after, I attended an interview with the careers master, Mr Edridge, who doubled as a geography teacher. He asked all the pertinent questions – what my interests, plans and ambitions were, what qualifications I hoped to gain, where I saw myself in two years' time (I had no idea) – and then listened attentively to a five-minute spiel from me in which I attempted to tell him all about myself. When I'd finished, he leaned forward in his chair, steepled his fingers under his chin and asked if I'd ever considered becoming a vet. The suggestion came so far out of left field that I assumed he was joking and started laughing, only to notice the deadly serious expression on his face.

While one arm of the school was trying to steer me towards a career in which I required A-level qualifications in biology, chemistry, physics and maths – all my favourite subjects, in other words – the other was desperately trying to instil some military discipline into me. Friday was the worst day of the week – the day when we reported for duty in the CCF (the Combined Cadet Force) or corps,

as it was better known. Every Friday, we learned to march, drill a
squad, read a map using a compass, strip down a rifle, put it back
together piece by piece and occasionally fire it. We wore an army
uniform and had to keep it spotless, polishing our boots, cleaning
our gaiters, shining the brass on our belts and ironing our uniforms,
if necessary, every Thursday in preparation for a parade-ground inspection the next day. That was all very well but nobody was going
to iron the kinks out of some of us, especially me. The slightest
mark, irregularity on our uniforms or act of indiscipline would land
us in 'defaulters' when we had to wear our stiff battle dress for a
week, reporting morning and night to the master in charge of corps,
Mr Garside.

A fit-looking man in his fifties, Mr Garside was a former soldier
who taught physical education and ran the school tuck shop, where
he resembled a genial sweetshop owner behind the counter. 'A Mars
Bar and a Bounty, that'll be twelve pence to you, sir.' Unfortunately,
the moment he stepped onto the parade ground in his army uniform, he mutated into a tyrant – a transformation so comprehen-
sive in every facet that he became completely unrecognisable to us.
It didn't help that because several of us were dyslexic and automatically turned left instead of right or vice versa – the commands 'eyes
right' or 'squad left wheel' induced the same confusion and chaos
– we kept him in a permanent state of meltdown. One boy, called
Stubbings, swung both arms forward at the same time on parade
and was incapable of swinging them alternately or keeping them in
sync with his feet. Marching directly behind him was a nightmare as
it was impossible not to follow his lead – as impossible as trying to
march in a straight line and maintain a straight face while Mr Garside roared himself hoarse. Smiling on parade was a grave offence
and unpardonable under any circumstances, let alone laughter.

He was joined on the parade ground by two professional soldiers from Brock Barracks in Reading. They made an unlikely double act. Sergeant Gidman was a hard-as-nails Scot with scarcely any teeth and fingers like blunt instruments, whose tight-fitting beret gave the impression it had been welded onto his head. His Glaswegian accent was so thick, we needed subtitles to understand him. His commands sounded like the death throes of an aeroplane nosediving to earth and suddenly righting itself at the last second. Captain Bateson was a tall, languid man, with ash-blond hair and a wispy moustache the colour of vanilla ice cream, who was so spectacularly disinterested in us he left Sergeant Gidman to do all his shouting and screaming for him. The first time I encountered Sergeant Gidman, I saluted him with my left hand; it was the most natural thing in the world for me but something that sent him into such a paroxysm of anger I feared he'd combust. 'You're not in the bloody Girl Guides now,' he raged. Once, after dismantling a rifle and spending an hour striving to reassemble it – it looked like some form of medieval hoe by the time I'd finished with it – he snatched it from me, examined it for several seconds and thrust it back into my hands. 'I don't know what that is, but it doesn't belong in the army.' Nor, more obviously, did I.

The only time I can honestly say I enjoyed myself during five years in the corps was when I drilled a squad of professional soldiers at Brock Barracks. Sergeant Gidman had explained to us that the squaddies were so conditioned to obeying orders, they'd march off the end of a cliff if commanded to. I was intrigued by this and couldn't wait to test the theory. I noticed the parade ground was bounded by a brick wall on one side, and when my turn came to drill the squad, I ordered them to march towards it. I continued to shout quick march at the top of my voice and, sure enough, they clattered into it – the men in the front rank pressing their noses against it, pounding their boots, while those at the rear leaned against them, swinging their arms. In their helplessness, they reminded me of a beetle stranded on its back, cycling its legs in the air. I left them like that for a few seconds before ordering them to about-turn and march back to the middle of the parade ground. When I'd finished, Sergeant Gidman strode up to me. 'Congratulations,' he said. 'You've just wiped out an entire platoon of British soldiers.'

• • •

I became a house prefect during my last term, though not a very good one. The thinking behind it was that by handing me some responsibility, I would be more likely to stay out of trouble. We had nothing in common with the prefects who had terrorised us when we were juniors, and I would have no more worn a knuckleduster than I would have agreed to get my hair cut. But, because I nursed a healthy disregard for authority and never felt remotely at ease as a prefect, my approach to imposing discipline tended to be more Monty Pythonesque than anything. Not surprisingly, my methods soon came unstuck.

One evening, while taking the juniors for prep, I found myself becoming increasingly exasperated by the non-stop antics of a boy named Orme – a troublemaker in my own image. Before I could stop myself, I told him that if he continued to misbehave, he would have to stand on a chair with the wastepaper bin on his head until he learned to be quiet. I was a fine one to talk, of course, and as if sensing this, Orme continued to prove a disruptive influence, leaving me with no choice but to act decisively or lose face. He'd barely climbed onto the chair and placed the bin over his head when the door opened and Mr Buxton walked in, accompanied by a man and a woman on a school tour. The sight of Orme stopped them dead in their tracks.

Rather than draw attention to Orme, who continued to stand on the chair behatted by the bin like a human lamp shade, Mr Buxton proceeded to studiously ignore him, though it was clear he couldn't wait to march the prospective parents out of the room fast enough. 'These boys are just finishing their prep, as you can see,' he explained, breaking the uncomfortable silence. 'So we won't disturb them a moment longer.' The couple had not taken their eyes off Orme since entering the room and remained staring at him in a mixture of puzzlement and disbelief before Mr Buxton steered them gently towards the door. I knew from the glare he gave me over his shoulder on the way out that the matter would not end there. Later, he knocked on the door of my single room. The glare had not left his face. 'I thought you'd like to know that the couple I was showing around earlier have decided against sending their son to Shiplake College,' he announced. 'They had concerns about our disciplinary methods. And, quite frankly, I can't say I blame them.'

You would have thought that lightning wouldn't strike twice, but a fortnight later, in the run-up to the end of term, Mr Buxton fielded another complaint about me from a parent. On this occasion, I had impulsively leaned out of a window and tipped a bottle of milk over a boy from two storeys above him. The boy, Lund, was ostentatiously directing the car parking during a school open day – his mannerisms and exaggerated flourishes making him appear like some Elizabethan courtier. If he had been wearing a cloak, he'd have thrown it over the puddles for the occupants to traverse. I couldn't bear it. I waited until he was beneath the window motioning a car forward and hurriedly drenched him from head to foot. Stupidly, I spent too long leaning out of the window admiring my handiwork before darting my head back in. I didn't care if Lund saw me, but the driver of the car, whose windscreen was splattered in the process, was quick to ask him for my name.

All Mr Buxton wanted to know was what had possessed me to do it: 'But why?' I was standing in his office, with its sporting cups and trophies, the portrait of him on the wall behind his desk mirroring the identical expression on the face in front of me. 'But why?' He must have asked the same question at least four times, drawing out the space between the two words on each occasion. However, I couldn't give him an answer – not one he'd understand anyway. 'There's only two more weeks to the end of term. Two more weeks before you leave us for good.' He tried not to sound too relieved at the prospect. 'Please see if you can stay out of trouble.' And then he caught me off guard. 'Have you given any more thought at all to what you want to do with your life?'

The truth was, I hadn't. I had no idea, no plans for leaving, no plans for the immediate future – other than the certainty that I knew I wasn't going to become a vet. Unlike my friends and contemporaries, some of whom were hoping to go to university, a few to art or technical colleges (exam results allowing) and could talk of little else, I had no career path to follow, no ambition to talk of, no direction and no job lined up. Despite my ongoing skirmishes with spelling and punctuation, I knew I wanted to write but had no faith or confidence in my ability to do so. Leaving school was my only plan.

Nevertheless, I was determined to mark the occasion in style and was far from being alone in that regard. Several of us had put our heads together and come up with an idea for a valedictory prank that involved tampering with the plaque above the entrance to the school library – or one letter of it to be precise. The library was named after Peter Carter-Ruck, the founder-governor and former chairman of Shiplake College, and our idea, naturally enough, was to change the R in Ruck to an F.

It later turned out, however, that Peter Carter-Ruck had more claims to fame than just his affiliation with Shiplake College. An eminent lawyer – his name was considered synonymous with libel law in Britain – he had also been variously described as a 'dedicated liar', a 'chancer out for the maximum fee', a 'scourge of *Private Eye*' and the bane of Fleet Street editors, who, in the words of *The Guardian*, 'did for freedom of speech what the Boston Strangler did for door-to-door salesmen'. Fair game, then – except that we knew none of that or had any clue who he was. I vaguely thought he might be some distinguished old boy, but what did I know? To us, Carter-Ruck was simply a name that we could have some fun with.

There were about twelve of us present on the last night of term – I had never seen the library so full – chipping away quietly by torchlight with a hammer and chisel, which was passed around among us. Each of us took a turn so that we could all say we did our bit and we left our mark, that it was a collective effort. I was not the first choice perhaps to wield the hammer and chisel, having spent much of my early life writing backwards, but I happily played my part. Among the boys alongside me that night, chipping away at the R in Ruck, was my great friend and fellow poet, Charlie Viney. Little did we know that, in effect, we were also carving out a friendship in stone, one that would endure another fifty years – which was more than could be said for my faltering prose. When we were satisfied that the R sufficiently resembled an F, we cleaned up, left no trace and stole back into the night to continue our celebrations... well away from the Carter-Fuck Library.

We later found out that the unfortunate name change went unde-tected for another five months, until the last week of the following term. I never learned the exact details or what happened after it was discovered, though it must have caused a furore. The culprits were long gone, of course. What I do know was that when I returned to Shiplake College a year later to play cricket for the old boys against the first XI – the only time I ever went back – Mr Buxton saw me coming down the corridor, hitched up his gown like a jilted bride and ran in the opposite direction. I'm sure he would have agreed with me that the F-word I had left in my wake that night perfectly summed up my journey through the education system.

PART II

PART II

CHAPTER THIRTEEN

I'M GLAD TO SAY YOU'VE PASSED THE AUDITION

I was offered my first professional job within three months of leaving school. No one was more surprised than me. For the next two weeks before I started it, I waited for a call or letter explaining that there had been a mistake, that I had been given the position in error. I imagined the grovelling apology, the secret sigh of relief I would emit at the news. This had become my default response whenever anything positive was about to happen to me, whenever a golden opportunity presented itself – thinking that I didn't deserve it or I'd fall woefully short of the mark. But no such communication came, and one grey Monday morning in October 1972, I arrived outside the offices of Spotlight Casting Directory in London's Leicester Square to begin the first day of my working life. On time, for once, but nervous.

I was Spotlight's new junior assistant editor – a title I was struggling to come to terms with. Typically, I ignored the qualifiers, junior and assistant, and focused almost entirely on the word editor. It excited and scared me at the same time, in the same breath. It excited me because it was a name to conjure with, and I thought it might sound impressive when I told people what my job was going to be; after all, I was only eighteen and had just left school. Mainly, though, it scared me. It came freighted with the weight of expectation and doubt – doubt in my ability, in me, doubt because I now knew I'd flunked my English A-level exam and I was therefore unworthy of the title. Although my hand was resting on the handle of the office door, ready to push it open, I could hardly bring myself to complete the simple act. A part of me wanted to turn around and hurry back down the street to the Tube station, to cut and run. And I might have done it too, had there not been so much riding on it, so much to be grateful for.

Spotlight was an A to Z of actors, often referred to as the 'Bible' for the casting profession and the entertainment industry as a whole. It was essential for any aspiring actor, or an established one for that matter, to have his or her photo in the directory, along with a few pertinent facts such as height (often a matter of conjecture), credits and agent's name, among other details. Virtually no major film, stage production, television or radio programme, advertisement or commercial project at that time was cast without Spotlight being consulted or accessed at some point in the process. In 1972, Spotlight was published annually, in two separate alphabetised volumes, as thick as a London telephone directory but glossier. I had even briefly expressed an interest in casting during my interview, which was not as much of a lie as it sounded. I was interested in it, but not to the extent that I made out.

The job had come about through a good friend of my mother's, Olive Dodds, a casting director for films and television and a regular visitor to our house while I was growing up. She had called in to see us at a time when many of my school friends were striking out in the world and I was still chewing over my exam results, at a loose end and unsure what to do with my life. I had learned, even before I left school in fact, that I'd failed my English A-level. The bleak news was delivered by Mr Priestley, in a voice that came whistling bluntly off the Yorkshire Moors. 'I see you neglected to complete the final question in the paper. That's an automatic failure, lad. I suggest you return to the school to re-sit it at the end of the winter term.' I had hoped to scrape home in history, only to discover that the one subject that had fascinated me all my young life had turned its back on me too – or, more probably, me on it. Olive Dodds's visit could not have been timelier.

She always gave the impression she had wandered off a film set: the cigarette holder she used when she smoked and her selection of floppy hats made her appear delightfully quirky to my eyes. The names of famous actors that regularly fluttered off her tongue came as naturally to her as the air she breathed. What little I understood about casting, I derived solely from her. She was also the only person I knew, aside from my long-suffering family, who'd sat stoically through the entire three chapters of *Murder on the River Dart* without having to be helped away in a state of near exhaustion. When I was fourteen, she presented me with a copy of *Roget's Thesaurus*. 'It's the one book you're going to need if you want to become a writer.' I had never heard of it, had no idea how to read it, let alone pronounce it, and didn't touch it for at least another decade. Now, in testimony to the service it has provided, the use I have made of it, its pages are frayed and yellowed like old newspaper, its binding loose, its cover having long perished. An object far too cherished to discard.

It was Olive Dodds who told me that Spotlight was advertising for an editorial assistant and suggested I applied for it. She gave me a quick rundown on the company. 'It would be an excellent opportunity for you, don't you think? I'll mention your name to them, and we'll see what happens.' She was as good as her word and the interview took place a week later.

It was so short that I barely had time to get comfortable in my seat before Nicholas Relf, a man in his late thirties who distilled the essence of calm authority, asked, 'When can you start?' The question was so sudden that my mind went blank. 'How about two weeks' time?' he proposed. I agreed – I didn't know what else to say – and gulped. Surely interviews weren't supposed to be this easy. I was to start on a salary of £18 a week – and as the average weekly wage for a man over twenty-one in 1972 was £36, and £20 for a woman, it was not as paltry as it sounded. Indeed, in today's money, £18 amounts to £206 a week or just over £10,000 a year – not to be sneezed at. 'That just leaves me to say congratulations then.' He rose from the chair and extended his hand. 'I'm glad to say you've passed the audition.'

On my first morning at work, I had no idea what to expect and hesitated outside on the pavement for a minute or more, my hand poised on the door handle as if waiting for my cue. Spotlight was housed in a tall, narrow building that looked as if it should have been wider somehow. It was little more than a stone's throw from Leicester Square Underground Station and bookended – dwarfed almost – by two bigger structures, one of which accommodated a record shop. Finally, I stepped inside. The lobby was cramped with a stone staircase to my right and an ancient iron contraption, which passed for a lift, in front of me. It had a latticed metal door that you had to open and close yourself. I fumbled it shut, pushed the button to the third floor and held my breath. It was like stepping aboard some kind of Victorian spaceship. Seconds later, it lifted upwards, rattling noisily before depositing me with a sudden lurch-ing jolt outside Spotlight's general office. What I hadn't expected on my first day at work, however, was to walk through the door and find myself confronted by a line of some twenty faces gazing in my direction. My first thought was that I must have been late. 'This is John, everyone,' Nicholas Relf announced. And before I knew it, I was shaking hands with each member of staff, their faces blurring before my eyes like the pages of a flip book, their names flying so fast over my head that I had no hope of catching them.

Eventually I was shown to my desk, empty apart from a green telephone, at the far end of the office next to a grimy window – all the windows, I noticed, were grimy. Mine was one of four or five desks, all positioned so that their occupants could see anyone who entered. A wooden counter ran almost the full length of the room, where the actors came in to renew their subscriptions, enrol in the directory or simply have a chat with the guarantee of a will-ing audience. The view from the windows was of the deadlocked traffic below and the Talk of the Town, a nightclub and live music venue once described as B-list Vegas, which sprawled the length of the pavement in faded red brick on the opposite side of the road. I always knew when it was time to go home because its spangly necklace of neon lights snapped on at the appropriate time every evening and shimmered in my window.

Home was now a bedsit in Belsize Park, which I shared with a school friend, Tom Hallam, who was working as a waiter at the Connaught in Mayfair and training to become a hotel manager. One of the few highlights of my time in the bedsit was the moun-tains of leftover food he smuggled back from his shift, and the midnight feasts we indulged in, usually quaffed down with a couple of bottles of cheap red wine. It did nothing to help my haphazard efforts at getting ready for work in the morning or arriving on time, unfortunately.

I was introduced to the intricacies of the job by a woman called Joan Gill, who was considered the 'mother' of the front office. Nothing happened at Spotlight without her knowing about it. Her hair resembled yellow candyfloss and her face was always heavily made up, as if she was about to take to the stage herself. She had worked at the casting directory as 'girl and woman', as she put it, and proudly explained that it had been in business since 1927. 'Not that I go back quite that far,' she trilled. The first piece of advice she gave me – actually, it was the only piece – was that I must never, under any circumstances, raise my voice when talking to an actor. 'You must always speak quietly. Most actors are shy, nervous people away from the camera or an audience and can't bear to be spoken to loudly. Softly, softly every time, please. Otherwise, they might run away. Don't laugh – I've seen a few do that before when spoken to in the wrong manner. Always remember, they are more frightened of you than you are of them.' And she smiled, as though I had just admitted to a phobia of spiders.

She also advised me that I would see plenty of famous faces while working in the office. 'Don't be too startled or put off by that, though overall I tend to look after the more famous ones. They know me, you see, and it's so much easier and simpler all round if I deal with them.' And that, in a nutshell, was my introduction to Spotlight. The rest, she informed me, I would have to pick up for myself.

The first famous face I recognised was the comedian Benny Hill, of all people. He was smartly dressed, in sharp contrast to the madcap array of characters he portrayed on his eponymous TV show, and carried a small zip-up briefcase under his arm. Of course,

Joan was out of her seat in a trice, notebook and pen in hand to take down all the necessary details. 'How lovely to see you again, Mr Hill.' He opened his briefcase, produced several headshots of aspiring young actresses, which he arranged along the countertop as if he was spreading a deck of cards, and confirmed he would pay for them all to be included in the latest edition of the directory. 'Oh, they are lucky to have you, Mr Hill,' she cooed, casting a practised eye over the photographs. Joan's squeals of delight and girlish giggles whenever a famous actor cracked a joke or made some witty aside became part of the soundtrack of the office, often drowning out the rumble of the traffic below.

It took barely a week before I realised that I didn't fit in and normal service was resumed – well, for me at any rate. I had nothing in common with the women in the front office, all of whom were several years older than me. After a lifetime at all-boys' schools, I found their discussions about their marriages, their health or the intimate details of their bodies, carried out as though I wasn't sitting next to them, faintly shocking. Any grand illusions I had of being a casting director, or a junior assistant editor for that matter, were swiftly extinguished. For a start, Spotlight already had a junior assistant editor – Andrew, the only other male in the office, who was in his early twenties and the son of the editor, Leonard Ambler. I knew that was his title because there was a sign on his desk that said so. At first, I thought my role might be the junior assistant editor to the junior assistant editor, if such a thing existed, but quickly gave up on that idea. The reality of the situation was that I was essentially the office boy, and my days soon curdled with boredom.

One of my jobs was to make the tea, every afternoon at quarter to four on the dot – though not with the teabag still in it, as I managed on my first day. Joan's deafening shriek when she took a sip and discovered the bag floating in her cuppa, as she always called it, brought the office to an abrupt standstill. I always drank my tea that way and couldn't understand what the problem was. I also looked after the petty cash, which, unsurprisingly, was not my strongest suit, if indeed I had any strong suits. I also regularly ran errands for the casting directors or managers and escorted the actors to the audition rooms when casting sessions were in progress. One girl begged me to stay with her and sat biting her nails and jiggling her legs furiously until her name was called – whereupon she walked into the audition without a backward glance, looking as bold as brass, as if the last few minutes had never happened.

I was responsible for the mail too, distributing the incoming letters to the various recipients in the office while taking the outgoing mail to the post office at the end of each day. Sometimes, I got the incoming mail muddled up with the outgoing mail and ended up merging the lot into one pile in the outgoing box, thereby sending the incoming post on yet another circuit of London. Inevitably the ingoing letters washed up at my door again, when it occurred to me it might be fun to set the whole process in motion once more and eliminate the tiresome task of having to deal with them for at least another couple of days. It was like trying to see how many rows of plates I could keep spinning; when the plates threatened to slow down, I gave them another turn and off they went again, winging their way around the circuit for the umpteenth time. Consequently, some important letters never got read. For all I know several of them are on permanent repeat, still trapped somewhere inside the system, endlessly doing the rounds. I was the worst office boy in London.

When I wasn't causing chaos with the office post, I was changing light bulbs – or one person's light bulbs in particular. That person was the director of Spotlight, Douglas Wheatley, a former actor who had been at the company longer even than Joan. He rang my phone once a month without fail, sometimes more, always with the same request: 'The light bulb above my desk has gone again. I wonder if you wouldn't mind coming downstairs to change it for me.' A somewhat mysterious figure, who rarely seemed to leave his spacious office on the floor below, I imagined him to be in his late sixties or early seventies. He had a full head of coiffured white hair and wore immaculately tailored pin-stripe suits, with a purple tie and matching pocket handkerchief. Entering his office was like stepping back in time – the curtains were half-drawn and the walls lined with framed posters, portraits and photographs of actors and films from another era, almost as if he came to work just to dream. To change his lightbulb, I had to climb onto his desk and reach up into the light fitting above while he remained seated beneath me. Usually, he would attempt to make conversation. 'How are they treating you upstairs? Well, I hope.' Or 'Are you still enjoying your work?' I always answered in the affirmative. 'That's good to hear. We like to run a happy ship at Spotlight.' After completing the task, I would jump off the desk and flick the switch by the door. 'Bravo,' he'd exclaim.

I must have done this on some eight or nine occasions during my first few months before Joan called me to one side. 'You do realise light bulbs don't fail quite that often, don't you?' At that point, I suddenly experienced my own light bulb moment. Joan didn't need to say any more – the knowing expression she gave me was self-explanatory, pitched somewhere between disbelief and resignation. A look that said *You're just not cut out for this, are you*? After that, the calls from Douglas Wheatley stopped and I never saw him again.

Joan was right. I felt as restrained by the four walls of the office as

I had in any classroom and just as isolated. The deadening routine of the job stoked my restlessness and I welcomed any opportunity, any excuse to leave my desk, to run an errand, take a walkabout in Soho or an excursion into Charing Cross Road, anything to chivvy along the hours. Starved of adrenaline and momentum – my rocket fuel – and unable to sit still, my days unspooled until they lost all meaning and I couldn't tell them apart. My timekeeping was abysmal too; I was regularly late for work or extended my lunchbreaks by as much as twenty minutes, sometimes longer. I was self-destructing but didn't know it. And in the middle of all of this, my old friend maths returned to haunt me.

No matter how hard I tried, I could not make the petty cash add up at the end of each week. Often, I put in my own money to top it up and prevent Barry Trove, the accountant, from making his frequent visits to my desk. On one occasion there was a significant shortfall and, as I didn't have the money to rectify it, I was summoned to his office. 'Take a seat, John.' The cash box was sitting on his desk in front of me with the lid up. 'You can be straight with me, you know. What you say in my office is just between us, no one else.' Instinctively, I didn't trust him and watched him push the cash box closer to me until it was almost resting on the edge of the desk, about to topple into my lap. 'You're not being honest with us, are you?' He kept his fingers on the box, inching it forward, watching me closely as if he was tempting me to snatch it off the edge and make a dash for the door. 'I'm right, aren't I? You're purloining the office cash.'

I didn't know what to say – mainly because I had never heard of the word purloining before and was thrown by it. I was expecting him to accuse me of pinching the office cash and had braced myself for it. I guessed purloin meant roughly the same thing, though to what extent I couldn't be sure. Perhaps it was a more polite way of saying I was a thief, of watering it down, or maybe it carried even more force. Either way, I knew I had to say something, so I replied 'No' and watched his face for any sudden change or movement. He remained staring at me. 'I will get to the bottom of this,' he said. 'And when I do, you'd better hope you've not been lying to me.'

The first place I went after leaving his office was downstairs to the modelling agency that shared the building with us. Some of the staff were the same age as me, or a year or two older, and were the only people I felt I could talk to. I usually bumped into them in the kitchen while I was spooning teabags into the bin or consulting my list as to who took sugar and who didn't. Occasionally they took pity on me and I was invited to one of their lavish teas that included scones and a selection of fancy cakes. I knocked on the office door and was immediately asked inside. 'You look like you need cheering up,' one of them said. 'Do you want to stay for tea?' After a while, I casually dropped the word purloin into the conversation, seeking its meaning, and my suspicions were confirmed. 'It means nicking something, love,' I was informed.

Halfway through tea, there was another knock on the door and one of the girls jumped up to answer it. I recognised Barry Trove's voice.

'You haven't seen John anywhere, have you? You know, the young boy who works for us?'

'Isn't he upstairs with you?'

'No, he's not at his desk. I just wondered if...' And his voice trailed away.

'Sorry, can't help you there... but I'll keep an eye out for him and let him know you're looking for him.' She returned to the table giggling and I quickly got up to go. 'Finish your tea first,' she instructed.

I left it for an interval of five minutes before returning to the office and keeping my head down. When I next looked up, Barry Trove was standing by my desk with the cash box in hand. Speaking quickly, he told me that one of my colleagues had bought some office supplies with the petty cash the other day but neglected to log it, which, as he put it, in a voice that betrayed no hint of remorse, 'explained the shortfall'. I waited for him to apologise, but there was nothing. 'So we won't say any more about it in that case.' And he handed me back the box.

For a day or two afterwards, I retreated further into myself, stung by the accusation, but then, out of nowhere, something equally unexpected took place: I was offered a role in a movie. The lead role, to be exact. What was left of my adrenaline suddenly reignited, cueing a feeling of shock and excitement and, if only for a moment, the rarest glimmer of hope.

I had noticed the man seated at the far end of the office for the past two days, intently sifting through copies of Spotlight. Intermittently, he would glance in my direction, more as if he were lost in thought than anything, before continuing his perusal of the directory. I paid him little or no attention until he walked over to the opposite end of the counter, next to my desk, and addressed me.

'Excuse me.' He had an American accent, and I instantly looked up from what I was doing, which was probably nothing, as usual. 'Are you an actor by any chance?' I explained I worked at Spotlight. He appeared not to understand at first. 'It's just that I've gone through the whole of this directory and can't find what I'm looking for. But then every time I look over at you, I discover it's been staring me in the face all along.'

'What has?' I asked.

'You have,' he said. 'You're perfect for the lead in the film I'm

268

about to make. You couldn't be more perfect, in fact. Please tell me you're an actor.'

For a split-second, I sensed an escape hatch start to open. Nonetheless, I stuck resolutely to the script and repeated that I worked here.

'Is that why I can't find you in this directory?'

'Yes.'

'And you've got no acting experience at all?' I shook my head. 'So what exactly is it you do here?' He made it sound as though whatever it was, it couldn't compare with the role he had just offered me.

I lowered my voice. 'I'm the junior assistant editor.' Somehow it didn't sound right.

'That's a real shame because let me tell you, you're so right for this movie.' By now everyone in the office had stopped what they were doing to listen to our conversation. Joan had even left her seat and was standing by the counter, pretending to look for something. 'Have you ever thought about being an actor?' He didn't let me answer. 'Because you should. You should consider it, I'm serious. This job isn't for you, I can see that. Listen, I'll tell you what I'll do, I'll give you my name and the number of my hotel.' He scribbled it on a piece of paper that Joan just happened to have to hand. 'And if you change your mind or you have any questions you want to ask, you can get me on this number. But you'll need to be quick – I fly back to the States the day after tomorrow.'

If the others in the office had any time for me at all, it dried up in an instant after that. Their expressions turned sourer by the second. 'I've been here for four years and no one's ever offered me a part,' one of them said, as if it was the only reason she had taken the job. 'He walks in here and hey presto, someone wants to put him in a film. Typical.' The offer of the part appeared to be the final insult for them. 'What's this film about anyway?' I told her I didn't know;

I hadn't thought to ask. 'That's the first question I'd have asked,' she continued, and they all nodded in agreement. 'Are you going to take the part then?'

Naturally, the answer was no. I never made that call. In the end, my old fear of not being good enough – a fear of failing that I didn't yet consciously recognise – resurfaced and reeled me back into my box. The box that kept me safe. It seemed that, no matter what was at stake, I could never rise above the boy who always finished fourteenth out of fourteen.

However, I soon wished I had been bold enough to make the call because a week later, Nicholas Relf asked me into his office for what he described as a quick chat. It turned out to be every bit as quick as my interview with him six months earlier. I toyed with the idea that he might want to talk to me about becoming a casting director or suggest I'd be better employed as an actor or say there was a part he wanted me to audition for. But he wrong-footed me from the moment I sat down.

'There's a question I want to ask you, John. Can you honestly say you're happy here?'

The tone of his voice was gentle and persuasive, and I was surprised how easily he drew the words out of me. 'Well, no, I suppose not,' I found myself saying.

'I don't think there's any suppose about it,' he said, suppressing the faintest of smiles. 'It's fairly obvious to everybody here that you're not happy in your work. People do remark on it. That's important to us because if you're not happy, then you're clearly not performing to the best of your ability and that means we're not happy either.'

I could see the direction in which the conversation was heading. 'What about casting?' I asked hurriedly.

'What about it?'

'If there was an opening there, then maybe I could...'

'I'm sorry to say that's not an option for you,' he replied before I could finish my sentence. 'No, I think we've given you every chance we could – I don't think we could have been any fairer with you under the circumstances.' His tone remained friendly but business-like. 'I think it best for all concerned, therefore, that we accept it hasn't worked out, for you or for us, and we part ways and move on. That way you get to discover what it is you want to do with your life, and we find someone who is, well... better suited to the job. I don't think you can say fairer than that.'

I nodded and waited for Nicholas Relf to tell me that I'd been sacked or fired, but he never did; he never used those words. It was as if we were discussing a mutual friend who had gone a little off the rails and we were merely exchanging our sympathies.

He stood up and extended his hand. 'I'm sorry that this hasn't worked out how we all hoped.' I shook it and shuffled awkwardly to the door, but he got there before me and held it open. 'Good luck, John,' he said. 'I hope you find what you're looking for.' It was an exceptionally polite sacking.

• • •

It was while I was working at Spotlight that I attended a Hilder-sham House school reunion in London and received another kind of shock altogether. I have no idea what induced me to go; it was not like me to want to remind myself of the most frightening time in my life or to return to the dark parts of my past. I kept telling myself it was better to leave it where it was. In the end, I was glad I went, because it provided a peculiar form of closure that I must have been unwittingly seeking.

The revelation of the evening turned out to be Mr Snowden himself. I had expected to see the same man who'd lived inside my head for the past eleven years – not the one who appeared to have shrunk before my eyes, startlingly diminutive, standing in the centre of the room. Except, of course, he hadn't shrunk; I had grown taller (no more than medium height) and he had stayed the same. I certainly hadn't expected to find myself looking down on him, the shadow of a man who had once towered over me but would never do so again. The same monster who had controlled my fear like a needle on a dial, who had leaned over me in class marking my work while I sat at my desk frozen in terror, waiting for the trigger release of his fist. There was the same sliver of hair over one eye, now pure white, and the same bristling moustache where his spittle had formed when he lost control. His hair was shorn, newly cut that day I assumed, as though it were the start of a new term. The more I looked at him, the more diminished he appeared, like time was playing some cruel joke on me.

I had spotted him the minute I walked into the room. It wasn't difficult; the room was half full and my eyes were automatically drawn to him, as if by instinct. Were the others subjected to this same cruel joke, I wondered, or was it just me? I could tell he recognised me instantly and a few minutes later, he marched over. The first thing he wanted to ask me was whether I was still playing cricket and if not, why not. It was as though the six years I had endured at Hildersham House had never existed. It occurred to me in that moment how easy it would be to knock him down, to follow him to the Tube or the taxi rank, to exact my retribution, to turn the tables on him – but quickly stamped on the thought, like a cinder spat out of a roaring fire.

I fidgeted restlessly from foot to foot, hoping my face didn't betray the thoughts that were racing through my head, until Mr Snowden recognised someone else and moved off. There seemed to be more parents than former pupils, which wasn't surprising, and no more than a couple of teachers whose names I remembered. I had long given up hope of seeing Miss Shepherd again. Maybe the rest had been too ashamed to attend. It was a small gathering, the conversation desultory, people already drifting towards the exit. I looked for my old friend James Teague but there was no sign of him, nor any of my contemporaries. They had remained several steps ahead of me, as ever, and sensibly stayed away. There was one exception, though – the asthmatic Andrew Stimpson, my fellow sufferer during French and Latin lessons. We soon caught each other's eye, just as we had in class. How curious that the two boys Mr Snowden had mercilessly picked on – the two boys who had forged a small alliance against him – should have shown up but the others hadn't. Victims to the end, perhaps.

I immediately recognised the young boy in him: he had the same wheezing laugh for one thing, the ever-present inhaler, the frail body and haunted eyes that made him look like he still needed rescuing. He recalled how much we dreaded French and the times I had tried to protect him by saying something stupid, thereby diverting Mr Snowden's attention. 'I haven't forgotten,' he said. 'Some of the things you used to say were so funny. But none of us protected you, did we?' I mumbled that I didn't need protecting, though we both knew that wasn't true. I didn't mention the occasions I almost feared for my life and his, when the line between normality and madness was so blurred it had all but vanished.

Before I slipped away, I introduced myself to Mrs Blackman, who steadfastly purported not to recognise me. She put on her glasses, still dangling on a cord around her neck, to study me in more detail.

'No, I can't say I remember you or the name,' she said. 'What was it again?' I couldn't believe that the seven-year-old she regularly admonished for being unable to tie his laces or knot his tie – 'We've never had a boy like you at Hildersham House before' – had simply evaporated from her memory. I repeated my name and explained that I'd left in the summer of 1967. This time she made an involuntary movement with her hand and placed it over her throat, keeping it there for several seconds. 'No, I'm sorry, it doesn't ring any bells, but jolly good of you to turn up all the same.' Puzzlingly, I could have sworn that she knew exactly who I was. I took one last look at Mr Snowden before leaving, as if to imprint him on my retina for ever; he was still holding centre stage while the numbers dwindled around him. All the way back to the Tube, I could hear time laughing at me over my shoulder.

• • •

After my dismissal from Spotlight, I returned home to Sussex to ponder my next move; the lease on the bedsit in Belsize Park was about to expire anyway. No one seemed unduly surprised when I turned up with my battered suitcase and told them the news – typically, Dow's 'Oh, Donty' was suffused more with humour than disappointment. My options appeared to be few, and it didn't help that I had no clue what I wanted to do with my life other than the immediate concern of passing my driving test. Once more, I was at a loose end.

For the most part I had managed to keep my dyslexic traits under control in the office – apart from the maths, obviously – but my attempts to learn to drive hastened its return with an untimely rush and I was soon back under its sway. I frequently mistook the brake for the clutch whenever I tried to change gear – making the car emit an alarming scream like the death throes of a pterodactyl – and the accelerator for the brake when slowing down or stopping, almost as frequently as I confused my left with my right. My only hope of distinguishing one from the other was to visualise writing with my left hand, carving the image as deeply as I could into my mind, or by taking my left hand off the steering wheel and squeezing it into a fist for a few seconds, though not even that was foolproof. Like me, my driving was reliably unreliable.

My instructor was an elderly man called Mr Cousens, who already looked well past the point of retirement – an impression he did nothing to deter by climbing into the passenger seat and placing a rug over his knees. Often, I had to sneak a quick glance at him while driving because of the long silences he was prone to falling into with a sudden lack of movement or urgency. Sometimes two or three minutes would pass before he gave an instruction, which, given the unpredictability of my driving, perturbed me. I had even started to suspect he might be nodding off during the lessons or, more worryingly, failing to maintain consciousness. I was concerned there might actually be something wrong with him. It was during my third or fourth lesson that my worst fears were realised. We were driving through the Broadway in Haywards Heath – a busy road that featured two zebra crossings and two roundabouts – when, out of the corner of my eye, I saw his body roll to one side, as if in slow motion, and heard his forehead strike the passenger window with a soft thunk.

My first instinct was to panic. 'Mr Cousens... are you all right?' I was trying to keep one eye on him and the other on the road. 'Mr Cousens,' I repeated. 'Wake up.'

I could see the signs for Cuckfield up ahead, but first I had to negotiate a zebra crossing bustling with pedestrians and, a little further on, another roundabout. Of course, I could have just stopped the car – that would have been the sensible thing to do – but my mind was awash and I kept driving, praying Mr Cousens would wake up. The zebra crossing raced towards me, on a slight slope. I thought about using the brake, but the foot pedals seemed to move and merge before my eyes, repeatedly changing positions, disorientating me – like a street hawker's three paper cups, one of which contained a hidden coin. But which one? I worried if I stamped on the brakes, I'd probably hit the accelerator or the clutch instead, so I drove around the pedestrians as if they were bollards and swept on. Oblivious to the danger, Mr Cousens remained asleep, his mouth open, his face pressed against the window, his breath fogging the glass. At one point, after a sudden, sharp right turn, his head lolled and slumped against my shoulder and, using one hand, I rolled him gently back into his seat.

How I managed to white-knuckle the car home – it was a journey of almost six miles of unprecedented terror – I don't know, but I did it, more by luck than judgement. It was nothing short of miraculous, really. When I pulled into the drive, thankfully hitting the brake and coming to a jolting halt in front of our gate, I could have shouted for joy. And I might have done, had it not been for the sight of Mr Cousens, whose face had turned a horribly pale, waxy colour.

I shouted for my mother instead, who took one look at him and immediately called for an ambulance. 'How did it happen?' I explained how he'd suddenly fallen fast asleep in the middle of Haywards Heath and I couldn't wake him. 'I think it might be a bit more serious than that,' she said. Indeed, it transpired that Mr Cousens had suffered a minor stroke and for a while, I worried that my driving had played some part in it. But my mother, who stayed in touch with Mr Cousens's wife after the incident, assured me she'd been pleading with him to retire for more than a year, fearful that something like this might happen. 'So it could have happened to anyone – not just you.' Except that it was me. Fortunately, Mr Cousens made a full recovery, though his days as a driving instructor were over.

His replacement, Mr Hislop, could not have been more different had he tried. A former sergeant in the army, tall and powerfully built, he had to virtually fold himself in half to climb into his orange Beetle as if it were a contortionist's box; once seated, his head stopped just short of scraping the roof. When my concentration wavered or his patience stretched thin, he ordered me out of the car and made me walk around it several times to let the air into my head, as he phrased it. Unfortunately, it didn't have the desired effect. I failed three driving tests in Brighton in rapid succession – spectacularly so on the second occasion, when I traversed a roundabout in the wrong direction. I had navigated countless roundabouts before without making that mistake, which made it even more perplexing. I weaved in and out of the onrushing vehicles in a state of panicked confusion, with a hundred car horns blasting my ears, while the examiner slammed his clipboard against the glovebox, so hard he nearly snapped it in half. 'For God's sake!' he shouted each time I narrowly avoided a collision.

Somehow, I eventually passed my driving test at the fourth time of asking. There was a waiting list of six months in Brighton – perhaps there was a sudden shortage of examiners – so I took it at Herne Bay in Kent instead. My mother drove us there, and I jumped behind the wheel for a brief practice run along the seafront before the test. What followed was one of those rare days when the planets aligned and, for once, everything slotted effortlessly into place. Well, almost.

I had parked the car near the driving test centre, after completing the first part of the examination, and was preparing to answer questions on the highway code when my mother, returning from a stroll on the seafront, happened to walk by. Of course, she spotted me straight away, leaned in and gave me one of her full-beam smiles and an enthusiastic wave of the hand. She didn't need any encouragement from me, and I smartly looked away as if to say *not now*. But she was back within a couple of minutes to repeat the same undipped smile, the same little dance of the fingers. I watched the examiner's eyes slide in her direction and my heart sank. 'Do you know that woman?' I reluctantly muttered that she was my mother and wondered whether I should apologise. He didn't comment but continued to scribble on a piece of paper attached to his clipboard. Finally, he unfastened the paper and handed it to me. 'This is your certificate,' he said. 'You've passed your driving test – well done.' I was so taken aback, I almost asked him to repeat it. At the same time, I could see my mother in the sideview mirror, returning for a third sortie past the car. I climbed out to wave the certificate at her and relay the good news, but there was no need. The expression on her face told me that she already knew.

Inexplicably, given my driving trials, I took a job at a second-hand car dealership in Cuckfield not long after passing my test. It was asking for trouble and, in the process, I continued the theme of false starts in the job market in a succession of roles for which I was entirely unsuited yet fatally drawn to. I lasted five days at the car dealership and all things considered, that was generous.

My requirements were to start the cars every morning and check they were in working order, wash them and keep them spotless inside and out, pick up and deliver cars to the yard whenever necessary, answer the phone and look after customers. 'There'll be a bit of mechanics thrown in from time to time – nothing too complicated,' the manager explained during the interview. 'I'm assuming you're well up with that kind of stuff.' I nodded and tried to look as confident as I could, while my heart dropped through the floor. Mechanics and maths, unfortunately, went hand in hand.

One of the cars I had to start every morning was a Citroën DS – known in the yard as the General after the former president of France, General de Gaulle. The first time I switched on its ignition, something peculiar happened. Without any warning, the rear of the vehicle rose off the ground and expanded like an accordion. For a moment I thought it was going to lift off, taking me with it, or tip me through the windscreen, or eject me through the roof, or just leave me suspended in mid-air. I must have sat there for at least a couple of minutes wondering what to do next, until I had the bright idea to turn off the engine. It was only then, to my relief, that the vehicle started to contract and return to earth, sinking slowly back into its resting position with what sounded like a contented sigh. I never went near it again after that and never discovered why, for no apparent reason, it rose off the ground. 'Don't forget to fire up the General,' the manager insisted every morning, as if it was the only car in the yard that mattered. I told him I'd already seen to it. Heralded in its day as a vehicle ahead of its time, futuristic and quirky, a masterpiece of French ingenuity that looked like it had 'fallen from the sky', I never understood its allure. To me, it looked like a fart on wheels and behaved like one too.

The yard was a strange, soulless place that lacked one core ingredient – clients. There were two salesmen, one of whom wore a cream suit and tinted glasses and looked like a hitman moonlighting as a second-hand car dealer. He spent most of his time in the field behind the main office, shooting at tin cans on a fence using an arsenal of handguns he stowed in the boot of his car. When he wasn't firing them, he was cleaning them or squinting down their barrels, usually with his feet up on the desk. Sometimes, I felt as if I was the only one who did any work. Yet I received my marching orders after somehow managing to scratch the door of a car I was polishing. I don't recall how it happened, except that it left a long gash like a claw mark on the paintwork. The manager noticed it at once. 'Don't bother coming back on Monday morning,' was all he said. In the background, I could hear the thud, thud of a pistol and the rattle of a tin can.

The jobs came thick and fast after that. I never stayed in any of them longer than a few weeks or a couple of months at best, when I was either fired or quit of my own accord, mostly out of boredom. They included everything from working on Brighton pier at a sweet store to building swimming pools, helping out at a chicken farm, and driving a tractor for the council; on one occasion I demolished the gates to a golf club with my trailer as if they were made of matchwood. I also taught games at a local school and was employed as a door-to-door salesman for a double-glazing company called Davies and Tate. In between that, I was thrown out halfway through a job interview after applying to be a sales assistant at an art gallery in Eastbourne... for smiling too much.

There were multitudinous low points and moments when I wondered whether I would ever hold down a job, until one incident happily redressed the balance. The first door I knocked at as a double-glazing salesman was answered by a friendly middle-aged woman. I introduced myself, gave the name of the company I represented and asked her if she was interested in having any double glazing fitted. I half expected her to shut the door in my face but, to my astonishment, she burst out laughing.

'I thought Tate and Lyle manufactured sugar,' she said.

I looked at her quizzically. 'Tate and Lyle?'

'Yes, you said you were from Tate and Lyle. I wasn't aware they'd branched out into double glazing.'

I apologised and told her they hadn't, as far as I knew; I'd meant to say Davies and Tate. I added, by way of explanation, that this was my first day in the job. By now, we were both laughing.

'You know, I really could do with some double glazing in my home office if I think about it.' She continued to laugh. 'That way, I can tell everyone I bought it off a sugar salesman.'

It was the only time I ever sold any double glazing.

The one job I drew the line at was that of a commodities broker. It was offered to me in a pub, of all places, by someone I vaguely knew, who assumed, after one beer too many, that I would be good at it: 'Let me tell you, you'd make a bloody good commodities broker.' It was the equivalent of being told I would make a good vet or that I should study maths and physics as my specialist subjects.

I told him he was either drunk or mad or both. 'I'd be a bloody disaster, more like.'

But he refused to take no for an answer. 'Come up to London and spend a day in the office with us – you might surprise yourself. I'm serious.'

I didn't explain that I had already rejected the job on principle or that I could think of nothing worse than being a commodities broker. 'You'll end up having to fire me,' I said. 'Just like everyone else.'

During our conversation, the inevitable question cropped up. *What are you going to do with your life?* It was the question that had dogged my footsteps since my last term at school, the question that always tripped me up or put my head in a spin, searching for an answer I couldn't provide. But not any longer, it seemed. The words were out of my mouth almost before I was aware I'd uttered them or had time to take in what I'd said. It was as if the answer had been there all along, lurking just below the surface, patiently waiting for me to have the confidence, the wherewithal, the belief to speak it out aloud. It felt oddly fitting somehow that it should take the offer of a job as a commodities broker, in the smoky haze of a pub, to bring me to my senses – to this jumping-off point, this realisation that I finally knew what I wanted to do with my life. It instantly felt like the right answer for me. The only answer.

Now all I had to do was make it happen.

CHAPTER FOURTEEN

CALLING CLAIRE ONE...
CALLING CLAIRE ONE

The moment I walked into a newsroom and encountered the havoc, the inky smell on deadline, the clatter of typewriters still sounding in my head long after they had fallen silent, I knew I belonged. I knew I had found what I was looking for – a profession with enough movement, momentum, excitement and fear to keep me interested, to indulge my constant hunt for adrenaline and feed it. It was as if I had to experience all the false starts, to ride the carousel of disappointment, just to arrive at another significant left turn in my life and finally discover the profession that was right for me. Journalism was the only job I ever visualised myself doing – from the writing of imaginary sports reports in my head, to seeing my name in print – and it didn't disappoint. It was what I should have been doing all along, instead of allowing my lack of confidence and the persistent doubts in my ability to always get in the way.

The first newspaper I worked on was a weekly, the *Surrey Advertiser* in Guildford. The minimum requirement to become a journalist on a provincial paper in those days was five O-levels or at the very least a pass in English language or literature – two A-levels, a diploma of journalism or a degree in English naturally opened doors much faster. Failing that, you could enter the profession via an in-house training scheme and hope someone took a chance on you, which was the route I eventually followed. It helped that there were many more regional newspapers and therefore many more jobs than there are now. As usual, I had left things late – I had already turned twenty-one – but not, it turned out, too late in this instance. My proclivity for putting things off had as much to do with my relish for chaos as it had with my limitations and un-sureness. No matter what it was, whether it was revising for exams, writing stories to deadline or making decisions that might have a bearing on the rest of my life, I always waited until the last minute before jumping into action, until I was virtually face-to-face with the stone-cold brick of the wall hurtling towards me.

My interview with the editor of the *Surrey Advertiser* was even shorter than the one at Spotlight – it lasted scarcely two minutes and was repeatedly interrupted by the phone on his desk. But there was enough time for him to proffer a word of advice that instantly chimed with me: 'I'll say to you what I always tell anyone starting out on this paper. Show us what you're made of.' Within two weeks of my arrival, I had written my first front-page story, proudly plant-ing my flag on top of the mountain, before learning, exactly a day later, one of the enduring truisms of a newsroom: you are only as good as your last story.

In this case, my copy was returned from the sub-editors' office with more lines and scribbled asides than I could take in, as if I had somehow entered a maze of my own making. It was the equivalent of plummeting from the summit to the bottom in the space of sec-onds. The story needed a new angle; the last line (the 'payoff' as it was referred to) had been moved to the top of the story with the intro crossed out; and some facts had been circled accompanied by question-marks, the words 'Surely not!' next to another. The spelling mistakes, of which there were any number, were underscored twice. It reminded me of how Mr Snowden would strike an angry array of red lines through my French prep at Hildersham House – but without the threat of violence, obviously. The sub-editor paused by my desk only to explain that it required a total rewrite and remarked bluntly that I should learn to 'bond immediately' with the office dictionary – a loose, coverless pile of tattered pages that unravelled like a ball of wool in your hands. All trainee journalists at some stage had their stories thrown back at them; it was part of the learning process. In a world before computers and spell-checks, you had to rely solely on a dictionary, but if you couldn't spell a word in the first place, tracking it down in one could prove equally problematic, as I often found to my cost. There was no excuse for a spelling mistake and no hiding place in a newsroom.

It was the first step on a fierce learning curve, and I quickly realised that if I was to survive on a newspaper, let alone progress, I had to stay on the right side of the sub-editors at any price. That price, I knew only too well on the evidence of my working life so far, was the sack. I spent the first few months worrying that I'd be summoned at a moment's notice to the editor's office and dreaded its sudden arrival like a knock on the door in the middle of the night. This was the first time I didn't want to lose a job – all the others I could take or leave – and, because of it, the fear loomed doubly large. The terror of being given the sack lived uneasily alongside another fear: my dyslexia. Or, more to the point, my horror of being exposed, of being found out for who I was: the seven-year-old boy who could write only one word, his name spelled backwards.

I had progressed since then, of course, but that did not dilute my anxiety, my fright. And barely a day went by when it was wasn't on my mind or when I didn't worry about it. I had good reason to be fearful. Being dyslexic in a profession like journalism meant I was opening myself up to all kinds of trouble, walking a path strewn with pitfalls, littered with obstacles – many of which I couldn't spot and any of which had the potential to bring my world crashing down around my ears. I always made sure I had an excuse handy – the typewriter keys kept sticking; I was trying to type and read my notes at the same time; the pages of the dictionary were missing; I was racing the clock on a razor-thin deadline – whenever I erred or misspelled a word. In reality, though, if anyone had my number, it was the sub-editors.

When I started in journalism, sub-editors were kings and not exactly benevolent rulers at that. It was no stretch of the imagination to say that they could make or break you. Most of those I encountered were vinegary veterans and sticklers for factual accuracy. They were the last line of defence, guardians against libel, grammatical errors, sloppy copy, clumsy or simple mistakes – in other words, the backbone of the newspaper. Many were a year or two away from retirement; some had already passed that point and were still working because, as they delighted in remarking, the paper couldn't exist without them. Mainly, I suspected, it was because they couldn't imagine doing anything else with their lives. They had seen it all and nothing could surprise them, not even my spelling or lack of punctuation, though that didn't stop them from regularly pointing out my missteps. If they called you into their cramped, smoke-filled office in the corner of the newsroom, you knew it was not to praise your work, dissect the merits of the news story you had just written or make you feel good about yourself. Once they had corrected your mistake, you repeated it at your peril; equally, you never forgot any pearls of wisdom they grudgingly tossed your way. When they weren't throwing my unvarnished copy back at me, they were sometimes rewriting it on the stroke of deadline in two or three minutes flat, because, as they frequently reminded me, 'it was quicker this way'. Usually, when it appeared in the paper, I struggled to recognise a single word I'd written, so complete was the rewrite. I never complained about that, for the simple reason that it made me look a far better reporter than I was or could ever hope to be. And, apart from anything else, it still carried my byline. I probably learned more from these grumpy past masters than I learned from anyone.

I soon realised I would never be anything more than an adequate news reporter at best and one whose attempts to master shorthand note-taking might last a lifetime. Sport was my true calling and I made no secret of that fact. I always kept an eye out for a vacancy on the sports desk at the *Surrey Advertiser*; I volunteered to cover a football match most Saturdays and filled in whenever a member of the department went on holiday. I hated having to cover county court or council meetings, where it would be hard to find anything more tedious. On one occasion, I attended court without any socks; in my hurry to get to work on time, I'd somehow managed to lose mine and just slipped on a pair of clogs instead, not thinking any more about it. Halfway through the session, a note from the judge was passed to the press bench. It simply stated that no member of the press would be allowed to attend court in future unless they were wearing socks. This proved a particularly puzzling decree for the female reporter seated next to me in a Biba dress.

I knew I wouldn't rest until I'd landed a job as a full-time sports reporter. For one thing, I regularly read my newspapers back to front – in keeping with most things I've done in my life. It's a habit I've never broken, nor wanted to, ever since I started reading them aged twelve or thirteen and became obsessed with sport and sports reporting. For me, the back page has always been the front page, and I turned to it first every time before idly working my way through the rest of the paper, often giving the lead story or the news section no more than a cursory glance. Finally, I couldn't resist the call any longer and answered an advertisement for a reporter at a south coast news agency to cover Brighton and Hove Albion Football Club's home games and Sussex's fortunes in the County Cricket Championship.

It was not exactly a rude awakening joining an agency, but I rapidly discovered that the dream of being a sports writer bore no relation to the reality of delivering a match report 'on the whistle', as it was known. This meant filing a story on the final blast of the referee's whistle or a few seconds earlier – not five, ten or twenty minutes later, for that was an unpardonable sin – by dictating it down the phone to a copytaker and hoping I could decipher the hieroglyphics that passed for my scrawled handwriting, my own version of shorthand. I spent the whole game scribbling or crossing out words, not daring to take my eyes off the action for a second, juggling facts and figures, pounding the story into some semblance of order, trying to block out the roar of the crowd while competing with the brain-frying immediacy of deadline. Sometimes my hard work was spectacularly undone by a winning goal in the dying seconds or a controversial penalty, and I suddenly found myself with a new story to write and the turmoil redoubled. If I managed to overcome that, I hotfooted it to the press conference, made a note of the pertinent quotes and started on a rewrite for the second edition – so punch-drunk at times that I could barely write, let alone think, straight. Usually, over the following days, the panic wore off, the fever dream dissipated and I was ready to go again for the next home game.

The stint at the agency foreshadowed much of what was to follow a few years later for me and provided the perfect opportunity to cut my teeth, to test myself at a higher level. It was gratifying to see my copy in print too, almost exactly as I had written it, in newspapers as diverse as the *Sunday Express*, the *Sunday Telegraph* and the *News of the World*. The cod bylines that accompanied my reports were not so rewarding though, and I appeared as anyone from Tom Hall to Colin Morley to Jim Fairclough to 'a special correspondent' and whoever else they cared to name me as.

A couple of years later I was offered a job as sports reporter at the *Crawley Observer*. The role offered more autonomy and I returned to the relative haven of provincial journalism. One of the comforts of working on local papers was that they were invariably staffed by characters with enough idiosyncrasies and eccentricities to suggest they, like me, would have struggled within the confines of a more conventional job, and the *Crawley Observer* was no exception. The editor unfailingly wore a pair of white gloves in the office like a snooker referee or a magician, though the only trick I saw him perform was a disappearing act for several hours every lunchtime. Another member of the editorial team elected to spend his nights sleeping in a coffin. I never learned the reason for either of these anomalies.

One of the most intriguing things about the newsroom was the intercom system that had been rigged up between editorial and advertising. The system was almost single-handedly run by the news editor, Malcolm Ingrams, and existed because the departments were situated at opposite ends of the building. Barely a day went by without Ingrams contacting advertising via the intercom, and the conversations ping-ponged back and forth with annoying regularity. 'Calling Claire One,' he would announce, 'calling Claire One.' Because of his pronounced Yorkshire accent, one sounded exactly like 'wan'. If there was no response, he would try again: 'Calling Claire Two… calling Claire Two.' Claire One was Claire Drummond, the advertising manager, and Claire Two was her deputy, Claire Broderick. Why he never used their surnames remained another mystery. Fortunately, the two Claires spent more time out of the office than in, but one or the other would get back to him at some point and a voice would crackle discordantly over the rattle of typewriters and ringing telephones. 'Calling Malcolm Ingrams… this is Claire One. How can we help?' Ingrams would respond with all the glee of a ham radio enthusiast. 'Ah, Claire One. Any chance you could pop over to editorial? Couple of things I need to discuss. Ta.'

Naturally, I couldn't wait to get my hands on the system but had to hold fire until Ingrams and the editor were out of the office. I often imitated Ingrams's voice and was surprised whenever I received a response from someone in advertising. I even started a pop quiz, which involved me opera singing a tune to make it harder to recognise, and invented a character called Claire Three. 'Calling Claire Three… calling Claire Three. Could you please move your tractor? It's blocking the entrance to the car park.' This went on for a while until one day, having messaged Claire One to 'collect her pipe and slippers from the receptionist's desk', I was startled to hear the editor's voice come booming back at me. 'Calling John Lazenby… calling John Lazenby. Get on with some fucking work.'

It was over and out for me a year later and I joined the *Eastbourne Herald* as deputy sports editor, swapping a typewriter for a computer terminal and laptop. In the process, much to my delight,

I discovered that new technology was nowhere near as daunting as I had feared. The *Herald* was one of the first provincial newspapers in the country to convert to 'new tech', at the same time as Britain's most famous papers were deserting Fleet Street to move their editorial and printing operations to modern, computerised plants in Wapping. To make it to Fleet Street one day had always been the allure for me – and it still beckoned brightly, even though I was now in my thirties.

I spent three happy years in Eastbourne and always knew I would be sad to leave it behind should I ever achieve my ultimate ambition, though there were several sporting institutions and certain individuals who would not have been sorry to see the back of me. Eastbourne United FC, for one, and the man who operated the Tannoy on their match days for another. He had needed a bathroom break near the end of an Isthmian League game against Maidenhead United one Saturday – a game that bore all the hallmarks of a dismal, goalless draw – and asked me to keep an eye on things for him. 'I doubt whether I'll miss anything – it's one of those games, isn't it?' When he returned about five minutes later, I inexplicably conjured a couple of imaginary goals out of the air and told him Eastbourne were 2–0 up. 'Blimey', was all he said and raced up the ladder to his box to announce the score before I could stop him. I regretted it the moment the words were out of my mouth, but as usual, I couldn't help myself. The false announcement brought proceedings to an instantaneous halt. Twenty-two players, and four match officials stopped what they were doing to stare in amazement in the direction of the Tannoy. The crowd responded with a volley of laughter and cheers, interspersed with jeers, and the Maidenhead player who had the ball at his feet hoofed it into the stand, as much in disgust as bewilderment. I ended up writing an apology in the match programme, printed in full, and was never invited back into the boardroom for a half-time cup of tea and sandwiches.

Maybe I was on the never-ending hunt for a greater injection of adrenaline, or maybe I realised that if I didn't make that move to Fleet Street soon, I never would and the chance would be lost for ever. So, undeterred by my age – I was thirty-five by this time – I applied for a job on the sports desk of the national news agency, the Press Association or PA, as it is more commonly known. PA shared a premises with Reuters, an elegant Grade II listed building at no. 85 Fleet Street, designed in 1935 by Sir Edwin Lutyens. When I arrived there in January 1990 for my interview, they were the last surviving bastions of journalism – along with an unlikely outlier, Dundee's *Sunday Post*. But better late than never, I told myself. Getting hired by PA, however, turned out to be nothing short of a marathon. After being interviewed by the sports editor and the deputy news editor, I also had to write a 300-word football round-up in ten minutes on a rickety typewriter, using the previous weekend's league results, and sit an exam designed to test my sporting knowledge. I did not hold out much hope for my chances. Two days later, I was astonished to receive a letter provisionally offering me the job, with instructions to return to Fleet Street for a medical and an interview with the editor, Colin Webb.

I later learned that the doctor who conducted the medical was the oldest practising GP in London. He was certainly the most can-tankerous, and for a moment I wondered if he wasn't part of the test, such was his marked lack of manners and obvious impatience. The medical followed the standard procedure – eyesight, chest, heart, lungs, blood pressure, urine sample – but, peculiarly, also required me to remove all my clothes and kneel in a chair with my head almost buried in its seat. This final examination occurred only after he had brusquely commanded me to pick my clothes up off the floor and fold them neatly on the surgery bed. It involved a torch and is best left there. Despite this indignity, I was deemed fit to sit at a desk and type at a keyboard.

By the time I knocked on the editor's door, I didn't know what to think any more. I should have guessed there was one more surprise to come. The office was light and airy and looked out at the art deco *Daily Express* building, with its ocean-liner decks of glass and chrome. I saw his arm move as soon as I entered the room and thought he was about to stand and shake my hand. But he remained seated and a small spherical object flew towards me instead. I noticed the revolving white seam instantly, the cherry-red of a cricket ball, and knew I had to catch it. I didn't question for a second why he had tossed a cricket ball at me but told myself not to snatch at it, to let it come to me. How my grandfather would have groaned had I spilled that chance – a groan that would have echoed loudly down the years. It was aimed at my midriff, at a perfect catchable height, and I didn't have to move a muscle. I heard the satisfying smack of leather as it connected with my palms and allowed it to nestle into my hands before enclosing my fingers around it. A part of me wanted to throw it up in triumph, in celebration, but I refrained for once.

Finally, I had sealed my selection.

CHAPTER FIFTEEN

RUNNING BLINDLY ALONG
A HIGH WIRE

I never expected to find myself talking to a room full of people about my dyslexia. After all, I had spent the best part of four decades trying to hide the subject from my colleagues, to keep it a closely guarded secret, to pretend it never happened. But then again, I had never expected to find myself living in New Zealand either.

We had visited New Zealand in late 2015 so that my Kiwi partner, Sharon, could have some time with her family. Originally, we hadn't planned to stay any longer than two or three months – but, in our lives, plans often had a habit of flying out of the window. I was freelancing for *The Independent* and the *Independent on Sunday* in London at this point, working four or five days a week on a rolling rota. 'I'll see you in about two months' time,' I told one of my colleagues, logging off at the end of my last shift there. 'You won't come back,' he replied without lifting his eyes from the keyboard. 'What makes you say that?' I asked. 'Well, put it this way, if I had the chance to go to New Zealand, I wouldn't be coming back. Not for anybody.'

Three months later, *The Independent* shut down its print editions, after launching with a revolutionary fanfare thirty years earlier, and started a new life as an online newspaper. My job no longer existed. As luck would have it, I received a small redundancy package and everything seemed to click automatically into place. Suddenly there was no reason to go back to the UK. We were already happily settled in New Zealand, living on the east coast of the North Island surrounded by beaches, a couple of hours by car from Auckland and immersed in the lifestyle. Secretly, I had been dreading the prospect of returning home, so we reversed our decision – it wasn't hard – and stayed on instead. Within a year, we had started a micro-publishing company, ghostwriting biographies and short-story collections.

In 2018, I was approached by a woman called Sandra McKersey to collaborate with her on a writing project. Sandra turned out to be a human dynamo, a philanthropist and the founding director of People Potential, an aptly named, much-garlanded adult educational training facility in Northland. We soon became friends and while working with her one day, I dropped dyslexia into the conversation and briefly explained some of my story to her, surprising myself in the process. Her immediate reaction was to ask if I had ever considered talking about it publicly. I told her I hadn't. 'I think you should,' she said. I was reluctant, uneasy about it at first, and realised I had become so conditioned by my anxiety to build a wall of silence around my dyslexia, to keep shoring up its defences, that I would make any excuse not to do it. I was still locked in a state of denial, entrenched in the mindset of a profession that prided itself on the survival of the fittest, its competitiveness, where the last thing you wanted to do was show your opponent your weaknesses. 'But you're not in survival mode any more, are you?' Sandra pointed out.

Rarely a visit went by when she didn't ask if I had made up my mind yet, and I knew she wouldn't rest until I had. 'Good,' she said when I finally told her I would do it. 'Because I've already arranged for you to talk at a women's business event I'm attending next week.' She might have had confidence in me, but I was still far from convinced that people wouldn't laugh at what I had to say.

And then something else happened that I never expected: the first time I spoke about my dyslexia, a woman in the audience started to cry, not laugh, and I was promptly booked to speak at another function the following week and another one after that, until it became a regular occurrence. What really surprised me, however, was the number of people who wanted to chat afterwards about their children's dyslexia, or their grandchildren's, or their own struggles in the classroom or why they had felt too frightened or too ashamed to do anything about it themselves at the time. And some just came to say thank you and no more. Sandra was delighted and couldn't resist saying that she had told me so. 'I knew you'd be great. You just need to have a little more faith in yourself, that's all.' There was a piece of advice for me too. 'Slow down and stop talking so fast – you're like a freight train up there.' Teaching had always been Sandra's vocation and perhaps, in a curious kind of way, she had become my later-in-life version of Miss Shepherd.

I shall always be indebted to her for persuading me to share my experiences with dyslexia, because nothing could have been further from my mind at that time. In many ways, I was just glad to have put it behind me at last – or so I thought. Sharon, a fellow journalist, had long encouraged me to write about my experiences. However, within the confines of the UK and straightjacketed by the past, I was simply unwilling to break cover. I often wonder whether I would have been able to make that change, to unburden myself of my dyslexia had I stayed in England. I was gloriously unaware that, in many ways, I was still doing what I had done as a small boy: dog-earing the pages of my hymn book and hoping no one noticed.

Perhaps it took sixty years to fully understand that whatever dyslexia takes from you in terms of the trouble and inconvenience it provokes – for instance, I still have difficulty remembering my own telephone number and invariably transpose the digits – it pays you back in full every time and sometimes even in gold. Whether I am writing, using my imagination, utilising my natural curiosity, my atypical thinking, shifting 3D shapes in my mind or seeing images or pictures so clearly inside my own head I can virtually touch them, I know it is being fuelled and fired by my dyslexic brain. Nowadays if people ask me about my diverse brain wiring, I tell them that I would rather have had it than not, that I wouldn't have wanted it any other way – which amounts to a huge and profound sea change.

When I started out as a young journalist being dyslexic was viewed as an 'affliction' you were likely to be castigated for and often mistaken for a character defect. My prime objective was simple: to instinctively mask it, before I even knew what masking was, and keep it under wraps. Consequently, I lived my whole career, more than forty years of it, struggling to escape from under the shadow of doubt and fear. Doubt that I wasn't up to the job, that I was an imposter who thought backwards; fear that I would commit some unforgivable howler for which I'd always be remembered or that I'd be rumbled, found out; fear that the shadow would eventually overtake me. It was no surprise that I brought the shame and ridicule of the classroom into the newsroom with me. And yet, somehow, I survived and even flourished.

Before I left the *Eastbourne Herald* for Fleet Street, one of the sub-editors there, another vinegary veteran called Jim Barton – he could be cussed and forthright or charming and kind, as the mood took him – gave me some advice I've never forgotten. 'You know you're about to jump into the shark tank, don't you?' I had been told nothing but that since announcing my departure, though not perhaps in those graphic terms. 'Then you'd better hope you've got eyes in the back of your head because you're going to need them where you're going.' It was unrealistic to think you won't make mistakes, he continued, we all do – it's the nature of the game – but the key to survival, he grimly pointed out, was simply to make fewer mistakes than the guy next to you. It was not the most subtle piece of advice I've ever received, nor the most earth-shattering, but it was honest and well-intended and it has always stuck with me. After all, he had probably hoovered up enough of mine.

Naturally, I sailed perilously close to the rocks on numerous occasions over the next twenty-five years, both as a reporter and sub-editor, in my battle to heed his advice, keep my dyslexic moments to the minimum and stay afloat. One of the worst of those moments occurred when, in the heat of deadline, I confused Pontypridd and Pontypool in a headline, thereby accidentally bestowing rugby's Principality Cup on the wrong team – in this case, Pontypool. That amounted to a sackable offence on that particular Sunday newspaper, and I'd regularly seen people kicked out for less. But no one in the office appeared to notice my mistake, including the hawk-eyed revise sub, the proofreader or the sports editor himself – though, inevitably, most of Wales would have. I didn't realise what I'd done until I was travelling home on the train that night and it struck me with the fury of a thunderbolt. I spent the next few days fretting endlessly about it before returning to the office. I still don't know how I got away with it. Perhaps the news cycle that week in 2002 was so eventful it was swept under the carpet along with everything else. Or perhaps I was just lucky – it happens sometimes, even on newspapers.

On another occasion, while working at *The Guardian*, I managed to turn the Hong Kong Sevens rugby tournament into the Hong Konk Sevens. Even worse, I had written it into the subhead and the blunder, therefore, stood out like an inebriated intruder on the pitch. Remarkably, the revise sub missed the typo, though to be fair to him, we were right up against deadline and he had no more than seconds to scan his eye over it before sending the story to the page. In my defence, I had to cut some fifty lines out of the story, write a headline, a standfirst and a picture caption in five minutes flat, with the production editor yelling 'I need that copy now' in my ear, until it felt as if I was running blindly along a high wire.

The revise sub, in this instance, was an unflappable character, the essence of calm, who rarely raised his voice above the din of deadline even at its most incendiary. His first response to the mistake after it was urgently flagged by the proofreader was to see the funny side of it. 'Hong Konk,' he laughed, deftly defusing the situation. 'How wonderful.' If only all revise subs were like him, but sadly they weren't. Another I used to work with would jump out of his seat on deadline and headbutt the wall behind him. One night he struck the wall so hard he cut his forehead open but returned to his seat with blood streaming down his face and refused to leave his post until the edition was put to bed. Being dyslexic, I worried that I was the one who had tipped him over the edge. Another revise sub would punch his computer screen repeatedly, then hurl the dictionary across the office in the direction of the culprit responsible. It wasn't unusual for low-flying wastepaper bins to go hurtling across the office either, often causing you to duck your head beneath the screen.

If I ever needed another reminder of my dyslexia, just to keep me on my toes, I could always rely on a copytaker to inadvertently provide it. Because of the almost constant roar of the crowd during matches, they couldn't hear you dictate your copy and you couldn't hear them – making for a perfect storm of mishaps, misunderstandings and mistakes. You could add mayhem and madness to that list. Sometimes, if a goal or try was scored, the noise became so intense that whole paragraphs disappeared into the ether or became so horribly lost in translation that they resembled a conversation between two drunks in a wind tunnel. Which undoubtedly explained why, in a rugby union international I covered between England and France, the line 'the English forwards set out their stall on the French line' became 'the English forwards set out their stools on the French line'. The Parc des Princes, the crucible of French rugby at that time, went out as 'a park in France', and the attempts by England's Mick Skinner 'to pull the ball out of a maul' ended up as 'Mick Skinner pulled a ball off them all'. All of which was sent out under my byline to hundreds of newspapers, news outlets and PA subscribers throughout the country.

There was another reason for this: Saturday afternoon deadlines were so tight that when a match report finally left the copytakers' desk and landed in front of a sub-editor, there was barely time to write a headline or check the scoreline before it had to be sent out. Copy riddled with typos and errors was infinitely preferable to no copy at all. The cricket version of this proved equally embarrassing for me. In a county game between Sussex and Hampshire, where the crowd noise was minimal, if there even was a crowd, the copytaking process contrived to turn Imran Khan's endeavours to skittle the Hampshire tail with 'some fiery, short-pitched bowling' into 'some furry, short-pitched balling'.

Today, it is comforting to know those days belong in the rear-view

mirror and I don't have to face down deadlines as punishing or gru-
elling as that again. I still miss aspects of it, of course, as you would
with anything you've done for forty-odd years – but I also remember every grain of energy and effort that I expended on preserving my survival. More comforting by far is the fact that, by finally
talking openly about my dyslexia, I accidentally reconnected with
my long-lost seven-year-old self – as if we'd suddenly bumped into
each other down some cobwebbed corridor. I couldn't remember
the last time I'd thought of NHOJ, not properly. Yet I have always
been that small boy, standing at the end of the drive at Hildersham
House after my parents had driven off and abandoned me, willing
them to turn their car around, the freezing sleet numbing my hands
and feet but not the fear and pain I felt inside. Although I had my
victories along the way, a part of me will always be ashamed that for
four decades or more, I abandoned him too.

CHAPTER SIXTEEN

WHEN YOUR TIME HAS TURNED TO DOG YEARS

I t was my partner who first dropped ADHD into the conversation – or attention deficit hyperactivity disorder, to give it its full title. We'd been in New Zealand for four years at this point, and she was in the middle of explaining some infinitely tedious but doubtlessly necessary piece of internet banking to me, for what must have felt to her like the hundredth time. Probably because it was the hundredth time. At that moment, ADHD meant no more to me than a quartet of letters I was almost certainly bound to transpose at some stage, letters I would have to assemble in the right order inside my head before I could say them aloud. I had heard of ADHD, obviously, but never thought to find out what it stood for or what it meant, because, as far as I was concerned, it wouldn't have anything to do with me. I was about to discover, however, that nothing could have been further from the truth.

Sharon's suggestion, pitched as lightly as if she was offering a day at the beach, was that when I had a moment, I could google, read some of the relevant online forums, acquaint myself with the facts and see what bells it rang or what conclusions, if any, I drew. She

made the request sound casual and unthreatening. 'Have you ever
wondered whether there might be something more to it than just
dyslexia?' she asked, having once again resolved my online banking
issue. 'It's only a thought, that's all.' But a thought that, once lodged
inside my head, I could not ignore.

Even I had to admit that within seconds of typing ADHD into
Google, the symptoms were startlingly familiar – and the more I
read, the more they kept on coming, leaping off the screen at me,
ambushing me one after the other. It was like overhearing someone talk about you in the next room in less than flattering terms.
Having overcome my initial surprise, my next reaction was one of
puzzlement, fused with a sense of frustration: why had no one ever
mentioned ADHD to me before? How had I managed to spend
most of my life without knowing about it? It felt as if I had lived in
the same house all my life, only to suddenly discover it contained a
secret room that I never knew existed until now. I didn't even know
my own home.

I soaked up the new information, learning that the symptoms of
ADHD can be divided into two distinct categories of behavioural
problems – inattentiveness and hyperactivity. And in each case, I
saw myself reflected back to me. I was easily distracted; I was for-
getful; I regularly mislaid possessions; I was unable to stick at tasks I
found monotonous; I had no organisational skills; I failed to follow
instructions; I did not recognise or remember patterns, including
how to work many household appliances; I had difficulty managing
my finances, an issue aggravated by my procrastination, disorgani-
sation and a lack of executive planning; I could not sit still; I could
not stop moving; I impulsively blurted things out; I acted without thinking, often with little or no sense of the danger involved;

and those were just the obvious ones. The same characteristics, I realised, that I had always previously associated with dyslexia.

It was no surprise to me, and even less of a surprise to Sharon, that forgetfulness or a knack for losing belongings was so prominent on the list. I had been absent-mindedly leaving items behind on trains, station platforms, in waiting rooms and shops all my life – certainly all my working life. Everything from coats, jackets, scarves, umbrellas, briefcases, glasses, books and notebooks to my lunch or even a bag of groceries, to the extent that it had become a standing joke between us. If I bought a new briefcase, the standard question was always, 'How long is this one going to last before you lose it?' Fortunately, I've never worn hats, otherwise they would have considerably swelled the aggregate. Once, I left my briefcase on the platform at Kew Station, travelled halfway down the line before I realised what I'd done, and turned back only to learn that there was a security scare at the station. My unattended briefcase.

The habit had not improved since moving to New Zealand – in fact, with less adrenaline to focus my mind, it had probably got worse. I routinely mislaid my sunglasses or reading glasses at our local supermarket and had consequently become well-acquainted with the woman who looked after the lost property. Sometimes she saw me coming and had the item in front of her, ready to hand it over, so I didn't have to say anything but thank you. 'Someone found these perched on a baked bean tin,' she said to me once, returning my sunglasses with a broad smile.

I continued to digest as much information as I could about ADHD and, after several hours of reading all I could absorb in one sitting, told Sharon that I was 100 per cent certain I had it, firing off a list of heavily researched facts and figures. Which was very

ADHD, of course. But each new fact only intensified my conviction. I learned there was no cure for it because it was a neurological difference rather than a disease, but there were medications and tricks and tools in abundance to mitigate the effects. I learned, too, that the submerged iceberg that is ADHD can wreck hopes, sink dreams, capsize plans and force you to alter the entire course of your life if it is not properly managed or treated. 'I'm one of more than 366 million adults worldwide who are affected by it,' I gasped, pausing only to look back at the screen and double-check that I'd quoted the figures correctly. 'I don't see how I couldn't be – it's that obvious, isn't it?' Sharon didn't answer but gave me a look instead that simply said *I know*.

And then I did something else typically ADHD: having read about it for days and discussed it for hours on end, I suddenly stopped talking about it, thinking about it, and returned it to the shelf – as if it was no longer important, as if the novelty, the newness, had just worn off. Sometimes, something's only exciting until it's not. And the momentum stalled.

Inevitably, as time passed and I did precisely nothing to remedy the situation, we had words about it: 'If you're so convinced you've got ADHD, why are you ignoring it now? It's like throwing away a lifeline.' I soon snapped to attention when she emitted the word 'mate' several times – the Kiwi equivalent of Dow's 'No, I'm very sorry, but...', an equally efficient warning mechanism that left me in no doubt she was at the end of her tether. I had read enough comments on forums by ADHD partners to know that I had been thoughtless in ignoring it. It was those closest to me who had to bear the brunt of it, to run the gauntlet, to live it every day. I had made multiple unkept promises too: to address it, to speak to a doctor. I had raised her hopes for positive progress, only to fail to deliver on each occasion. Later that day, after our awkward exchange, I went to the supermarket to be reunited with my sunglasses again. The woman handed them over to me and jokingly suggested it was time I had my own drawer next to the tills. Amusing as that seemed, I knew I had to stop pretending and take some action. Enough was enough – it was a case of now or never – so I rang my doctor and made an appointment on the spot.

A GP cannot conduct a formal diagnosis or assessment of ADHD – that's a job for a psychiatrist, a clinical psychologist, a paediatrician or a specialist – but they can ask you to sit a test or answer a series of questions that will determine whether they should refer you to any of the aforementioned experts. My doctor asked ten questions in all, none of them difficult to answer, and I remember thinking if only every test or exam was that straightforward, how much simpler my life would have been. 'Well, that's about as conclusive as you can get,' she said once I'd finished the test. 'I don't think there will be any doubt that you have ADHD and I'm going to refer you to a specialist right away.' Usually, she explained, the test throws up grey areas and points of contention, where a patient might be only 50 per cent likely to have it or 60–40, which makes for a difficult judgement call. 'But not with you,' she added. 'I've put a tick beside every question you've answered.'

I couldn't remember the last time I'd received ten out of ten for anything.

• • •

I cannot bear waiting – whether it's waiting in line, waiting in a queue, waiting for news, for something to happen or, as in this case, waiting to be diagnosed with ADHD. So, when my doctor warned me that it might be several months before I saw a specialist and I might have to sit tight for a while, I automatically feared the worst. After all, time was not on my side. More relevantly, I cannot sit still for the life of me. For example, if my phone rings or I call someone, I rarely stay seated; I like to walk around the garden instead or urgently pace the floor of whatever room I happen to be in. Anything but remain stationary. If I had to sit still, I'd probably throw the phone into the air or, worse, against the wall. Which is why I've always thought that a job in a call centre would be my idea of hell – not that I'd ever stick to the script, of course, or be polite to people. Movement is my life force and waiting is an anathema, a place where, if you stay marooned for any length of time, frustration, hopelessness and despair converge.

'I can't put an exact figure on it, I'm afraid,' my doctor explained when I asked her how long the wait might be. 'It could take anything up to six months or longer – there's just no way of knowing. I can't bump you up the waiting list, unfortunately, but I can mark your case as urgent and hope that makes a difference.' I had virtually zoned out by this time and could see an endless corridor stretching ahead of me, unswervingly straight. 'I must warn you it's not much better in the private sector either, if you're thinking of going down that route. I'm sorry. It's a long haul, whichever way you look at it.' The walls of the corridor were already closing in.

In the end I waited twelve months before I received a call (naturally, I took it moving around the room) informing me, almost a year to the day since I'd first spoken to my doctor about it, that the publicly funded system was no longer assessing adults for ADHD and the department was closing. The only choice open to me was to go private, but I would still face a long wait. No, they couldn't put an exact figure on it. It occurred to me that it would have been easier to wash my hands of the whole thing at that point, rather than wait six months or another year or be told there weren't enough psychiatrists, clinical psychologists or specialists at the end of it. But that was not the path I wanted to take – despite the messages the system was sending me.

Issues with access to ADHD diagnosis and support are not just confined to New Zealand, however; systems are overloaded and overstretched worldwide. As awareness and information about ADHD has grown in the past few years, so the number of sufferers and those who believe they possess the symptoms has increased, particularly among middle-aged adults, and the perception that it is a domain predominantly for children no longer holds true. In the UK, for instance, *The Lancet* and the National Institute for Health and Clinical Excellence (NICE) estimate that the number of people diagnosed with ADHD is 2.6 million, with a childhood incidence rate of 5 per cent and an incidence rate for adults of between 3 and 4 per cent. The average wait for an assessment is six months to a year.

In some parts of the UK, though, wait times are considerably longer and rising rapidly, as are the stakes. In November 2023, the Central and Northwest London NHS Trust was forced to close its waiting list because of the 'extremely high number of referrals'. The wait time there currently stands at thirty-six months – for those who successfully manage to get on the waiting list in the first place. NICE guidelines assert that no one should have to wait longer than three months between being referred for an ADHD assessment and being seen. Astonishingly, the BBC reported in March 2023 that a diagnosis for ADHD can take 'longer than five years in Sussex and up to four years in Surrey'.

In New Zealand, approximately 280,000 people – 5 per cent of the country's population of 5 million – have ADHD, but only between 1 and 2 per cent are diagnosed, according to the latest research, while a further 20 per cent are not even aware they have it. The situation has been compounded in both countries by the prohibitively expensive cost of a private diagnosis, which is £1,200 for an adult in the UK and $1,600–$1,800 (about £860) in New Zealand – money that is beyond the scope of many people's budgets. Others, cast into the void by the system, have reportedly resorted to bridging the gap by seeking advice and medical help from social media or have just given up through lack of hope. One solution under discussion in New Zealand is to provide GPs with specialist training in the field so that they can diagnose and treat ADHD, thereby relieving the pressure on specialists and releasing more psychiatrists and psychologists back into the fold. At the time of writing, only psychiatrists, and paediatricians in the case of children, can endorse the use of stimulants to treat ADHD patients. But the books of many psychiatrists are so full they are unable to take on new patients. The fear is that in the short term, things are likely to get worse before they get better – a situation I heard one doctor attribute to the failure of the medical system in New Zealand to treat ADHD as an emergency and offer a service worthy of the severe challenges this condition often presents.

In my case, I doggedly and uncharacteristically waited it out, until finally I was fortunate enough to have my assessment made via a video call and to be told what I already knew: I had ADHD and had therefore spent most of my life encumbered with the dual demands of dyslexia and attention deficit hyperactivity disorder. It is one thing to be diagnosed with ADHD but it is quite another to receive the assessment in your mid-sixties, when you've reached state-pension age, when your time has turned to dog years and everything is marching remorselessly in the wrong direction. In that moment,

I discovered I had travelled through life without knowing about this unseen outrider at my side, hiding in plain sight all along, just as my dyslexia had done.

Dyslexia and ADHD are contrasting brain disorders, but they can overlap and coexist and frequently do. The figures show that about three in ten people who suffer from dyslexia also have ADHD. It is often hard to tell them apart, to distinguish one from the other, as some of the characteristics – reading difficulties, frustration, distraction, attentional disengagement – are so similar they can easily intertwine and coincide or feed off each other. They are like a pair of mountaineers roped together dangling above a precipice, who, with one sudden movement, can be thrown off-kilter or knocked off-course or sent crashing back to where they started. Sometimes it requires no more than tension on the rope to send me into a downward spiral or unexpectedly impact my life. And not just my life either, but the lives of those around me, especially those close to me.

Yet no sooner was I diagnosed than I underwent a re-evaluation of my life, a kind of rethink, and experienced what thousands of other sufferers describe on learning they have ADHD – intense relief. It's a feeling of calmness that, after so much struggle, things suddenly start to make sense; everything seems less complicated, less cluttered inside your head; the missing piece to your jigsaw suddenly falls into place; you have an instruction manual to yourself, a road map; and a lifetime of quirks and traits can finally be explained and interpreted. Now I could start to draw a shaky boundary line between my personality and my brain wiring. All along, I had thought I *was* my neurodiversity.

It may not be quite that easy, of course, and a diagnosis is only the first important step on the long road ahead. But you feel for the first time that you are armed with some understanding and insight into who you are, not to mention the knowledge that there are a range of therapies and treatment options available, lifelines to reach for. It had never occurred to me that there would ever be a way of making life easier for myself and, by extension, for those who came into contact with me. It was like being gifted something precious: a new start in life, regardless of my age.

It explained why the fast pace of the newsroom, with its irresistible adrenaline peaks, was tailor-made for my ADHD brain. It explained why I lived off the fumes for a few hours afterwards but dreaded the doldrum-like lows that inevitably followed. It was why I was often thrown the last story to edit in the furnace of deadline, when speed was of the essence. Sometimes I had more production staff gathered around my desk than a football referee, all shouting in my ear at once. There was an odd imbalance, an awkward dynamic between what I was good at in the workplace and the things I struggled with. I was viewed as being quick and clear-headed on deadline, a safe pair of hands, which was not how I saw myself – but, in a strange way, the chaos of it all played to my ADHD strengths, my ability to hyperfocus on anything that interested me. It gave me access to the adrenaline and momentum I craved and brought the best out of me, even though fear and anxiety were almost always the propellants. Luckily, no one knew what was driving me – more to the point, nor did I at that time.

Now that I do, I can start to come to terms with the shadow side of ADHD – particularly my urgent need to sabotage things if they are going too well, too smoothly. When that happens, I cannot stop myself from creating chaos and upheaval where none exists, to compensate for the lack of adrenaline and momentum in my everyday life by replicating the dopamine hit of deadline. At least now I can attempt to shut down the urge before it takes hold.

And then there is the default communication style I resort to whenever I'm under stress or feel threatened or embarrassed in any way – what my partner aptly calls my 'Lord of the Flies communication style', which can be combative and confrontational and occasionally tip over into exasperation. It was a style forged and sharpened during eleven granite years at boarding school, designed to protect me, to repel and rebuff bullies at every turn – but one that, practised outside the school walls, has sometimes proved to be the bane of relationships. It is usually triggered by rejection, a feeling of failure, perceived criticism or disapproval of something I've said or done and is so ingrained in me that most of the time I don't realise I'm doing it. What I know is that it is a muscle I have flexed too often for my own comfort, as if I am back at school again – a line that has been thrown at me on numerous occasions – defending myself, fighting for survival or my reputation.

Recently, I was introduced to a new condition – well, new to me – called RSD (rejection-sensitive dysphoria), which many experts describe as a disabling feature of ADHD. It is almost as though every time you open the box, another initialism tumbles out – in the same way that whenever you open one door in life, they all start to fly open. RSD occurs when you experience severe emotional pain or acute discomfort because of rejection, criticism, failure or embarrassment and you are unable to respond in a measured, balanced way to those feelings, which often overpower you. One of the complications of being diagnosed with ADHD so late in life is the difficulty I have in trying to separate my character and personality from my neurodiversity. I cannot pretend to be an expert in any of this, of course, and sometimes it leaves me with more questions than answers.

It is all too tempting to look back with regret, to wonder what might have been if I had only received a diagnosis earlier, but by the same token, I keep reminding myself that my cognitive condition has made me extraordinarily resilient, that I have a different way of looking at the world and I have come a long way on it. Even if for most of that journey I've felt as if I've been driving a car with dodgy brakes and faulty steering.

The more I learn about ADHD, however, the more I am reminded of my mother and become more certain that she carried many of the same symptoms as me – impulsivity, forgetfulness, inattention, continually talking over other people, difficulty with maths and accounting. It helps me to see her in a different light, and I can identify the signs from afar in her own mother too, with her dressing gown pockets stashed with unpaid bills. Mum often told me that my dyslexia came from her – 'You can blame me for that one' – though I suspect that in fact, she was suffering from what is known today as dyscalculia, a learning difficulty that affects a person's ability to comprehend numbers and understand maths. ADHD and dyslexia both have a genetic component and if a parent has one or the other, there is more than a 50 per cent chance of it being passed on.

As much as I loved visiting Mum in her later years, our conversations could be wearying at times. Part of the frustration for me, I now recognise, was that we shared the same tendencies and triggers and therefore many of those conversations ended in a kind of stalemate – mainly because we were both talking at the same time or thinking about what we were going to say next while the other was speaking. In fairness to her, she could also be an accomplished listener, more so than me. Sharon, who was sometimes reduced to the role of spectator during our exchanges – it was virtually impossible to get a word in edgeways – found it amusing, nonetheless, likening it to an impenetrable maze or a switchback of rail tracks, continually criss-crossing or veering wildly from side to side.

Yet it was Sharon who Mum chose to confide in when she shared a revelation about my early days at boarding school. She admitted she had cried the whole way home after leaving me at Hildersham House and had never wanted me to go in the first place. She explained that she went along with it because she believed it was for the best: 'It was a tradition you didn't question. It was the way things were done in those days.' It never occurred to me that she might have been heartbroken too, or that she was as much a victim of the time and place as I was. She certainly never mentioned it to me.

For his part, my father spent five of the happiest years of his life at prep school, where his abiding memory as a junior boy was being read bedtime stories by the headmaster's wife. He wanted the same environment for me, to receive the same kindness he was shown. I don't doubt they would have removed me in an instant from Hildersham House had I told them the reality of my situation. But the code of silence was so strong that I never broke it, and they each died without learning the full truth of my boarding school experience.

My mother remained a force of nature well into her nineties, even after my father's death in 2002, aged eighty-five with advancing Parkinson's, and never lost her appetite or zeal for life. I had visited Dad in hospital in Brighton a few days before he passed and told him I would try to get down again to see him at the weekend. 'I won't be here,' he replied and continued to stare into the corner of the ward, as if he were about to answer the call of the ocean one last time or was searching for a beckoning horizon somewhere in the distance. 'Well, anyway...' I mumbled aimlessly, looking at his tiny head on the pillow, at the last pathetic strands of hair. 'As I say, I'll try to make it down.' But he remained transfixed by whatever it was he saw in the far corner of the room. 'I won't be here,' he repeated, more softly this time. And, sure enough, he was right. He died in the small hours of Sunday morning. After his near-death experiences during the war, his refusal to fear the end of life had remained as steadfast as ever.

Dow followed him in 2007 having suffered from Alzheimer's for several years, passing away at a nursing home in Peacehaven, East Sussex, aged eighty-seven. But Mum soldiered on, at times so racked by the pain of arthritis she could barely move. She retained her enthusiasm for books, films and music – all kinds of music – and liked nothing more than holding court at her flat in Lewes, a dazzling conversationalist still. Her inquisitive nature never deserted her and she always had a fund of questions for me whenever I turned up. 'Who's this Brian Sprinklesteen I keep hearing so much about?' she asked me once. 'Is he any good?' She meant Bruce Springsteen. She could never remember people's names and regularly got Christian names and surnames in the wrong order. Apparently, I'm the same.

She maintained a small cohort of loyal friends until the end, who regularly called in for a quick chat and a small drink with her. Except that there was no such thing as a small drink with Mum – or a quick chat. She still mixed a fearsome gin and Dubonnet and would repeatedly fill her guests' glasses to the brim, refusing to listen to their protestations or notice they had placed their hands over the rim in a futile gesture to stop her pouring another. When you drank with Mum, you played by her rules. A few hours later, she sent them stumbling out into the night, incapable of finding their way home or fumbling their front-door key into the lock. Finally, after a fall at her flat and a month in hospital, followed by a short spell in a nursing home in Worthing, she died in late April 2011, missing her ninety-fourth birthday by a matter of days.

As I don't have children of my own, I'll never know whether the twin challenges of ADHD and dyslexia would have stopped with me or been passed on. Fortunately, my sister, Gina, and her husband, David, produced two highly intelligent, creative boys, Will and Jack, and made up for my sparsely populated branch of the family tree by also having three grandchildren.

• • •

And so, finally, here I am, juggling ADHD and dyslexia – after being juggled by this double act for more than sixty years. It is early days yet and I am still at the curious phase of my diagnosis, but I'm learning something new every day. I'm learning to welcome and accept my ADHD, to stop feeling sorry for myself and not to listen too closely to the voice inside my head that constantly berates me for losing my sunglasses for the fiftieth time, for misplacing my phone or forgetting to shut the lid on the freezer. I'm learning to stay resolute, not to judge myself too harshly and to cut myself some slack instead.

I tell myself I am entering my next decade with a feeling of fresh hope, and I'm happy with my life, with the fact that it continues to unfold layer by layer. I'm not degenerating into some crusty, older version of myself or descending into a state of ennui; I'm re-energised, reinvigorated and moving forward with purpose and direction. And so, in a way, my life begins again. I have the chance to make good – to repair some of the damage I've caused, to look at ADHD from the outside in, to scroll back and understand the impact it has had on others. After all, my partner never applied to become a household manager, a personal banker, a tax expert, an IT helpdesk operator and general factotum all rolled into one when she met me. I know I have much unpicking still to do, to accept I am facing a lifelong challenge with ADHD and dyslexia, and at no point will the game ever be played out. But I also tell myself that I have got a handle on it and, because ADHD has lost its element of surprise and therefore a significant portion of its power over me, it can no longer seize the wheel or send me skewing off the side of the road the way it used to.

I remind myself that I have more than sixty years in the rear-view mirror and I've got this. I can recognise the danger signs, my own patterns; I can read the scrambled signals in my brain whenever my thirst for adrenaline demands to be slaked, whenever I feel the impulse to sabotage things because they're going uncomfortably well. I know that when the brakes feel mushy, it is time to stop the car, to sit still and turn off the engine, to consult my road map and wait for the squall to blow over before moving forward again.

It amuses me and makes me smile that, after spending so much of my early life travelling backwards, it has taken me as long as another lifetime to write that I am finally moving forwards or that the signposts are no longer pointing the wrong way and I am heading at last in the right direction. And I am. I am moving forward hopeful that there are no more surprises to come, safe in the knowledge that I have all my tricks and strategies in place and awareness is now my watchword.

It doesn't mean I know where my sunglasses are, though.

EPILOGUE

They say it takes only one person to change a life for the better, but in my case, it needed at least two, if not more.

It is almost certain that had I been left to my own devices, I would never have realised my boyhood dream of writing a book and becoming an *a-published* author. However, my great friend Charlie Viney – one of my fellow partners-in-crime at Shiplake's Carter-Fuck library that night in July 1972 – reignited that dream in 2002 when he became a literary agent after a long and successful career in general trade publishing. I was nearly fifty at the time and was convinced that the opportunity had passed me by. The thirteen-year-old me, author of *Murder on the River Dart*, would have believed with all his heart that I could write a book, but I had lost my way somewhere down the line. I might have accomplished becoming a journalist but being an author now appeared to be way out of my reach. It was almost as if Charlie carried that belief for me. His offer to act as my agent, although I'd never come close to writing a book in the thirty years since leaving school, was testament to his unshakeable and remarkable faith in my ability.

The truth of it was that he wanted me to write a book more than

I wanted to write one – far more, in fact. As usual, my old fear that I wouldn't be good enough had jumped all over it. But Charlie refused to take no for an answer and persuaded me to start work on an idea I had hatched a year earlier, a book that would combine travel with sport – but then, typically, allowed it to remain just that, the germ of an idea. 'I can sell a non-fiction book to a publisher on two chapters and a synopsis,' he said. 'Just write it and we'll see where it takes us.'

Charlie provided what was the elixir of life to a dyslexic: belief. And powered by that belief and encouragement, I took my book idea back off the shelf and started writing. When I faltered halfway through the second chapter, he was on the phone to me in a flash. 'You've got to do this, John – you'll kick yourself for evermore if you don't.'

My first book, *Test of Time*, was published by John Murray in 2005 when I was fifty-one – a late bloomer, as ever. And despite a ten-year hiatus between my first and second books, Charlie never gave up on me. I broke the drought in 2015 and my third followed just two years after. I had finally got the hang of it. Naturally, I had turned the hyperfocus of my undiagnosed ADHD onto my pet subjects of sport and history.

Miss Shepherd never gave up on me either, and I often wonder what would have happened had our paths never merged, if I'd never been diagnosed with dyslexia or her hand had never guided mine across the page. I suspect my life would have taken a very different direction. Sometimes I imagine a parallel timeline where I never learned to read or write and where drawing and painting remained my only outlet for expression. The chances of her coming to teach at an independent boarding school like Hildersham House were slim indeed – a rarity under normal circumstances but a wonderful happenstance, nevertheless, for me. Especially as she specialised in teaching dyslexic children – another rarity – and knew everything there was to know about the subject. What were the odds? It was almost as though she had taken a wrong turn and arrived there by accident, it was so improbable.

The bulk of teachers at boarding schools in 1962 were hidebound and hard-line, with few exceptions. They were defined by their uniformity and rarely stepped out of character. They would no more have had an original thought or idea in their heads than they'd have been persuaded to accept the existence of dyslexia. It was teaching by numbers, where they expected every pupil to be the same and the worst thing you could be in their eyes was different, or not fit in or be wired differently – not that they'd have recognised the term. Luckily, Miss Shepherd moved among them and although our time together was brief – it lasted two years and passed with the speed of a rocket – she set my life in motion. I will be forever grateful to her.

I am grateful also to the generations who have followed behind me and to those who've helped to rewrite the language, remove the barriers, remove the shame and ridicule and invent a whole new vocabulary around neurodiversity, to make it possible to have a conversation that now thrums with compassion and energy. We have been liberated. We no longer need to seek permission to talk about our ADHD, our dyslexia, dyspraxia, dyscalculia, autism, and more, to make our voices heard. In fact, the word neurodiversity was coined only as recently as 1997 when Judy Singer, an Australian sociologist, first introduced it to the world in an undergraduate thesis. In an interview with *The Guardian* in 2023, she described her word as a concept, as 'an umbrella term for a movement'. She explained, 'As a word, "neurodiversity" describes the whole of humanity. But the neurodiversity *movement* is a political movement for people who want their human rights.' The Oxford Dictionary defines it as someone who exhibits 'patterns of thought and behaviour that are different from those of most people though still part of the normal range in humans'. It feels as if it has been around for ever.

I marvel too at the number of role models there are for dyslexics to draw strength from today, to inspire and urge us on at every turn of our journey. What I wouldn't have given for such an esteemed list when I was young and starting out as a journalist. People such as the film director Steven Spielberg, who was diagnosed with dyslexia at sixty; the entrepreneur Sir Richard Branson, diagnosed with dyslexia and ADHD; Erin Brockovich, the environmental activist, who identified reading as her greatest challenge; Jamie Oliver, the celebrity chef and author, who revealed in the *Daily Telegraph* that he didn't read a complete novel until he was thirty-eight; the legendary Welsh singer Sir Tom Jones, who was 'branded' lazy by his teachers and criticised for not trying hard enough. 'They didn't diagnose dyslexia when I was at school, they just thought you were thick,' he told the *Daily Express*. Then there is also the late Benjamin Zephaniah, the creative polymath who was expelled from school at thirteen unable to read or write because of dyslexia but went on to become an author, poet, musician, actor and campaigner, recognised by *The Times* in 2008 as one of the top fifty post-war writers in Britain. And there are many, many more, from all walks of life, of all ages, including artists, photographers, sportspeople, business leaders, scientists, engineers, architects, doctors, designers and inventors. The world is full of us.

ACKNOWLEDGEMENTS

Many thanks to Biteback Publishing, especially to Olivia Beattie for her belief in the project from the outset and to Catriona Allon for her brilliant copy-editing. I'm grateful to both for instantly 'getting' *NHOJ* and for their dedication at every stage. As always, I am indebted to my agent, Charlie Viney, for his continued support and encouragement, for unforgettably going the extra mile for *NHOJ* and for his enduring friendship.

Special thanks to Sandra McKersey for her kindness and support, notably for taking that first leap with me and helping me to finally open up about my dyslexia; to Jean Meyer for her inexhaustible generosity, positivity and interest (and for being the only 93-year-old to supply me with essential computer equipment and advice about BookTok); to Jeannie Cochrane for giving her time and encouragement so generously and for providing key insights and advice from a specialist teaching perspective; and to Ron Meyer for his ever-imaginative ideas, good-humoured support and always being there when times are tough, particularly during the early stages of *NHOJ*. Thanks to David, Henriette and Koura for providing the perfect sanctuary for writing, for fuelling the project with endless doorstep deliveries and much laughter and friendship, and to Gina, David, Will and Jack for a lifetime of memories and, more recently, for their support from afar. My heartfelt thanks, of course, to Sharon for your patience, honesty, humour, wisdom and invaluable creative input at every turn – not forgetting it was your suggestion that I write about my tangled life in the first place. *NHOJ* owes much to your unstinting resilience and belief. As ever, I could not have done it without you.

Finally, all my thanks to Dorothy Shepherd, wherever she may be, for her kindness, optimism and pioneering presence in my young life. Although I have had to change many of the names in the telling of *NHOJ*, hers, for obvious reasons, is among the handful I've remained faithful to. My fervent wish for all those struggling in classrooms, battling to overcome the odds or discover your true place in the world, is that you too find your Miss Shepherd.